The Church Leader's
MBA

What Business School Instructors Wish
Church Leaders Knew about Management

EDITORS

Dr. Mark Smith, Ed D
David W. Wright, Ph D

Dr. Mark Smith and David W. Wright
Ohio Christian University
1476 Lancaster Pike
Circleville, Ohio 43113
877.762.8669
www.OhioChristian.edu

Graphic Design: Lyn Rayn

Contents

Introduction

You must be honest, but you must not offend
You must correct, but you must not discourage.
You must hold accountable, but you must not dishearten.
You must achieve greatly, but with little or no formal authority.
You serve as example, foil, advocate, friend, counselor, and teacher.
You are a prophet.
You are a leader.

Few other tasks offer either the demands or the rewards.

When you fail, you are as irrelevant as last year's outvoted politician.
When you succeed, you become as dear as family.

You work in a social context that no longer understands nor respects your role.

But in those special moments when everything works, you bring hope where there is despair, love where the grim reality of broken life presses people down, and purpose to the lost and aimless.

You stand as God's ambassador to a world of desperate secularity, a reminder of the timeless, the sacred, the spiritual, the eternal.

No calling is nobler. No work is more fulfilling.

You are a minister.

To succeed as a minister, you need some uncommon characteristics—a divine calling, a thick skin, a sense of humor, and a stubborn streak, to name a few. Oh, and a bit of good luck now and then never hurts either.

A study by Robert Herman and Martin Butler looked at twelve qualities that characterize effective religious leaders.[1] Their research employed three instruments: The Managerial Practices Survey (MPS), which is a well-known survey instrument with strong reliability and validity;[2] the Leader Behavior Questionnaire (LBQ), which is also broadly utilized and considered highly reliable;[3] and a lesser known survey titled the Ministerial Effectiveness Inventory (MEI).[4]

Herman and Butler's research revealed that effective ministerial leaders are

- managers
- problem solvers
- planners
- delegators
- inspirers
- change agents
- shepherds
- communicators
- multitaskers
- students
- servants
- persons of integrity.

Clearly, to succeed in that range of roles and responsibilities, a minister will need a good set of professional tools. That's what this book is for—to offer professional tools for ministerial leadership drawn from a set of management and leadership disciplines to which most ministers receive scant exposure during their preparation.

How We Created This Resource

We took a pretty straightforward approach in creating this book.

1. We identified several key disciplinary areas from the standard management curriculum taught in most masters of business administration programs.
2. We gathered faculty and business leaders we respect, those who exhibit strong expertise in each of these key areas. We asked them this question:

   What four or five concepts from your area of management and leadership expertise would you like your minister to know?
3. We distilled their responses into the key principles that form the basis of what we have come to call *The Church Leader's MBA*.
4. Surrounding those insights with supporting research and clarifying them with examples from real-life situations, we delivered them to you in the chapters of this book.

The Nature of Management and Leadership in the Church

Before you dig into the heart of this *Church Leader's MBA*, permit me a few reflections on the nature of management and leadership in the church.

All of us who have contributed to this book have been involved in ministry for many years. We've worked with church congregations, para-church organizations, educational institutions, and business organizations. We are ministers and organizational managers.

Unfortunately, most ministerial preparation programs do little to provide these tools for ministers. One of our students recently told us that she has learned more valuable information about managing the church in her first few management classes than she learned in her entire ministerial preparation program.

Before you respond, let me assure you that we've heard and respect the arguments that the church is a divine organism. We believe, as do most church leaders, that God's Kingdom grows and succeeds through God's blessing, not through human "management." But the last time we checked, all of the churches and all of the religious organizations we know about are made up of human beings. Furthermore, in our experience, every one of these congregations and religious organizations exists in a social context. Or, the church may be a divine organism. But it is also a human organization.

In his recent book, *Staying Power: Why People Leave the Church Over Change and What You Can Do About It*, Bob Whitesel says this about the dual nature of the church:

Early in my seminary career, Emil Brunner acquainted me with the church in two manifestations. He pointed out in *The Misunderstanding of the Church* (trans. Harold Knight, London: Lutterworth Press, 1952) that historically the church was looked upon as an institution or organization, but that the reformers such as Luther and Calvin saw something more: a community built on relationships which Brunner called the "hidden" or "invisible" church (p. 10-19). This understanding of the church, as both an organization, which needs to be managed as well as a spiritual community, which thrives through divine guidance, has been the dual thrust that this and my previous writings have attempted to unite.[5]

The church is both a human organization and a spiritual community. Our point in this book is that successful ministerial leaders understand *both* elements of this identity and master a set of tools related to the leadership of *both* these elements.

The Role of Organizational Leadership in the Church

No human organization that we know of has the inherent ability to manage itself well. Human organizations need leaders who understand the dynamics of creating, leading, and managing successful organizations.

Sadly, over and over again, we've watched good people descend into fits of conflict. We've seen God's agenda in a community falter. And we've seen the name of the church sullied, simply because those with the responsibility of leading did not understand how to employ even the most rudimentary leadership principles that are commonplace in avowedly "secular" organizations.

The church is not a business. It cannot be run that way. But it *is* a human organization. And many of the principles of human organization and leadership that mark the success of other kinds of organizations can be applied successfully to religious organizations.

There isn't really a good place for ministers to get this education. If you're a good learner and you pay attention, you may learn on the job what you need to survive. But there should be a better way.

Our aim is to offer tools to help you better manage the human organization represented by your ministry, to see what might happen when you bring management principles to ministerial leadership. But we'd also like to be clear that just managing the organizational machinery won't be enough.

Leading the Church Well

Most church leaders have a vision. It may not be the right vision for the place and time, but at least on some level, that really doesn't matter. An organization actively pursuing a vision is healthier than one without any vision. The problem is that ministers often don't know the practical steps necessary to turn vision into reality. They don't have the organizational tools needed to accomplish what their vision calls them to do.

Talk about a recipe for frustration and disillusionment. What a tragedy! It doesn't have to be so. The missing link is the ability to develop and lead a healthy, dynamic, purposeful organization.

At this point we must also recognize that different church traditions place congregational leadership roles at different places within the church organization. For example, in some churches the senior or solo pastor is expected to lead the organization much as a CEO leads secular organizations. In other churches, the pastor is not expected to act as a CEO, but is expected to be a counselor, a shepherd, a prophet, or a priest representing God to the people and the people to God.

Further, different church traditions empower congregational leadership differently. Whether a church has a board of elders, a board of administration, or a vestry, leadership in the church is often shared across groups of professional and volunteer leaders.

The point is that no matter where the task of organizational leadership lies, every church has its leaders. Those leaders need to know how to serve competently in that role. This resource is for them.

The Church Leader's MBA focuses on four areas of professional management skills that we believe ministers must develop:

- The ability to develop an organization
- The ability to lead people effectively
- The ability to manage the operational elements of the organization
- The ability to manage one's own ongoing professional development.

We offer one final insight, a simple plan for your professional development as leaders of successful organizations:

- You are great at something. Invest most of your personal development effort in this area.
- You can be competent at two or three more things. Keep learning in these areas.
- You must be capable at everything the job requires. Borrow all the brains it takes for your organization to succeed in these areas.

David Wright, Ph.D.
Indiana Wesleyan University
Department of Graduate Studies in Ministry

Endnotes

1. D. Martin Butler and Robert D. Herman, "Effective Ministerial Leadership," *The Journal of Nonprofit Management and Leadership* 9 (1999): 229-39.
2. Gary Yukl, Stephen J. Wall, and Richard Lepsinger, "Preliminary Report on the Validation of the Managerial Practices Survey," *Measures of Leadership*, ed. Kenneth E. Clark, Miriam B. Clark, and Robert R. Albright (West Orange, NJ: Leadership Library of America, 1990).

3. H. Newton Malony and Laura F. Majovsky, "The Role of Psychological Assessment in Predicting Ministerial Success," *The Review of Religious Research* 28 (1986): 29-39.
4. Bob Whitesel, *Staying Power: Why People Leave the Church Over Change and What You Can Do About It!)* (Nashville: Abingdon, 2003).

1

What Church Leader's Need to Know About . . .

Organizational Leadership

Pastor, Be a Leader!

"The servant-leader is servant first . . . It begins with a natural
feeling that one wants to serve, to serve first.
The conscious choice brings one to aspire to lead."[1]

—ROBERT K. GREENLEAF

SPECIAL NOTE: Some Portions of this chapter are also featured in Dr. Lindsay's
and Dr. Smith's book on leadership.

Watch Out, Jesus, Here I Come!

Pastor Jose had a vision. He wanted to see growth in the church he pastored. Many of his members supported his vision. Jose wrote it down, created a plan, and developed some goals. He even included strategy on how to measure goal achievement in order to determine success. The plan was ready and he now could go change the world. His motto was, "Watch out, Jesus, here I come!" But as time passed, nothing happened. He became more frustrated; depression and failure became his companions. As church members watched from the sidelines, they saw what Pastor Jose was unable to see: he did not know how to lead forward with his vision. He always referred to the project as "his" project. When a group discussed new initiatives, he dominated the discussion, giving only token appreciation to others who shared viable ideas. At times he dismissed these ideas before the speaker had finished talking. In his mind, he alone knew how to make his vision a reality. After all, it was "God's vision." He worked even harder and harder. After two frustrating years, he resigned, certain that his parishioners "weren't interested in change." He considered leaving the ministry altogether. This story is played out over and over in the church. Why do visionaries fail? Why do church projects fail even when the top leaders support them? There are many answers, but one rises above the others—poor leadership strategies.

A Blueprint for Failure

When talking about their pastors, many Christian leaders express strong support for "the man of God." However, these business leaders are quick to point out several traits that cause pastors to fail.

1. The vision is the pastor's vision only.
2. The vision is not clearly communicated.
3. The vision does not include others.
4. The vision lacks careful planning.
5. The vision is poorly implemented.
6. The vision is never revisited.

Today, there is a critical need for pastor/leaders to work with others to form a God-given vision and then lead the church forward in its implementation. These leaders must be principled and trustworthy. Six billion people have a desperate need for compassionate, trustworthy leaders. Pastor, are you willing to be a world-changing leader? Are you open to changing *your* world? Our families, communities, churches, and organizations need a valiant response to this call if we are to make a world-changing difference in the next decade. This chapter offers you some strategies to use in changing your world.

Defining Lead

Business leaders have a wide variety of lea(
which to choose. To better understand the bu:
should review key principles from the world of ⸻
Leadership is the act of modeling, serving, a⸻
vision, and goals of a community, team, or organi⸻   ⸻⸻u.
In their overview of leadership strategies, leadership   ⸻⸻ren Bennis and
Burt Nanus describe these qualities of effective leadership:

- Leadership is authority
- Leadership is vision
- Leadership is mobilization of forces
- Leadership commits people to action
- Leadership involves hard work
- Leadership is associated with the strong
- Leadership is both born and developed[2]

This list shows that leadership not only involves numerous characteristics, but also is difficult to define. Richard Chewning defines leadership: "Good leadership is an art. It provides direction and purpose for an organization. It elicits trust and helps employees focus on the big purposes of the organization. Leadership must be earned and it is voluntarily given by those who follow, not taken by those who lead. Followers perceive that leaders can work with them to provide opportunities to meet their personal goals while making a contribution to the goals of the business."[3]

Perhaps one of the most important aspects of leadership, Chewning adds, is understanding that "each of us can grow and develop leadership skills."[4] This should give hope to pastor/leaders. Knowing how critical it is to be an effective leader, the pastor then should aspire to develop leadership skills.

Daniel Goleman approaches leadership from a slightly different perspective but in a similar vein of thought. "Leaders set strategy, they motivate, they create mission, they build culture." Further, he says, the "singular job of the leader is to get results."[5] Pastors often are frustrated by this "results focus," but much of their frustration can be reduced by establishing a clear agenda—one that is capable of producing results. An agenda of results should include not only numerical and monetary growth, but also spiritual growth. Ironically, most pastors do not like the image or the pressure associated with a corporate inclination. Rather than see a dichotomy between the spiritual and the business mind-sets, it is more productive to view these two approaches as different means to the same end. Pastors need to understand that the church essentially is about results, and the primary result is to build the Kingdom of Christ.

Leadership Styles

To avoid the pitfalls of ineffective pastoral leadership, pastors should understand the benefits and pitfalls of various leadership styles. Using a style that does not fit a particular project or group of people will only defeat the pastor's good intentions. Sometimes, elements of different styles can be combined for optimum results. Goleman reviews six leadership styles.[6]

1. Demands Immediate Compliance: Coercive Leadership

To coerce means to achieve something by force. A stylistic phrase would be "Do what I tell you." The underlying emotional intelligence competencies of the coercive leadership style are the drive to initiate, control, and achieve. For some reason, coercive leadership seems to be a preference with some pastors. Although a pastor must demonstrate strong leadership, coercive leadership is rarely helpful and more often than not causes congregational discomfort. In extreme situations such as a church split or a case of defiant sin in the church, coercive leadership may prove useful if it is used with love and discretion. The coercive style is always appropriate during a genuine emergency, such as a natural disaster or terrorist attack. However, Goleman suggests that if a leader relies solely on this style or continues to use it once the emergency passes, the long-term impact will be ruinous.[7] While the coercive leadership style has merit in certain narrowly defined circumstances, it seldom should be used as an everyday model.

2. Mobilizing People Toward a Vision: Authoritative Leadership

An authoritative leader might be characterized by the phrase, "Come with me." This leader is a self-confident, empathetic change catalyst. This style works best when changes require a new vision, or when clear direction is needed. Goleman describes authoritarian leadership as the ability to maximize "commitment to the organization's goals and strategy." He explains further:

> By framing the individual tasks within a grand vision, the authoritative leader defines standards that revolve around that vision. When he gives performance feedback—whether positive or negative—the singular criterion is whether or not that performance furthers the vision. The standards for success are clear to all, as are the rewards. Finally, consider the style's impact on flexibility. An authoritative leader states the end but generally gives people plenty of leeway to devise their own means. Authoritative leaders give people the freedom to innovate, experiment, and take calculated risks.[8]

The pastor who employs authoritarian leadership is respected and goal focused. However, in being too goal focused, this leader may overlook or forget people in the process of accomplishing goals.

3. Creating Harmony and Emotional Bonds: Affiliative Leadership

An affiliative leader often will use the phrase "People come first." This leader's strengths are empathy, relationship building, and communication. Affiliative leadership works best to heal rifts in a team or to motivate people. Goleman describes this leader as one "who strives to keep employees happy and to create harmony among them. He leads by building strong emotional bonds and then reaping the benefits of such an approach, namely fierce loyalty. The style also has a markedly positive effect on communication. People who like one another a lot talk a lot. They share ideas; they share inspiration."[9]

The pastor who is an affiliative leader works constantly at relationships. While this leader may frustrate some who are goal focused, this pastor will be respected for harmony of vision and purpose.

4. Forging Consensus through Participation: Democratic Leadership

The democratic leader's catch phrase is "What do you think?" This leader exemplifies collaboration, team leadership, and communication. The strength of this style is that many people are involved in the decision-making processes. This tends to broaden the church base and include many people; some will view this style with concern because decisions are not made quickly or efficiently.

5. *Setting High Standards: Pacesetting Leadership*

"Do as I do—now," characterizes the pacesetting leader. Setting high standards of performance, the pacesetter is noted for conscientiousness, initiative, and the drive to achieve. This works best when the goal is to get quick results. "The pacesetting style has its place in the leader's repertory, but it should be used sparingly," Goleman advises. "After all, the hallmarks of the pacesetting style sound admirable. The leader sets extremely high performance standards. He is obsessive about doing things better and faster. He pinpoints poor performers and demands more from them."[11]

The pastor who is a pacesetting leader tends to come into the church organization for specific purposes and stay for short periods of time. Because of a get-it-done attitude, this pastor may be applauded by business leaders. The same attitude, however, may frustrate others in the congregation.

6. *Developing Future Leaders: Coaching Leadership*

The coaching leader's underlying competencies are empathy, self-awareness, and the ability to develop others. The coaching leader's catch phrase is "Try this." This style works best as a way to help employees improve performance or develop long-term strengths. The pastor who uses this strategy must build a trust relationship with a few. This relationship is built on admission of needed improvements and a willingness to resolve the issues. This style is primarily used with staff in one-on-one sessions.

Which Style is Best?

Goleman believes that the most effective leader will master four or more styles, "using the right one at just the right time and in the right measure. The payoff is in the results."[13] Pastors should study their individual leadership styles in light of these six, modifying and adapting various elements in order to improve interaction skills and be more effective. A pastor must ask which style is best in a given situation. The following questions should initiate reflective thinking about which style is appropriate:

1. Does the problem identified need immediate action with strong leadership?
2. Does the situation require motivational leadership?
3. Does the situation need consensus?
4. Does the identified need area require high performance standards?

The Servant Leader

We are biased toward a servant leadership. The term "servant leader" has captured the attention of the workplace. A servant leader influences people to collaboratively work toward mutually shared visions and goals in order to produce results for the common good. It is the act of modeling, serving, and communicating the values, visions, and goals of a community, team, or organization in response to a need.

In *Assessing the Servant Organization*, Jim Laub describes effective servant leaders as those who

- display authenticity,
- value people,
- develop people,
- build community,
- provide leadership,
- share leadership.[14]

Although they do not call it servant leadership, James M. Kouzes and Barry Z. Posner support the underlying philosophy. Summarizing extensive research in *The Leadership Challenge*, they note five key leadership practices that promote change:

1. Challenging the process (status quo)
2. Inspiring a shared vision
3. Enabling others to act
4. Modeling the way
5. Encouraging the heart[15]

These five practices embody servant leadership. The spirit of this style transmits a sense of trust and respect while influencing people to produce the intended results. This evokes a sense of appreciation, optimism, freedom to improve and advance, motivation, involvement, and ownership. Effective and caring leaders can stifle or liberate the talents and skills of the team or organization. The effective pastor should strive to unleash the talents and creativity of those under his/her leadership.

World-Changing Servant Leadership

After reviewing leadership definitions, styles, and strategies, and after talking with numerous business leaders, we offer this definition of world-changing servant leadership for pastors:

> **Pastoral World-Changing Servant Leadership** is the ability to identify compelling needs, to initiate the collaborative action required to envision solutions, and to influence people and resources to serve others for a better future. This leadership is an active, purposeful, skilled, service-led influencing of others to further facilitate change or growth, enabling the team or community to achieve both corporate and individual goals.

Check Your Leadership Inventory

The process of becoming a world-changing servant leader requires action. Leaders must assess their inventory of key characteristics. The first characteristic is to see a compelling need. I see so many pastors who fail to notice the needs around them. Effective pastoral leadership is improved by studying the community and identifying its needs. Once you identify the needs, you must develop an action plan.

The pastor also must be a compassionate public leader. Great leaders transmit a compassionate spirit and the behaviors of a servant leader. In so doing, they provide

1. love and devotion as they encourage and strengthen others;
2. wisdom and good judgment as they guide and counsel others;

3. authority (caring and helpful influence) as they protect and support others;
4. goodness as they supply and comfort others;
5. equality as they work with others in the spirit of love and unity.

Servant leaders are promoted to a position of authority over those under their care. Servant leaders must not use coercive and positional power to lord it over people, nor should they act tyrannically. Instead, they are called to love, care, serve, train, and empower those they lead. The focal point of leadership should be meeting the needs of those being served.

Inspirational Servant Leaders

The following stories illustrate how servant leaders have changed the world.

Listen Up, Men! Esther: A Woman Pastor

Esther is a biblical figure who changed her world. When she appears in the Bible, she is an orphan Jewess named Hadassah, "also known as Esther" (Esther 2:7). Within four years she is a queen, the wife of Xerxes, the Persian king. Although this position gave her power, she managed it wisely. From her humble beginnings, Esther became God's instrument to save the entire Jewish population.

Want to be a world changer? Many consider her to have been Israel's best pastoral leader overall. Author Edith Deen highlights some leadership strategies that Esther modeled as she led the Jews.[16]

1. She gained favor with the people.
2. She used sound judgment.
3. She always thought of others first.
4. She was willing to sacrifice her position and even her life to save others.
5. She was dedicated and loyal.
6. She exhibited character.
7. She was fearless.
8. She was prudent.

Esther is a pattern for us to follow. Perhaps one of the greatest problems in the church is the lack of leadership strategies and involvement from the church organization's "common folks." Why is it that so few speak up when a church seeks to resolve problems? Among the reasons are these:

- Some are afraid to speak up.
- Some feel they have nothing valuable to offer.
- Some are not involved in the church, so feel voiceless.
- Some feel their ideas are not valued because of past rejection.
- Some simply do not care.

And, even more tragically, some pastors are too controlling and closed to new ideas. Esther changed her world. Which of Esther's leadership strategies would work for you?

Mother Teresa: A Church Leader with a Servant's Heart

Mother Teresa of Calcutta is a leader who impacted the world through servant leadership. She brought the plight of Calcutta's street people to the world's attention. When she walked onto Calcutta's streets, the poorest of the poor were living and dying there. No one seemed to be doing anything about their desperate situation or deplorable conditions. Her heart was so moved that she decided to take action. She began to work as a "missionary of charity," ministering to the lepers.

In his book *Something Beautiful for God*, Malcolm Muggeridge describes Mother Teresa as epitomizing servant leadership by choosing "to live in the slums of Calcutta, amidst all the dirt and disease and misery."[17] He describes her as having a "spirit so indomitable, a faith so intractable, and a love so abounding, that he felt abashed."[18]

Mother Teresa is known for having changed the plight of many lives. It is important to remember that she went about changing the world one heart at a time. Love was her modus operandi.

Mother Teresa exhibited these qualities:

1. An outstanding work ethic
2. Love for others

3. The ability to see the need
4. A vision to change the plight of the needy
5. A plan to implement her vision
6. The ability to organize resources
7. The ability to galvanize an effective vehicle for change; i.e., the Mothers of Charity[19]

It is apparent that Mother Teresa saw a need and committed herself to changing the world. The characteristics of great leadership seem to converge in the key behaviors she modeled and taught throughout her life. She clearly saw the relationship between leadership and God's kind of love.

President Ronald Regan: Visionary Leadership

President Reagan's vision for a nation to end the cold war and promote democracy was an example of visionary servant leadership. He is remembered as one of America's greatest presidents and one of our finest leaders. He said that our goal as Americans was "to have the vision to dream of a better, safer world, and the courage, persistence and patience to turn the dream into a reality."[20] He believed one man can change the world. History is validating that belief, as information emerges revealing President Reagan's part in the fall of communism. Democracy prevailed through his visionary leadership. Author Dinesh D'Souza concludes that President Reagan was governed by three basic elements of leadership:

1. **Vision** - the ability to frame conviction and visualize destination
2. **Action** - the ability to get from here to there
3. **Consent** - the ability to articulate vision and rally the people[21]

World-Changing Leadership as Exemplified by Jesus Christ

Embodying World-Changing Leadership

In looking at some well-known servant leaders in this chapter, we have identified certain characteristics and practices pivotal to successful servant leadership. Additionally, to effect substantive change in the world—key strategies are necessary. We would also do well to study the Person that writers on leadership acknowledge to be perhaps the most influential leader of all time: Jesus Christ.

World-Changing Leadership Involves Sharing Vision

One writer suggests that "Jesus knew his mission statement, and he did not deviate from it. He declared that his mission was, in essence, to teach people about a better way of living." Jesus was "a leader who, like many of us, had to depend on others to accomplish a goal."[22]

Jesus Christ had a vision. That vision was to change the world with a message of love. A healthy, creative mind produces vision. Individuals and organizations are always in critical need of vision. Outstanding, world-changing leaders possess great vision. They change the seen and envision the unseen. Their creative vision convicts, inspires, and enables people to achieve peak performance and attain extraordinary goals. That is exactly what Christ did as a leader. This was Jesus' vision statement:

> *"I have been given all authority in heaven and on earth! Go to the people of all nations and make them my disciples. Baptize them in the name of the Father, the Son, and the Holy Spirit, and teach them to do everything I have told you. I will be with you always, even until the end of the world."* (Matthew 28:18-20 CEV)

With this simple vision statement the world was changed.

World-Changing Leadership Involves Developing Others

Jesus developed others by reproducing Himself in them. Great pastors transmit excellence by loving, serving, and teaching their followers. As leaders develop those around them, they first must "manage themselves" by discipline. Followers will trust someone in a leadership role who is disciplined and consistent in behavior. World-changing pastors are preparing world changers. Great leaders reproduce the leadership strategies of Jesus Christ. The improvement, growth, and spread of world-changing endeavors will occur in direct proportion to the supply of world-changing pastor/leaders.

World-Changing Leadership Depends on Integrity

Stephen Covey espoused the idea of "principle-centered leadership." He suggests that "principle-centered leadership introduces a new paradigm—that we center our lives and our leadership of organizations and people on certain true north principles."[23]

Pastors who commit themselves to world-changing endeavors will be faced with several issues:

- How do I use power?
- How do I use wealth?
- How do I use positions of influence?

The Legacy of Servant Leadership

Why was Jesus Christ the greatest servant leader of all time? After being with His disciples only three years, He had so profoundly ingrained His principles in them that an entire world was changed—and continues to be changed. Therefore, as leaders in a world-changing effort, we must constantly instill in those around us the desire to complete the job even after we are gone.

Perhaps the greatest test of pastoral leadership is what happens after the leader is gone. Does the vision continue? Is the church developing other leaders to take the place of the pastor in the future? Just as Jesus Christ led twelve disciples to fill leadership roles, the pastor who is an inspirational servant leader must do the same. In the case of Jesus Christ and Christianity, the ripples continue to spread!

One man.
Twelve men.
And the world is changed.
Wow! What a leader!

Endnotes

1. Robert K. Greenleaf, *The Servant As Leader* (Indianapolis: Robert K. Greenleaf Center, 1991), 7.
2. Warren Bennis and Burt Nanus, *Leaders: The Strategies for Taking Charge* (New York: Harper and Row, 1985).
3. Richard C. Chewning and others, *Business Through the Eyes of Faith* (New York: Harper-Collins, 1990), 133.
4. Ibid.
5. Daniel Goleman, "Leadership That Gets Results," *Harvard Business Review* (March/April 2000): 78.

Endnotes 6 through 13, Ibid.

14. Jim Laub, *Assessing the Servant Organization: A description of the six key areas and eighteen characteristics of the Servant Organization,* © 2000 Jim Laub.
15. James M. Kouzes and Barry Z. Posner, *The Leadership Challenge: How to Keep Getting Extraordinary Things Done in Organizations*, from The Jossey-Bass Management Series (San Francisco: Jossey-Bass Publishers, 1995), 1-2.
16. Edith Deen, *All of the Women of the Bible* (San Francisco: Harper Collins, 1988), 148-51.
17. Malcolm Muggeridge, *Something Beautiful for God: Mother Teresa of Calcutta* (Garden City, NY: Image, 1977), 17.
18. Ibid.
19. Ibid.
20. Dinesh D'Souza, *Ronald Reagan: How an Ordinary Man Became an Extraordinary Leader* (New York: Free Press, 1997), 228.21.
21. Ibid.
22. Laurie Beth Jones, *Jesus CEO* (New York: Hyperion, 1995), xvii.
23. Stephen Covey, *The 7 Habits of Highly Effective People: Powerful Lessons in Personal Change* (New York: Fireside, 1990), 18.

2

What Church Leader's Need to Know About . . .

Managerial Ethics

Becoming a Leader after God's Own Heart

"Today we are having the most lively ethics discussions
since ancient Greece more than 2,300 years ago . . ."

—GEOFFREY P. LANTOS
PROFESSOR OF BUSINESS ADMINISTRATION[1]

A Well-intentioned Misappropriation?

Jim, a pseudonym, was leaving the community food bank where he had served as director. His career had been shaky from the start, but Jim felt he had grown into the position over time. Just a year earlier he had told me, "This (job) is where I think I'll stay until I retire." Now, only in his mid-40s, Jim was leaving to pursue a career in business. He had been stung by perceived ethical missteps, which had eroded both his credibility and his support among the food bank's board. "They didn't train me for this in seminary," he complained. "The rules for parsing verbs were explained clearly enough. But the rules about ethical business decisions were never addressed."

The ethical landscape can be a minefield for the Christian leader. Differentiating between what is appropriate and what is illicit can be daunting. Like all too many church leaders today, Jim had learned an important lesson the hard way: High expectations are placed upon church leaders, and ethical missteps, even minor ones, can be ruinous.

What was the fiscal blunder to which Jim had succumbed? In the midst of trying to keep a floundering food bank afloat, he had appropriated money designated specifically for food purchases and used it for office expenses. When the benefactors learned that money they had intended for food stuffs was going to buy a copy machine instead, they demanded a refund of their donation. Standing upon shaky ground, Jim could not refund the money without jeopardizing the daily operations of the center. The board decided that in order to make ends meet, Jim's salary would have to fill the gap. Thus, he was unceremoniously dismissed.

Jim considered his decision a judgment call, reasoning that if he didn't apply the designated money to the non-designated needs of the office, the food bank would lose its few already overworked employees. Certainly, he rationalized this is not what benefactors would want. However, the wealthy benefactors felt that Jim's ethical decision crossed the line of propriety. What Jim needed was some sort of system or procedure for effectively grappling with these kinds of ethical questions.

Defining Ethics

In his seminal book on planning, Fred David tenders a common definition of ethics. He writes, "Ethics can be defined as principles of conduct within organizations that guide decision making and behavior."[2] Even in its brevity, this definition is good, for it reminds us that ethics are not a set of hypothetical decrees, but principles that actively affect daily action and attitude. Ethics are powerful and dynamic ways of thinking that determine our choices, our actions, and our future.

How Business People Answer Ethical Questions

To arrive at a procedure for making ethical decisions, one might think the solution would be to look at how businesspeople address ethical dilemmas, and then copy their lead. However, in his classic study of business ethics, Raymond Baumhart discovered that even in the business world there is no clear system for ethical decision-making. Baumhart interviewed over one hundred businessmen in *An Honest Profit: What Businessmen Say About Ethics in Business*. Expecting to find some ethical concord, Baumhart was surprised when the results fell into three unexpected categories (see Figure 2.1).[3]

Figure 2.1 • "What does *ethical* mean to you?"

- **50 percent** of the respondents defined ethical as *"what my feelings tell me is right."*
- **25 percent** defined ethical as *"in accord with my religious beliefs."*
- **18 percent** of the businessmen defined ethical as *"according to the Golden Rule."*

Source: Raymond Baumhart, *An Honest Profit: What Businessmen Say about Ethics in Business* (New York: Holt, Rinehart and Wilson, 1968), 11-12, results of a survey of over 100 businessmen.

On the surface, two of these options seem to hold promise for formulating ethical guidelines in the business world. Upon closer inspection, however, all three fail as reliable guides to ethical decision making.

"In accord with my religious beliefs." This second option for framing ethical decision-making sounds good on the surface. Like feelings-based ethics, however, religious beliefs can be imprecise, unstable, and even volatile. Infanticide, genocide, and ethnic bigotry have been perpetrated and continue to be perpetrated in the name of religion. What one religion considers profane may be sacred to another religion. Even in the same denomination, there may be disagreement as to what denotes ethical behavior. In the shadows are even larger issues: What constitutes religion? How does religion differ from faith? Which religion is "right"? Relying on religious beliefs, especially when people embrace so many divergent views, is not an adequate or consistent guideline for ethical decision-making.

"According to the Golden Rule." The third response to Baumhart's survey seems to be the most promising guide for ethical behavior. Before making that assertion, however, look at Figure 2.2 and compare how the Golden Rule is worded by those to whom it is attributed.

Figure 2.2 • Versions of the Golden Rule

- **Buddha** "Hurt not others with that which pains yourself."(neg.)
- **Confucius** "What you do not want done to yourself, do not do to others."(neg.)
- **Hinduism** "Do nothing to others which if done to you would cause you pain."(neg.)
- **Jesus Christ** "Do to others what you would have them do to you."(pos.)

In these four renditions of the Golden Rule, we see that the first three are stated in the negative (neg.) or reactive form. In other words, they tell you only to refrain from those negative actions that you might not want done to you. While admirable, they fail to take into account positive or proactive behaviors—those that would benefit others. In a sense, then, they do not serve as a proactive guide to right behavior.

Jesus' positive rendition of the Golden Rule (see Matthew 7:12 and Luke 6:31) gives us a guideline that is more in tune with ethical behavior. It tells us essentially to "do good" to others (not just to refrain from those negative actions we do not want done to us). Thus, at its heart, Jesus' positive rendition of the Golden Rule could serve as a viable guideline for ethical decision-making. However, because the Golden Rule can be interpreted in negative as well as positive forms, it alone is inadequate in helping to formulate ethical guidelines in the business world.

The "Right, Just, and Love" Approach

To this ethical conundrum comes Alexander Hill, professor of business and economics at Seattle Pacific University. Hill offers some of the most original recent thinking on ethics we have encountered. In fact, Hill states that ethical decision making is the equivalent of sitting on a three-legged stool.[5] Hill envisions three biblically derived foundational principles as essential underpinnings for all Christian ethical decisions. Figure 2.3 illustrates Hill's three-legged foundation for ethical decision-making.

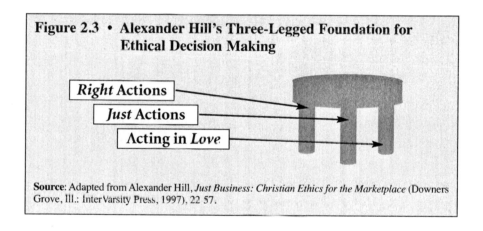

Figure 2.3 • Alexander Hill's Three-Legged Foundation for Ethical Decision Making

Right Actions

Just Actions

Acting in *Love*

Source: Adapted from Alexander Hill, *Just Business: Christian Ethics for the Marketplace* (Downers Grove, Ill.: InterVarsity Press, 1997), 22–57.

Hill's three-legged stool reminds us visually that if any one of the three supports is missing, the ethical process will become unbalanced. Let's look at each foundational support to understand what it teaches.

Right Actions

Hill equates right actions to "holiness," and sees in God's holy and separate character an admonition for Christians to undertake right actions through four avenues:

1. ***Right* actions begin by setting priorities that include "God – Family – Career" in that order**. Hill sees many of today's ethical challenges occurring because businesspeople (and even church leaders) subtly begin to elevate their careers above family and, ultimately, God. To root out

actions based on self or career, Christian leaders first need to determine whether or not their perspectives and actions are in accordance with what should be their highest priority—pleasing God.

2. **Right actions include being ethically pure—being physically, emotionally, and routinely separate from impure or tainted business practices**. The Apostle Peter reminds Christians to live "lives of holiness and godliness . . . without spot or blemish" (2 Peter 3:11, 14 RSV). This should extend to our business dealings. Hill feels that a part of what it means to be "holy" is a genuine aversion to and avoidance of any action that is ethically tainted.

3. **Right actions are accountable**. Here Hill sees right actions as resulting from the business leader's accountability to mature and ethical colleagues and/or managers, as well as to God. We will discuss accountability in more depth later in this chapter.

4. **Right actions are rooted in humility**. Hill stresses the importance of seeing oneself as a facilitator, team builder, and coach for those we serve. Through humility, we recognize our weaknesses and seek to improve them. In the process, we accept others and seek to empower them. In *Good to Great: Why Some Companies Make the Leap . . . and Others Don't*, best-selling author Jim Collins describes several great leaders who are excellent facilitators and mentors. In the course of his study, he discovered that typically "a spectacular rise (of a company) under a tyrannical disciplinarian (is) followed by an equally spectacular decline when the disciplinarian stepped way."[6]

Just Actions

Hill considers just actions to be the second leg of the ethical decision-making stool. Just actions have four aspects: equal procedures, protecting rights, fair reward for merit, and honoring promises. Let's look briefly at each of these aspects:

1. **Equal procedures** means that regardless of a person's standing in the company hierarchy, that person is to be treated equally. The New Testament speaks to this in Paul's admonition to avoid social, ethnic, and religious

discrimination in the Christian community. In Galatians 3:28, he says, "There is neither Jew nor Greek, slave nor free, male nor female, for you are all one in Christ Jesus." In the strongly patriarchal and ethnocentric society of two thousands years ago, Paul's statement was a revolutionary concept. Historically, this revolutionary concept has been and continues to be a Christian hallmark, one that should be reflected in business and modeled by business leaders.

2. By **protecting rights** Hill means safeguarding against erosion of a person's inalienable, God-given rights. These include the right to practice religion, the right to bodily safety, the right to be told the truth, and the right to freedom from harassment. Hill stresses that ethical decision making takes into account the free exercise of every person's rights, whether or not the law is involved.

3. **Fair reward for merit** is an important component of Hill's "just actions" leg of the three-legged stool, It is especially relevant today when executive salaries continue to skyrocket, while pension accounts are raided (see Figure 2.5 later in this chapter for more examples). Fair reward for merit requires adherence to compensation that is "fair" and evenhanded. In other words, lavish executive salaries, multimillion-dollar pensions, and exorbitant stock options are not "fair" rewards for executives in a corporate milieu when, at the same time and in the same corporation, rank-and-file employees are laid off, prevented from selling their own stock, or consigned woefully underfunded pension plans.

4. **Honoring promises** means that even in the competitive world of business, honoring one's word and keeping promises are necessary for engendering respect and mutual reliance. The University of Minnesota's Norman Bowie found that businesses known to honor their word actually operate more efficiently. This is because suppliers and consumers know they can depend on promised performance and/or delivery schedules.[7]

Acting in *Love*

The third leg of Hill's three-legged stool stands for demonstrating Christ-like love in ethical decision-making. Acting in love, according to Hill, involves shouldering others' pain, taking action on their behalf, and subjugating one's own rights in order to help others.

1. **Shouldering others' pain** means that good ethical decisions are based on solidarity with all stakeholders. This should result in the desire to help them deal with their problems. When employees, customers, suppliers, and other stakeholders experience difficulties, Christ's example requires us to bear their pain as if we were in pain with them (even when we are not). The writer of Hebrews says, "Remember those in prison as if you were their fellow prisoners, and those who are mistreated as if you yourselves were suffering" (13:3). This verse speaks clearly to solidarity with those who are hurting or disenfranchised. Management author Tom Peters points out that such "genuine concern for stakeholders" leads to productivity and long-term business relationships.[8]

2. **Taking action on their behalf** describes an atmospheres of mutual interdependence, one in which stakeholders actually take steps to assist others in what they cannot do for themselves. An example of this involves "Danny," who served as a receptionist for a large firm. Danny's frequently argumentative nature and insecurity led him to sometimes deal roughly and brusquely with customers. Rather than firing Danny, his manger took action on Danny's behalf and found a more suitable position for him in the company. The manger acted with love and on Danny's behalf to protect Danny's livelihood.

3. **Subjugating one's own rights to help others** describes what occurs when a worker practices self-sacrifice. For example, when a fire destroyed the textile factory of Malden Mills, CEO Aaron Feuerstein refused to lay off his workers, instead paying $20 million of their salaries from his own pocket. Malden told the news media the workers were "part of the enterprise, not a cost center to be cut. They've been with me for a long time. We've been good to each other, and there's a deep realization of that."[9]

False Exits

False exits are popular ways out of ethical dilemmas. Although widespread, customary, and/or clever, they are erroneous. Let's look at two of the most prevalent kinds of false exits.

The Danger of Dual Morality

According to some people (notably, many Christians), John D. Rockefeller Sr. was the most admired man of his time. However, he also was one of the most hated men in the business world. This occurred because morally he seemed to live in two different worlds.

At home, Rockefeller was a loving father who attended church regularly, taught Bible studies, and contributed substantially to Christian colleges. But at work, he was one of the most shrewd and unscrupulous businessmen of his era. Not above sending gangs of thugs to punish striking employees mercilessly, Rockefeller was once described as "a conscientious Christian who struggled to end the livelihood of his every rival."[10]

Rockefeller's proclivity to behave one way at home and another way at work has been labeled "dual morality." This is because he appeared to live by two separate moral codes—the morals he modeled at home and in church, and the morals he practiced in business.

Dual morality can be tempting, for businesspeople often will lament that "it's a dog-eat-dog world out there, and you have to bend the rules to compete." This perspective often is described as a "false-exit" because it offers a false and misleading exit to an ethical dilemma.

One consequence of dual morality is the muddy conception of right and wrong that emerges from those who witness the divergent worlds of a dual moralist. John D. Rockefeller Sr.'s son, John D. Rockefeller Jr., spent much of his life trying to undo his father's dual legacy. Continuing his father's generosity to Christian charities, Rockefeller Jr. attempted to treat his employees and competitors more fairly than his father had done. In the end, his heritage as a Rockefeller nullified most of his good work. The reputation of Rockefellers as ruthless and unscrupulous businessmen followed John D. Rockefeller Jr. for most of his life.

Losses That Result from Dual Morality

Dual morality often results in losses in three areas:

1. *Loss of respect*. As we saw from the story of John D. Rockefeller Jr., those that witness a dual moralist's world often become disenchanted and lose respect for that individual. Jesus' harshest words were reserved for the Pharisees. These religious leaders practiced dual morality to such an extent that Jesus said, "Woe to you, teachers of the law and Pharisees, you hypocrites! . . . on the outside you appear to people as righteous but on the inside you are full of hypocrisy and wickedness" (Matthew 23:27-28).

2. *Loss of consistency*. With dual morality, a person becomes ethically bipolar. The concern is that a dual moralist will lapse into the other side of their moral universe at inopportune times. This may be inadvertent or intentional. John D. Rockefeller Sr. often shortchanged his sons' weekly allowances to teach them to be vigilant. He said, "I cheat my boys every chance I get. I want to keep them sharp."[11]

3. *Loss of pleasing God*. Dual morality displeases God. Jesus left no room for doubt when He said, "Do not do what they do, for they do not practice what they preach" (Matthew 23:3).

The Erroneous Avenue of Agency

A second false exit is known as agency. Agency occurs when an individual claims to be an "agent" of another person and, thus, cannot be held accountable for an unethical action required by a superior.

Agency was regarded as a legitimate excuse in feudal times and as interpreted by early English law. Over time, agency became less acceptable as an excuse for unethical behavior, especially as abuses proliferated. Probably the most heinous example of agency as a false exit occurred during the Nuremberg Trials following World War 2. When Nazi officers excused their actions under the guise of agency, the general consensus ushered in the end of agency as an acceptable exit for ethical dilemmas. Agency violates Christian principles on at least two levels.

"The soul who sins is the one who will die."

Individuals are responsible for their own actions, even if these actions are conducted at the behest of others. The Bible makes that clear. An adage popular in biblical times states, "The fathers eat sour grapes, and the children's teeth are set on edge" (Ezekiel 18:2b). Roughly paraphrased, this means that persons customarily blame their actions and/or weaknesses on their ancestors and those who raised them. God adamantly counters, "As surely as I live, declares the Sovereign LORD, you will no longer quote this proverb in Israel. For every living soul belongs to me, the father as well as the son—both alike belong to me. The soul who sins is the one who will die." (18:3b-4). Thus, God directly and firmly declares that individuals, and not scapegoats, will be expected to bear the full weight of their choices.

"We must obey God rather than men."

When human directives are contrary to Scripture or natural law, individuals are required to obey God instead of humans. Daniel and his colleagues refused on numerous occasions to contradict their religious beliefs, even when ordered by their captors (Daniel 1:8-21; 3:1?4:3; 6.1-28). Likewise, as he stood before the Jewish High Court, Peter began his defense with this statement: "We must obey God rather than men!" (Acts 5:29)

Three Management Theories

To understand how to avoid false exits, we first must grasp three broad categories of management style.

Theory X: Scientific Management

At the turn of the nineteenth century, as an interest in scientific investigation increased, a parallel interest also arose—how to apply science to management. Popularized by mechanical engineer Fredrick Taylor, this management approach attempted to "engineer" better productivity. In other words, for the sake of efficiency, management was to focus on accomplishing a job in the most expeditious manner possible. Labeled "scientific management," this strategy is best summarized in Taylor's words: "The worker must be trimmed to fit the job."[12] This implied refitting the employee to a more efficient way of doing things.

Scientific management was later dubbed Theory X, an approach that placed job efficiency above employee satisfaction. In addition, rigorous analysis was applied to gauge employee performance and confirm efficiency. In many scenarios, the work hour was divided into six-minute periods, allowing management to closely monitor and measure employee performance. Enthusiastically embraced by factories across America, Theory X management essentially viewed the worker as just another cog in the machine, a cog that must be continually analyzed and adjusted to elicit optimum performance.

As a result, the value and clout of the employee suffered. Taylor referred to employees as "more or less a type of ox, heavy both mentally and physically."[13] He stressed that while in the past "the man had been first, in the future the system must be first."[14]Needless to say, Theory X undercut the Christian principle of justice, and led to widespread employee absenteeism and dissatisfaction.

Theory Y: Human Resource Management

Into this milieu came researcher Elton Mayo, whose experiments demonstrated that whenever employees were shown genuine care and encouragement, their productivity increased.[15] Mayo's conclusions were expanded by psychologist Fredrick Herzberg, whose own experiments demonstrated that responsibility, recognition, and opportunity increased employee satisfaction and productivity.[16]

By the 1960s Douglas McGregor coined the terms Theory X and Theory Y to stress the differences between the Taylor and Mayo-Herzberg approaches. Theory Y, as the Mayo-Herzberg position was dubbed, viewed the employee as a valuable resource that must be managed and handled in much the same way as any other precious resource. The importance of "human resources" in Theory Y management eventually led to what we now know as Human Resource (HR) management.

Although the HR approach is embraced by most companies today, nonetheless it views humans as something less than *imago Deo* (being created in the divine image of God). In the HR world of Theory Y, humans are still commodities—resources to be managed, developed, and even discarded if necessary.

Theory C: Covenantal Management

Into this tussle between management styles came the gregarious and well-liked leader of the Herman Miller Company, Max DePree. As CEO of this successful furniture manufacturer and Fortune 500 company, DePree was known for advocating "covenant relationships" between the company's employees and managers.[17]

Alexander Hill calls this management style "covenantal management," for at its root is the idea of mutual agreements, promises, or covenants between two entities. In a "covenantal management" scenario, the employee and employer demonstrate "right, just, and love" actions by making and keeping mutual promises in their dealings and strategies. In Hill's words, "Covenantal management . . . (calls) on employers to demonstrate *holiness* through purity, mutual accountability and humility; *justice* through rewarding merit, compensating for harm done, recognizing substantive rights and honoring procedural rights; and *love* through empathy, mercy and sacrifice" (italics Hill).[18]

An Eye-Opening Comparison

If we look at the justice component of Alexander Hill's three-legged stool of ethical decision-making, we will gain a better idea of how covenantal management works in relationship to the fair treatment of salaries. For example, fair reward for merit was evident in executive salaries at Herman Miller. Lynn Sharp Paine, the John G. McLean Professor at the Harvard School of Business, noted that "while at Herman Miller, Max DePree capped his annual income to 20 times the amount earned by his average factory employees. Contrast this with other Fortune 500 CEOs whose salaries averaged 117 times more than their workers."[19] In Figure 2.4., Lee A. Craig, Professor of Economics at North Carolina State University, presents an eye-opening comparison of executive compensation packages.[20]

Figure 2.4 • A Comparison of Executive Compensation Packages and the Workforce Environment

- **Jack Welch**, former CEO for GE. Welch receives a $10 million per year pension payment, even though GE has not contributed to its employees' pension plan since 1987.
- **Kenneth Lay**, former CEO of Enron. Lay cashed in $12.3 million in stock options in 2000, while other company workers were forbidden to sell the Enron stock in their retirement 401(k)s.
- **Gary Winnick**, former CEO of Global Crossing. Winnick cashed in $123 million in stocks in 2002, while other company workers were forbidden to sell the Global Crossings stock in their 401(k)s.
- **Dennis Kozlowski**, former CEO of Tyco. Kozlowski and his chief financial officer cashed out $500 million in stock shares, as the company slashed 11,000 jobs.

Source: Lee A. Craig, "Capitalism Isn't Always Pretty," *The Raleigh/Durham News and Observer* (Raleigh, NC: Raleigh/Durham N&O, 2003), August 11, 2002.

A Concept of Persons

Covenantal management exemplifies empathy and self-sacrifice by helping employees develop their gifts and talents. DePree puts it this way:

"It is fundamental that leaders endorse a concept of persons. This begins with an understanding of the diversity of people's gifts and talents and skills. . . . Trust and human dignity provide the opportunity for personal development. . . . Leaders owe people the sense of freedom of enabling gifts to be exercised."[21]

The principles of covenantal management are embraced by organizations such as Marriott International. As a hotelier, Marriott relies on low-wage workers who typically spend less than a year on the job. Donna Kline, director of work/life initiatives for Marriott, looked for a way to reduce this turnover. She discovered that most employees left their jobs due to personal problems. To address their needs, she set up a multi-lingual 24-hour hotline staffed by social workers to help employees. As a result, in five years Marriott's' one-year turnover rate had decreased to 35%, in an industry where the average approaches 100%.[22]

Heroic Leadership

The idea of covenantal management is not new, although the term is fairly recent. In his presidential address to the Society for Business Ethics, John Boatright called covenantal management the "Moral Management Model."[23] Lynne Paine calls it an "integrity strategy" in which ethics and empathy are the "driving force" behind an organization.[24] Joanne Cuilla and Al Gini assert that ethics are the real heart of leadership.[25] And John Hood, former president of the John Locke Foundation, a nonprofit think tank based in Raleigh, North Carolina, even argues that the moral/covenantal model is the fundamental spirit of what he calls "heroic" leadership.[26]

If ethicists call for such empathetic and covenantal management to be at the heart of strategic business practices, how much more should it be at the heart of the Church and her para-church offspring?

The Value of Ethical Behavior

Norman Bowie, the William L. Andersen Chair of Corporate Responsibility at the University of Minnesota, has correlated some of the benefits of ethical behavior and business success.[27] While this study examines secular businesses, the potential impact on religious endeavors is clear. If these principles bring heightened respect, growth, and unity to disheveled secular corporations, how much more should ethical behavior be reflected in a church or church organization? Let's look at four distinct benefits of ethical behavior, as Bowie sees it.

1. Ethical behavior reduces the cost of doing business.

By this, Bowie means that payments are made on time, supplies arrive on schedule, and a person's word is considered dependable. Thus, when a secular or religious organization states it will pay its bill on a certain date, the vendor can rely on the truthfulness of that promise. The vendor will not need to artificially add interest or service charges to cover anticipated delays in payments.

An editorial in *The Economist* points out that ethics lead to more trust and interdependence, which allows organizations to grow and flourish:

Most academic studies of the association between responsible corporate ethics and profitability suggest that the two will often go together. Researchers have managed to show that more ethically sensitive sales staff perform better . . .; that shared prices decline after reports of unethical conduct; and that companies which state an ethical commitment to stakeholders in their annual reports do better financially."[28]

2. Ethical behavior builds trust among stakeholders.

Bowie points out that people want to be part of an organization they can trust. This expectation may even be more pronounced in the church, where people expect a higher level of loyalty and interdependence. This atmosphere of trust created by ethical behavior extends to all levels of the organization. This means that frontline workers do not have to be rigorously monitored, since responsible behavior is modeled for them by superiors. Manuel Velasquez, the Dirksen Professor of Business Ethics at Santa Clara University, states, "Because trust flourishes in the caring organization, the organization does not have to invest resources in monitoring its employees and trying to make sure that they do not violate their contractual agreements. Thus, caring lowers the cost of running an organization."[29]

3. Ethical behavior avoids the free-riding problem.

The free-riding problem, sometimes called social loafing, occurs when certain individuals do not carry their weight because they know others on the team will pick up the slack. As a result, certain individuals may "free ride" on the energies of more motivated employees. W. L. Gore & Associates, Inc., manufacturer of the well-known "GORE-TEX" fabric, has almost eliminated free riding by utilizing "sponsors." Sponsors work closely with individual employees to help them develop their full potential as human beings and workers. These sponsors even act as "advocates" for employees before a compensation team (comprised of fellow employees) who recommend compensation levels.[30] W. L. Gore & Associates, Inc. has found, as have many other businesses, that when team members are encouraged to embrace the humility, fair action, and empathy of the three-legged stool model, then free riding can be eliminated.

4. Ethical behavior preserves social capital.

By "social" capital, Bowie means the goodwill generated by a company. And since "capital" designates a surplus, "social capital" connotes an organization in which a surplus of goodwill toward all stakeholders makes the organization an enjoyable place to work and do business. Social capital also should be readily evident in the church.

The Value of Accountability

In the *Journal of Business Ethics*, Clint Longenecker, the Stranahan Professor of Leadership and Organizational Excellence at the University of Toledo, and D. C. Ludwig argue that all leaders need accountability because of what they call the "Bathsheba Syndrome."[31] By this, Ludwig and Longenecker mean that a byproduct of a leader's success is usually unrestrained control and access to the company's resources. This too often leads to temptation, which can result in a subsequent action to misappropriate company resources. Ludwig and Longenecker see a biblical parallel in 2 Samuel 11:1—12:25, which details how King David of Israel was tempted by Bathsheba and then acted on that temptation by committing adultery with her.

Ludwig and Longenecker point out that unrestrained access to a company's resources and the temptation to behave unethically can be eradicated in part by an accountability system. An effective accountability committee or ethical audit can help thwart unethical behavior by warning the leader of the temptation's ramifications before the unethical behavior occurs.

In the business world, oversight and accountability committees can take many forms: ethics committees, social responsibility committees, ethics advisory boards, or judicial boards. Other control devices are social and ethical audits. However, the common denominator of these various forms is to provide advice and oversight in ethical accountability.

A Moral Compass

In the church context, a committee structure is customarily employed to manage the organization. However, the committee often abdicates its duty to provide ethical advice, guidance, and accountability. This is because the pastor (or pastors) is often regarded as a moral thinker, model, and champion. Thus, the committee eschews the thought of offering moral accountability—after all, isn't the pastor supposed to be the moral compass of the congregation?

Earning the Public's Trust: ECFA

To create or reengineer a capable accountability team, it is first advisable to examine how other organizations have successfully integrated accountability systems. One of the finest patterns for Christian accountability can be found in the Evangelical Council for Financial Accountability (ECFA). ECFA was founded in 1979 to help ensure the integrity of Christ-centered organizations that are qualified for nonprofit, tax-exempt status. Today, over 1,000 Christian organizations submit to the annual evaluation and approval process established by ECFA—resulting in a powerful collective testimony of accountability before God and man.

To support this mission, ECFA requires its members to adhere to seven "standards of accountability." These standards are applicable as guidelines for churches and many other religious organizations. We will list the ECFA Standards below, followed by our commentary:

STANDARD #1 – Doctrinal Statement: Every member organization shall subscribe to a written statement of faith clearly affirming its commitment to the evangelical Christian faith and shall conduct its financial and other operations in a manner that reflects those generally accepted Biblical truths and practices.

Commentary: As an organization that aligns itself with the "evangelical" wing of Christianity, the ECFA logically requires assent to an evangelical doctrinal statement.

STANDARD #2 – Board of Directors and Audit Review Committee: Every member organization shall be governed by a responsible board of not less than five individuals, a majority of whom shall be other than employees/staff and/or those related by blood or marriage, which shall meet at least semi-annually to establish policy and review its accomplishments. The board shall appoint a functioning audit review committee, a majority of whom shall be other than employees/staff and/or those related by blood or marriage, for the purpose of reviewing the annual audit and reporting its findings to the board.

Commentary: Here is a key lesson for any church seeking to thwart the "Bathsheba Syndrome." ECFA requires a sizable board ("not less than five"), a majority of whom are independent ("other than employees/staff and/or those related by blood or marriage"), which regularly meets to establish and review policy, and who oversee a "functioning audit review committee" with similar constraints on makeup and responsibility. Although this committee is designed to ensure financial accountability, its structure and makeup also can serve as a model for ethics committees.

STANDARD #3 – Audited Financial Statements: Every member organization shall obtain an annual audit performed by an independent certified public accounting firm in accordance with generally accepted auditing standards (GAAS) with financial statements prepared in accordance with generally accepted accounting principles (GAAP).

Commentary: In the financial world, a fiscal audit is routine. In the ethical realm, a social or ethical audit is becoming more commonplace. However, in the church, a social or ethical audit is rarely considered. Just as businesses have discovered the value of having an outside and independent organization audit or review their moral decisions, churches too can benefit from the value of yearly ethical or social audits. More and more denominations are offering these services, and a growing number of consultants affiliated with the American Society for Church Growth (ASCG) offer independent and effective social and ethical audits.)[32]

STANDARD #4 – Use of Resources: Every member organization shall exercise management and financial controls necessary to provide reasonable assurance that all resources are used (nationally and internationally) to accomplish the exempt purposes for which they are intended.

Commentary: The nonprofit status of many religious organizations can be jeopardized by unethical or erroneous behavior. Accountability committees must ensure that the church complies not only with moral law, but with legal requirements as well.

STANDARD #5 - Financial Disclosure: Every member organization shall provide a copy of its current audited financial statements upon written request.

Commentary: Disclosure of auditing procedures, both financial and moral, gives congregants and the community a sense of security, confidence, and authenticity.

STANDARD #6 - Conflicts of Interest: Every member organization shall avoid conflicts of interest. Transactions with related parties may be undertaken only if all of the following are observed: (1) a material transaction is fully disclosed in the audited financial statements of the organization; (2) the related party is excluded from the discussion and approval of such transaction; (3) a competitive bid or comparable valuation exists; and (4) the organization's board has acted upon and demonstrated that the transaction is in the best interest of the member organization.

Commentary: Conflicts of interest occur in all areas of business and church life. They often take the form of prohibited relationships and/or collaboration between employee-employee, employee-employer, subordinate-superior, etc. These relationships undermine clearheaded thinking due to the enticement and allure of the "Bathsheba Syndrome."

STANDARD #7 - Fund-Raising: Every member organization shall comply with each of the ECFA Standards for Fund-Raising.

Commentary: EFCA concludes with eleven subsections on fund-raising, an easily abused practice. Due to space limitations, we are not including these subsections here. For more specific information on ECFA's fund-raising guidelines, as well as additional information on ECFA and its goals, visit the ECFA web site.[33]

Mission Driven – Values Centered

Elsewhere in this book, we discuss the need for organization to be driven by mission/vision statements that encapsulate corporate attitudes and aspirations. Most companies (and churches) cannot flourish without being able to articulate their mission and/or vision. The same also can be said of those companies and churches without core values at the center of their mission/vision.

Medtronic of Minneapolis, Minnesota, is continually recognized as one of today's most ethically conscientious and morally responsible companies. Chairman and CEO William George states, "The subject of building a mission-driven and values-centered organization is near to my heart. I call this leadership with purpose, meaning leadership with vision, passion, and compassion"[34] George goes on to summarize Medtronic's six core values:

- contribute to human welfare
- focused growth
- unsurpassed quality
- fair profit
- personal worth of employees
- good citizenship[35]

These values are expressed in Medtronic's ethical decisions. According to George:

The mission weighs heavily on our ethical decisions, such as my decision to terminate the president of Europe for covering up a 'promotional fund' for an Italian distributor, or our decision to cease operations at a small acquisition in California where we had uncovered fraud.[36]

Such deployment of core values into concrete action has ingratiated Medtronic to both Wall Street and Main Street. Medtronic is an example of what happens when an ethical mission drives an organization. These same strategic lessons, principles, and guidelines can help a church or church-based organization more competently and successfully navigate the murky but unavoidable waters of ethical behavior.

Endnotes

1. Geoffrey P. Lantos, "Motivating Moral Behavior," *Journal of Consumer Marketing* 16, no. 3 (1999): 222.

2. Fred R. David, *Strategic Management: Concepts and Cases* (Upper Saddle River: NJ: Prentice Hall, 2003), 20.

3. Raymond Baumhart, *An Honest Profit: What Businessmen Say About Ethics in Business* (New York: Holt, Rinehart and Wilson, 1968), 11-12. For the student interested in a more recent update (and confirmation) of Baumhart's conclusions, see Steven N. Brenner and Earl A. Molander's article, "Is the Ethics of Business Changing?" in *Harvard Business Review* 55, no. 1 (January/February 1977): 57-71.

4. As quoted by Ed L. Miller, *Questions That Matter: An Invitation to Philosophy,* 4th ed. (New York: McGraw-Hill, 1996), 206. See also Alvin Plantinga's excellent deconstruction of Richard Rorty's relativistic beliefs in "The Twin Pillars of Christian Scholarship," *The Stob Lectures of Calvin College and Seminary* (Grand Rapids, MI: Calvin College Press, 1990), 1989-90.

5. Alexander Hill, *Just Business: Christian Ethics for the Marketplace* (Downers Grove, IL: InterVarsity Press, 1997), 22-57.

6. Jim Collins, *Good to Great: Why Some Companies Make the Leap . . . and Others Don't* (New York: Harper Collins Publishers, 2001), 133.

7. Norman E. Bowie, "Companies Are Discovering the Value of Ethics," *Annual Editions 02/03,* ed. John E. Richardson (Guilford CT: McGraw-Hill/Dushkin, 2002), 158-60.

8. Tom Peters, *The Pursuit of Wow! Every Person's Guide to Topsy-Turvy Times* (New York: Random House Publishers, 1994), 130.

9. Manuel G. Velasquez, *Business Ethics: Concepts and Cases*, 5th ed. (Upper Saddle River, NJ: Prentice Hall, 2003), 122-24, 491-92.

10. George A. Steiner and John F. Steiner, *Business, Government, and Society* (New York: Random House, 1985), 333.

11. Ibid., 27.

12. As quoted in Daniel J. Boorstin, *The Americans: The Democratic Experience* (New York: Vintage Press, 1974), 368-69.

13. Ibid., 363.

14. Ibid., 368.

15. Ibid., p. 369.

16. John Haggai, "Biblical Principles Applied to Organizational Behavior," in *Biblical Principles and Business,* ed. Richard Chewning, 3 vols. (Colorado Springs: NavPress, 1991), 3:131.

17. Max DePree, *Leadership Is an Art* (East Lansing, MI.: Michigan State University Press, 1987), xi-xxiii.

18. Hill, *Just Business*, 156.

19. Lynn Sharp Paine, "Managing for Organizational Integrity," *Harvard Business Review* (March 1994): 115-16.

20. Lee A. Craig, "Capitalism Isn't Always Pretty," *The Raleigh/Durham News and Observer*, August 11, 2002.

21. DePree, *Leadership*, 9, 16.

22. Bennett Daviss, "Profits from Principle: Five Forces Redefining Business," *Annual Editions 01/02*, ed. John E. Richardson, (Guilford, Conn.: McGraw-Hill/Dushkin, 2001), pp. 207-212.

23. John R. Boatright, "Does Business Ethics Rest on a Mistake?" (San Diego: Society for Business Ethics Presidential Address, August 6-9, 1998).

24. Lynn Sharp Paine, "Managing for Organizational Integrity," 106-117.

25. Joanne B. Ciulla, ed., *Ethics, the Heart of Leadership* (Westport: CT: Praeger Press, 1998), and Al Gine, "Moral Leadership and Business Ethics," in *Ethics, the Heart of Leadership*, 27-45.

26. John Hood, *The Heroic Enterprise: Business and the Common Good* (New York: The Free Press, 1996).

27. Norman E. Bowie, "Companies Are Discovering the Value of Ethics," 158-60.

28. Editorial, *The Economist* (New York: New York Times Publishing, 2000), April 22, 2000:66-67.

29. Velasquez, *Business Ethics*, 492.

30. Ibid., 493.

31. Dean C. Ludwig and Clinton O. Longenecker, "The Bathsheba Syndrome: The Ethical Failure of Successful Leaders," *Journal of Business Ethics*, no. 12 (1993): 265-73.

32. For more information on social or ethical audits conducted by members of the American Society for Church Growth, see their web site at www.ascg.org .

33. For more about the Evangelical Council for Financial Accountability, see their website at www.ccfa.org .

34. William W. George, "Mission Driven, Values Centered," *Annual Editions 01/02*, ed. John E. Richardson (Guilford, CT: McGraw-Hill/Dushkin, 2001), 186.

35. George, 187.

36. Ibid.

3

What Church Leader's Need to Know About . . .

The Legal Environment

Understanding the Basics

"Let the wise listen and add to their learning,
and let the discerning get guidance."

—PROVERBS 1:5 NIV

At a Loss for Words

Pastor Joe Benson has been in the ministry for the past twenty years. Over the course of his ministry, numerous people have consulted him about a variety of issues, some of which involve legal implications. Two attorneys attend Pastor Joe's church. One is an assistant district attorney; the other is a local practitioner with a small law firm. Pastor Joe never took a law course during his undergraduate or graduate studies. Whenever he converses with the attorneys—either in casual conversation or when consulting them about a church-related matter—he often feels at a loss to understand their terminology. Given Pastor Joe's many ministry responsibilities and the church's plans for expansion, he wonders if it would be wise to learn more about the law.

An Overview of the Law

P astor Joe's situation is not that uncommon. Many church pastors have never learned the basics of the law, the American legal system, and legal terminology. This chapter will provide an overview of these areas, helping to familiarize pastors with some key aspects of the law. There is one important caveat, however. No chapter or book can ever substitute for counsel from a licensed attorney. When confronted with a legal matter, pastors should always seek legal counsel. These are the topics discussed:

- the legal system
- ethics
- alternative dispute resolution
- civil procedure
- torts
- criminal law
- contracts

- sales
- forms of doing business
- real property
- insurance
- bankruptcy
- employment law

My discussion of these topics includes frequent references to Scripture. Where these Scriptures are not spelled out in the text, I urge the reader to look up and study these passages.

The Legal System

"Everyone must submit himself to the governing authorities, for there is no authority except that which God has established. The authorities that exist have been established by God" (Romans 13:1).

Romans 13:1-6 teaches the primary function of government is law enforcement. Exodus 18 explains that Moses was instructed by his father-in-law to establish a justice system to decide disputes that arose. I Corinthians 6:1-8 provides instructions to Christians who are considering suing other Christians.

Generally speaking, the American legal system is a tripartite system. On both a state and federal level, litigation begins in a lower court, progresses to an appellate court, and ends at a supreme court. In the federal legal system, these courts are called District Courts, Courts of Appeal, and the Supreme Court. In the various states, the names of the courts vary.

When the United States Supreme Court issues an opinion, it is generally binding on all citizens. When a federal Court of Appeals issues an opinion, it is only binding on the citizens in that particular circuit. When a federal District Court issues an opinion, it is only binding on the citizens in that particular district. When a state court issues an opinion, it is binding on its citizens only.

When a judge issues an opinion, it becomes precedent. If a case arises that is similar to a case that already has been decided, a court will usually follow the opinion in the prior case. This principle is known as *stare decisis*, which literally means "to stand on the decided case."

Much of our law is statutory and it derives from a federal, state, or local legislature. If a municipality enacts a law, it is called an ordinance. Other sources of law include case law, the United States Constitution, state constitutions, and administrative agency (federal, state, and local) rules and regulations.

The law can be classified in a number of ways: civil and criminal; national and international; and substantive and procedural. Most individuals categorize the law in the civil/criminal classification scheme: anything outside criminal law is civil law. *Criminal law* usually involves the commission of a crime against a person, although the matter is dealt with by the government against the alleged perpetrator. *Civil law* involves matters between individuals, in which one individual sues the other.

According to 1 Corinthians 6:1-6, Christians are forbidden to sue other Christians. One of the downsides of such suits is that the heathen will end up judging the matter (v.6). Paul admonishes the aggrieved party to take the loss instead. What, then, should Christians do? The answer lies in Matthew 18:15-18, which outlines a three-step process for handling disputes.

1. Step one involves having the aggrieved individual (party #1) confront the individual who caused the harm (party #2).
2. If this doesn't work, then party #1 should proceed to step two, which involves confronting party #2 in the presence of a witness.
3. If party #1 is still not satisfied, then the matter should be brought before the congregation.

Pastors should teach these scriptural principles to their congregations and apply them when they are asked for pastoral advice.

Ethics

"We will never find any basis for charges against this man Daniel unless it has something to do with the law of his God" (Daniel 6:5).

The Bible is replete with ethical dilemmas. One of the best known is recorded in Daniel 6. When Daniel assumed his position in the Babylonian government, some government officials became jealous and tried to subvert his authority. They were successful in their efforts to get the king to issue a decree that would outlaw prayer to any god or man except King Darius. The consequence for violating this decree was to be cast into a lion's den. Daniel was well aware of the decree. He had a choice: either obey the decree and cease praying to God, or pray to God in violation of the decree. Daniel defied the decree.

Torts

"You have laid down precepts that are to be fully obeyed" (Psalm 119:40).

A *tort* is a civil wrong that causes harm to another. Civil wrongs usually involve a request by the party bringing the action for monetary relief, such as compensatory damages. The purpose of tort law is to restore a person to the position before the tort occurred. The person committing the tort is known as the tortfeasor.

The Old Testament is filled with examples of torts. Leviticus 19:16 offers an injunction against slander. In Nehemiah 6:5-8, Nehemiah responds to Sanballat's libelous message.

There are three main categories of torts:

- intentional
- negligence
- strict liability

Intentional Torts

Intentional torts involve situations in which the tortfeasor intends to bring about the consequences of his/her action. Intentional torts are wide ranging. The most common intentional torts are defamation, appropriation, fraud, intentional infliction of emotional distress, and trespass.

Defamation involves slander (spoken defamation) and libel (written defamation). Defamation involves the wrongful injuring of a person's reputation and requires that the statement be made to a third party. In most cases, if what was said is true, defamation has not occurred.

Appropriation occurs when someone uses a person's name or likeness for commercial purposes, without first obtaining that person's permission. If a well-known shoe company uses a famous athlete's picture in its sneaker advertisements without asking the athlete for permission to run the ad, that shoe company is committing appropriation.

Fraud involves deceit that causes injury to another party. A car dealer who sells a used car with its odometer rolled back 20,000 miles could be liable to the purchaser of the vehicle.

Intentional infliction of emotional distress occurs when the tortfeasor commits an act that causes severe emotional distress to someone. The law requires the act to be so outrageous as to be beyond the bounds of civilized society. If an individual posing as a police officer calls a woman and falsely informs her that her husband has been fatally injured in a work-related accident, the individual is intentionally inflicting emotional distress.

Trespass normally involves land. A trespass occurs when someone enters another person's property without obtaining the owner's permission. Driving on someone's land is another example.

Negligence

The second category of intentional torts is negligence. Negligence occurs when someone's conduct falls short of what is expected and subsequently causes injury to someone else. Car accidents and medical malpractice are common examples of negligence.

Strict liability

The third category of intentional torts is strict liability. Strict liability is liability without regard to fault. In other words, the court will find a tortfeasor automatically liable for his/her actions. If, for example, your neighbor's pet panther were to escape, the neighbor would be strictly liable for any harm caused to your child. A more common example of strict liability involves product liability. In general, if you were to purchase a defective and dangerous product, and you were harmed by the product during normal use, the manufacturer would be strictly liable for your damages.

Criminal Law

"Consequently, he who rebels against the authority is rebelling against what God has instituted, and those who do so will bring judgment on themselves" (Romans 13:2).

The primary function of government is law enforcement (Romans 13:1-6). God has ordained government to punish evildoers. The purpose of criminal law is punishment. Punishment includes fines, imprisonment and even death. A crime is prosecuted by a prosecutor. Locally this person may be called the district attorney. At the state and federal levels, this individual is often called the attorney general.

The standard by which the government must prove its case is high: guilt beyond a reasonable doubt. Crimes are classified as felonies and misdemeanors. What distinguishes felonies from misdemeanors is the seriousness of the crime. Felonies usually involve imprisonment of more than a year.

To be convicted of a crime, the alleged perpetrator must commit an act that is prohibited by the statute. The perpetrator also must have the requisite state of mind. In the past, corporations were not considered individuals and, thus, did not have the requisite state of mind to commit a crime. Under modern criminal law, corporations may be held liable for certain crimes.

Common defenses to crimes include citing intoxication, insanity, duress, justifiable use of force, and status as a minor. The Constitution contains various criminal law safeguards, the most common can be found in the fourth, fifth, sixth, and eighth amendments. State constitutions provide similar safeguards.

4

What Church Leader's Need to Know About . . .

Globalization

Managing Change with Authenticity

"Globalization is the spread of . . . innovations around the world and the political and cultural adjustments that accompany this diffusion."[1]

—MICHAEL A. HITT, R. DUANE IRELAND, AND ROBERT E. HOSKISSON
STRATEGIC MANAGEMENT: COMPETITIVENESS AND GLOBALIZATION

It was Sunday morning in early December and Community Church was on a countdown to Christmas. Children from the first and second grades were to present a program during the service. Pastor Bob had prepared a sermon on the Bible as truth, aimed at the children's parents. He knew that most of these parents did not attend church and had very little in the way of a church background.

Unfortunately, the children sang songs that were old, boring, and slow. The lyrics included "thees" and "thou," outdated terms that were beyond the vernacular of these unchurched parents. In his twenty-ninth year of ministry, Pastor Bob was considered to be an excellent preacher. It was obvious that the fifty-six-year-old seminary graduate didn't grasp how postmoderns think. He preached about how some believe in relative truth. He claimed the Bible is *the* truth. He talked about the Bible as the only way to understand God. He explained the need for repentance, confession, and following Jesus.

Postmodern people do not accept unconditional authority from anywhere or anyone unless this authority can be clearly defined and defended. They are looking for something in which to believe but saying it is so doesn't make it so. Pastor Bob was right . . . and wrong. He was right about the truth; he was wrong about how his postmodern, unchurched audience would receive his message. These concepts were as foreign to his special guests as if he were speaking Swahili.

The Church Fell Asleep

Where did Bob go wrong? Has the church been asleep for the last forty to fifty years? Bob is intelligent, a great pastor, and a wonderful guy. The parents and relatives of children were people for whom the church was meeting a need. They showed up. They brought cameras. They were open to hear what Bob had to say. But he didn't even come close in content or style to speaking their language.

In the area of preaching, Bob appears to be unaware that it is no longer 1972. Like many churches, Community Church is operating in a time warp. Unchurched people who come to a quick, subconscious conclusion: the church is irrelevant.

In the last half century, the world has experienced the most dramatic pace of globalization in human history. However, the church too often has not kept up with this rapid change. Instead, it has been caught napping—and so has Bob. What can you as a pastor do to get out of the time warp?

An Incarnational Prerequisite

Know your audience. Most church guests are irreligious people who don't know the language of the church. Some are new Christians who have a relationship with Jesus, but don't know the language either. These people need a cultural translation. Divine truths must be translated into everyday language. Theologically, it's an incarnational prerequisite. We must teach our people to absolutely understand that Jesus Christ of Nazareth was the full embodiment of God.

Your audience consists of postmoderns. Postmodern people think differently and process information differently. The entry point for the Gospel is not to prove to them the Bible is true. That doesn't work because most postmoderns don't believe in absolute truth. What is true for one person is different for someone else. And both are acceptable, because truth is defined by the individual.

Do we reach postmoderns by telling them that the Scripture is just one truth of many? Of course not! But because they will view any discussion about Bible truth as irrelevant, that is not an *entry point* to them. The entry point for postmoderns is to answer questions like these: "Does it work? Does it make any difference in my life?" To this they will listen. This will grab their attention and help them begin their journeys. Later they will discover what all mature Christians know: The Bible is *the* truth.

Part of your audience is the millennial generation, those born after 1985. What grabs them? They want to see Christians demonstrate a genuine and authentic faith. They want to see Christianity in action. When people say "God is love," are they demonstrating that love with the less fortunate? The postmodern side of your audience wants to *know* that Christianity works. The millennial side wants to *see* Christianity at work. Our rapidly changing world requires you as a pastor to become an aggressive student of reality. Not only do you need to be aware of the changes that are taking place on the planet, but you also have to process this information so that you begin to architecturally impact the way you "do church."

This Changing World

In the past fifty years, the world has moved from a mysterious, little known, faraway, large, and overwhelming entity—to something different. The term "global village" has become real. The Internet and mass media have obliterated space, time, and distance. That foreign, strange, mysterious place is now what you watch and learn about on the Discovery Channel. You see it on CNN News. You correspond with someone through E-mail. You call someone on the other side of the globe and speak to them as if they were in the next room. The world has changed. It will never be the same.

The Components of Challenge

The Mission Field is Everywhere

The portal to the mission field used to take the form of the denominational mission department, the sent missionary, or the para-church mission agency. These avenues are still in operation, of course, but increasingly that portal for mission is you. You can communicate directly with a missionary anywhere in the world and you can do it in real time. You can go on a ten-day mission trip, simply by getting on a plane and spending a few hours crossing this globe. You are also a missionary as you interact every day with irreligious, unchurched unbelievers in your own community, at work, and at school. Some of them may even be your friends and relatives.

Secularization Has Transformed the West

The secularization of the West means that Christianity no longer dominates cultural values. Christians are now in the minority, but people in the West continue to have a very high interest in spiritual matters. These unchurched people consistently share their perception that the church is irrelevant.

In his book, *The Church in the Postmodern World*, John E. Phelan claims that for years Christians have been slowly eroding into people whose "faith" is nominal and cultural. He claims this is why the church is disappearing so quickly. "Now American Christendom is dead. The State will help the Church do its job . . . the culture no longer wears even a patina of piety. People no longer go to church because it is the thing to do or because people would talk about them. Culturally, we no longer even make a pretense of having a moral consensus. Pluralism, both cultural and religious, is the order of the day. . . . The United States and Canada now constitute one of the world's largest mission fields."[2]

Religious Conflicts Are Global

During this same period of time, world religions have globalized. Most Christians knew little of Islam before the World Trade Center attack on 9/11. Today, religions are seen as the source of world conflicts. Phillip Jenkins details this in *The Next Christendom: The Coming of Global Christianity*:

At the turn of the Third Millennium, religious loyalties are at the root of many of the world's ongoing civil wars and political violence, and in most cases, the critical division is the age-old battle between Christianity and Islam. However much of this would have surprised political analysts a generation or two ago, the critical political frontiers around the world are not decided by attitudes toward class or dialectical materialism, but by rival concepts of God. Across the regions that will be the most populous in this new century, vast religious conflicts and contests are already in progress . . .[3]

Unfortunate but true, Bob and Community Church wouldn't know what to do with Muslim neighbors even if they showed up at church.

Cultures Are Porous

Another dimension of this changing world is that cultures are now porous. They are co-mingled. On every level, people work, play, marry, interact, socialize, and share space with people of other cultures. You may have heard it said, "Everyone has gone everywhere to live." That is true today. This means that Bob and Community Church have a mission investment through their denomination in many countries around the world. It also means that they have an opportunity for world missions in their own city.

The "Isms" the Church Must Address

Another key feature of this changed world is represented by the "isms" that have reconfigured the world as we know it. These are isms that the church cannot ignore and to which the church must speak. Although they are daunting challenges, they present limitless opportunities.

The Changing Landscape: Pluralism

In the last five decades, religious pluralism has dramatically changed the social strata of the West. Countries that previously had many Christian denominations now have many religions. Diana L. Eck says, "The exponential growth of cultures and ethnicities in America has dramatically expanded our diversity, including the diversity of our religious traditions. Yet some of the most vocal secular analysts of America's growing multiculturalism leave religion completely out of the discussion, as if this new period of American immigration had no religious dimensions. . . . Any analysis of civil and political life will have to include religion along with race, ethnicity, and language."[4]

Even in America's heartland, the landscape has changed so dramatically that most pastors and churches would be shocked to see the current demographic profile of, for example, Minneapolis/St. Paul. Traditionally, the Twin Cities were 34 percent Lutheran. Now, these same cities are home to more than 80,000 Asians and Pacific Islanders. Approximately half of those people are refugees, including 14,000 Hmong, 10,000 Vietnamese, 8,000 Lao Buddhists, and 7,000 Cambodians. Their temples are a significant part of the religious texture of the Twin Cities today—along with Islamic Centers, Baha'i communities, and the temples of Minnesota Hindus and Jains.[5]

Choice Mentality: Consumerism

Wealth in the West has resulted in a choice mentality. In a wealthy society, people have more choices. For example, a sixty-five-year-old man who chooses to turn on a television. Next, he can choose to watch a network broadcast, or a cable or satellite feed. Then he must choose from among hundreds of channels. This man's grandfather did not have hundreds of program choices when he was young. In fact, he couldn't make even the first choice—whether or not to turn on the television.

This choice mentality results in what might be called customized lifestyles. Each individual is customizing a personal dream tailored to his or her individual interests.[6] This growing consumerism reflects a change in American life. The one-size-fits-all strategy of producer-driven culture during the first 350 years of U. S. history is being replaced by the consumer-driven demand for customized alternatives.[7]

Reconfiguring Family: Communalism

Another characteristic of our changing world is the redefinition of the basic social unit—the issue of what is a family. Talking about families is confusing at best. Today, people speak not of families, but of households. This is the changing definition and the reconfiguration of "family." Today, the basic unit under one roof is described in many ways. Such factors as divorce, cohabitation, single parenting, blended families, and grandparents raising grandchildren have caused some of these new household forms.[10] The implications for Community Church and others include developing ministries to address child care, parenting classes, relationship counseling, and groups such as Parents Without Partners.

Redefining Safety: Terrorism

The world has changed in a dramatic way because of the recent transitions in the reality of war. Terms like "hot war," "cold war," and "smart bomb" are to the pernicious fear of global war. The efforts of terrorism around the world have redefined war and have caused people to examine the dividing line between religious enthusiasm and religious fanaticism. Terrorism bridges the gap between good and evil. Terrorism has resulted in a redefinition of where and when a person can experience safety. "

While the brutality of terrorism may challenge those who counsel people driven by fear, it also affords opportunities for sharing the Gospel. People under stress are more receptive to the gospel.

Alone in a Crowd: Isolationism

How has technology changed the way people live? Answer that question in light of these realities: microwaves, voice mail, pizza deliveries, Internet, cable/satellite television, DVDs, and video games. What do they have in common? They have equipped people for cocooning. In today's world, you can be alone in a crowd. People live in isolation, even though they may be in a well-populated area.

Many of these people look at the church as being isolated and having little to do with their lives. When the church proclaims a message about salvation, people don't know what that means. They have no interest in finding out. They are consumed with the challenges in their own lives. The church must speak to people at the point of their need. The hearing that the church gains "will be greatly improved if we are able to stay in the life of the listener from beginning to end."[11]

In *Culture Shift,* author David Henderson explains what it means to focus on the receiver. "A man does not come to church asking about the connection between Romans 8 and 9. He comes saying, 'My daughter's going out with a yo-yo and I'm afraid he's going to get her pregnant.' If we talk to secular people about the Bible, we lose them. If we talk to them about themselves from the pages of the Bible, we grab them. Effective communication is not merely telling biblical truth. It is bringing biblical truth to bear in the life of the hearer. Otherwise, the words of the Bible remain dead."[12]

Testimony and Postmodernism

To deal with postmodernism, the church must demonstrate that Christianity makes a difference in peoples' lives. This is a tremendous opportunity for the church to practice what the early church found to be instrumental in spreading the Gospel: the powerful use of testimony. A testimony is simply sharing what God has done to impact your life. It may be an answer to prayer. In Bible classes or fellowship groups, it may mean spending time asking people to share what God has done in their lives during the previous week. This means that evangelism is not a challenging, complex, learned discipline that is restricted to a few people with a special gift. The best evangelism is actually witnessing. It is not memorizing Bible passages or understanding deep theological arguments. It is, instead, in the best sense, a simple, from-the-heart, unrehearsed, nonprofessional telling of your story—what God has done in your life, particularly as it relates to a specific problem or challenge. The good news is that once congregations grasp the significance of this, the evangelism committee in this postmodern age now becomes the entire church simply telling its stories.

Discipleship and Anti-institutionalism

Since Watergate, institutions of all types have become suspect in the eyes of just about everyone. Anti-institutionalism raises challenges for the local church that insists on identifying those connected to an institution. The web of inclusion in the Christian community may require a different paradigm like discipleship or relationship(s), in place of the member-based paradigm associated with institutions.

In his book *Postmoderns*, Craig Miller explains the role of the pastor in the postmodern world in this way:

> . . . to provide the vision, setting, and system in which discipleship can take place. The pastor's job is to be like the webmaster on the Internet, who manages a particular website. The webmaster's job is to create new websites, maintain the sites, and update them continually. In other words, the role of pastoring in the postmodern congregation is not simply to get people to join and then place them on committees and in places of ministry, such as teaching church school. The main task is to create opportunities for discipleship and to develop leadership among the laity, who will in turn lead others to faith and growth as disciples of Christ. . . . The modern approach was to make sure someone was a good member. The postmodern approach is to encourage those who are considering following Jesus Christ to get involved in a lifelong process of personal salvation.[13]

Bridging Ethnocentrism

With an increasing number of immigrants, many immigrants form smaller communities within the larger society. As a result, ethnocentrism can develop in each one of those subcultures. Ethnocentrism results from the socialization process people experience while growing up in their particular culture. The essence of ethnocentrism is the belief that certain things in a culture are right and good, and that behavior that expresses those beliefs is appropriate.[14] In a society with an influx of immigrants, multi-ethnocentrism can be complex and problematic. How does a church reach all these ethnic groups?

Many opportunities arise from this complexity. First, a number of groups have a desire to learn the dominant language. In the U.S. that language is English. English as a Second Language (ESL) classes are great opportunities to help people reach their intended goal and, at the same time, share Christian faith, fellowship, and support. New ethnic groups are receptive to new paradigms, including the Christian faith.

When people are strongly ethnocentric, a bridging strategy is necessary, such as placing an indigenous worker in that ethnic group. However, the opposite strategy is called for when people are enthusiastic about assimilation into the dominant culture and want to mingle with people of other cultures. Diagnosis of the target group is extremely important. That diagnosis will dictate the outreach strategy. Another aspect of the influx of immigrants and ethnocentrism is the high priority that many of the groups place on education for their children. This provides opportunities for churches to operate preschools and elementary schools, also making use of the schools as an evangelistic bridge to share the Gospel.

Reinventing of the Church

What Bob and Community Church need most is a basic reengineering of how they understand church. It is the greatest challenge of church management. Primarily, reinvention means getting back to the basics of what it means to be the church. As John Phelan points out, "Christian hope is not hope in the economy, or hope in the government, or hope in the stock market. . . . Christian hope is hope in Jesus Christ crucified, risen, and coming again. To speak with integrity to this culture, we must put aside 'cheap hope' born of the western ideology of optimism and place our hope in Jesus Christ alone."[15]

The Great Commission

"All authority in heaven and on earth has been given to me. Go therefore and make disciples of all nations, baptizing them in the name of the Father and of the Son and of the Holy Spirit, teaching them to observe all that I have commanded you; and lo, I am with you always to the close of the age" (Matthew 28:18-20 RSV).

Understanding what it means to be the church means taking the Great Commission seriously. When Jesus commissioned His disciples, He called people to go and make disciples of *panta ta enthne*. The *panta ta enthne* are "all the peoples" or "people groups." He then said that the way you make disciples is to baptize them and *to teach them all that I (Christ) have commanded* (v. 20). The challenge to the church is to teach the people in the church all that Christ has commanded. Research has pointed out that among Christians who are active in their churches, only 35 percent understand their purpose as making disciples. The larger group, 67 percent, identify the primary purpose of the church as providing a fellowship for themselves and their fellow members.[16]

Darrow Miller is Vice President of Food for the Hungry, International. Miller spends much of his time teaching about biblical worldview as it relates to the basic purpose of the church and the discipling of nations. Miller says this about the modern church and the biblical paradigm:

> There have never been more Christians, more churches, and more large churches in the world than there are today. We have been successful at doing what we set out to do: save souls and plant churches. And yet our nations continued to be very broken. Why? The church in the 20th Century has largely operated from a dualistic (Gnostic) paradigm. This Gnostic paradigm has shaped what it means to be a Christian, what it means to be the church, and what the role of the church is in society. The church has not been functioning from a biblical paradigm. If the church is not discipling the nation the nation will disciple the church. The church around the world is being defined by its surrounding culture. The church in the West looks not much different than the rest of modernity. The fundamental need of pastors around the world is to begin to understand the power of paradigm and seek to begin to function from a biblical worldview.[17]

Romans 12:2 says, *"Do not be conformed to this world but be transformed by the renewal of your mind"* (RSV). This transformation comes about by teaching, which was commanded by Christ in the Great Commission. This teaching is to be, to a radical extent: "teaching them all, *whatsoever I have commanded you."*

How to Reach a Post-Christian Society

This is particularly challenging, since your church faces a post-Christian culture. Dr. Eddie Gibbs, professor at Fuller Theological Seminary, says, "The church in the West must learn from the church in many other areas of the world to live on the margins, for we are now part of a post-Christendom society. It is not such a bad place from which to operate if we have mission zeal, a prophetic voice, and humility of spirit!"[18] This post-Christian environment provides many challenges and opportunities for the church. Your management task is (1) to be aware of these opportunities, and (2) respond with resources that increase the effectiveness of your congregation.

Move from Institution to Mission

Church growth advocate Elmer Towns says that church leaders need to realize that God wants a large growing church in every ethnic community of the world. The church has the opportunity to redesign itself. Jesus' command was to make disciples of all nations. They then were to be baptized and taught the Word of God. "When they are baptized they are added to the church (Acts 2:41), and when they are taught all things, they in turn become soul-winning evangelists who will teach others. That is the secret of the Great Commission, which is a secret of evangelizing the world."[19]

Focus on Outreach

Churches need to be evangelistically driven. This is the church's opportunity to reignite a passion for outreach. Christians and churches must focus not so much on the fact that they are second- or third-generation believers, but they are missionaries on a mission field. When Christians recast themselves as missionaries in their own country, they will represent a church that has become a mission station.

Understand Cross-Cultural Evangelism

A third way to reach a post-Christian society is to better understand cross-cultural evangelism. Elmer Towns explains: "Church leaders must understand cross-cultural evangelism. The methods that work in the southern United States do not work in a Korean community in Orange County, California, nor do they work in a Japanese community in Vancouver, British Columbia, Canada. The Gospel is eternal, and it never changes. We do not change the Gospel for any ethnic group, but we must learn the 'Bridges of God' to reach into every ethnic group so they become believers in Jesus Christ."[20] This means that churches must understand the cross-cultural nature of the Great Commission.

Be Prepared for Cultural Clash

You really can't plant a church anywhere in the world without being aware of the need to reach all people in your mission field. Many different ethnic groups may respond to the Gospel. Culturally, they may share the same lifestyles, hopes, and dreams. When people share an affinity with one another they can form a local church. This is part of the cosmopolitan and complex world in which we live. As Eddie Gibbs points out, "Church leaders must recognize that we are living in an increasingly pluralistic society, which means that pastors need cross-cultural missionary training!"[21] Your ability to understand other culture groups and design appropriate evangelistic strategies is a key to ministry management. Among those who have not experienced the Gospel, cultural tensions continue and may escalate in the future. "We have to be prepared to bear our witness with grace in a world in which the clash of cultures is likely to become more fierce and widespread."[22]

Denominational Labels

Another reality of the post-Christian era is the need for Christians to "hang together." Those who visit traditional missionaries on foreign soils often find that spirit of cooperation. Denominational isolationism for those on the mission field is not an option.

In his book *Challenging Quotes for World Changers*, David Shibley says, "For many of us, our denominational tags are becoming less important. We simply wish to be world Christians. Our first line of identification is with the entire Body of Christ worldwide, especially those in every nation who share our passion for closure on the Great Commission."[23] This is growing phenomenon. People from various denominations are gathering for a variety of efforts and activities. Their commonality and affinity for one another is defined more in mutual values concerning the mission of the church than in differences. On the mission field, Christians have little choice. In order to survive and thrive, they must work together. Also, it is very confusing for unchurched people to see Christians diversified and fractured in so many ways. Dr. Eddie Gibbs has said, "We have to be able to step outside of our particular tradition to appreciate the distinctive contributions of traditions other than our own. For instance, Pentecostals [in the mission field] now number more than all of the other Protestant denominations combined."[24]

High-Tech: Hindrance or Help?

The post-Christian era is occurring simultaneously with the information age. This has both a positive and negative impact on the church. On the positive side, the church has the opportunity to communicate the Gospel through various forms of electronic media with more innovations on the horizon every day. The downside of this is the danger of alienation. Pastors spend too much time behind a computer screen instead of interacting with people. Twenty years ago, John Naisbitt's *Megatrends* predicted this high-tech/high-touch world in which we now live.[25] The high-tech aspect of our society insulates people from direct touch with one another. This high-tech world generates a strong felt need for high touch. However, with the time constraints in a world that runs in the fast lane, people today are relating to fewer and more carefully chosen friends. Those kinds of relationships are more important than ever.

Networking

Interestingly, electronically connected people also are becoming network-oriented in their personal relationships. High-tech extremism is attaining high levels of high touch. This provides great opportunities for the church working through small-groups. A network of relationships demonstrates an opportunity for the message of the Gospel to penetrate by way of a web movement. Since networking is so much a part of the culture the potential for rapid evangelization actually increases.

The electronic age also means that we live in an era of instant and largely unregulated global communication. When an American church leader makes a comment about Islam, it is immediately reported, in real time, in Saudi Arabia, Pakistan, and throughout the Middle East.[26]

Employing Age-Specific Methodology

Because of technological advances in the twenty-first century, the media have been able to target specific groups. This age-specific methodology enables them to speak in a genre that is part of that age or group culture. MTV and *South Park* are examples of genres that target specific groups. Children's church is an example in the church culture.

Children's Church

Today, churches are combining technological breakthroughs with age-specific methodology. King of Kings Lutheran Church in Omaha includes a sanctuary for children. The worship service is led by children, and the worship seating is built to fit their bodies. Parents who want to worship together with their children are invited to worship in the children's church setting. Children's Pastor Dr. Roger Theimer explains it is more likely that parents can relate to the communication level of children. It's impossible for children understand the communication for adults in "adult worship." This reverses the trend of adult chauvinism.[27] This has biblical precedent. Those more spiritually mature always subordinate their strategic approach to those they are trying to reach. In Luke 10:8, Jesus was speaking about much more than dietary guidelines when He told His missionary-to-be disciples to eat what was set before them.

Biblical Truth Does Not Change

In a world of constant change—a rate of change never experienced before—the substance of Christianity does not change. The truth of Scripture, the good news about Jesus Christ, is the same today as it was yesterday. It will be the same tomorrow. But the look of the church, its methods and styles, its *modus operandi*—everything else must change. Bill Gates, Chairman and Chief Executive Officer of Microsoft Corporation, has said it this way: "If we are reactive and let change overwhelm us or pass us by, we will perceive change negatively. If we are proactive, seek to understand the future now, and embrace change, the idea of the unexpected can be positive and uplifting."[30] One of the keys to the effectiveness of the Christian church in the world in which we now live is recapturing the brilliance of Jesus' strategy: discipleship.

The Learning Society

Peter Drucker has reflected upon our changing world. He says, "Some of the greatest changes in social structure in the history of the human race have taken place this century. These changes have been non-violent, which is perhaps why few people pay them any attention. Yet had any of the great economists or sociologists of the last century been apprised of them, they would have laughed in disbelief."[31]

Drucker goes on to talk about some occupations that are no longer on the radar screen. Today few people hold the primary occupation of "farmer." He points out that in the British Census of 1910 a lower middle-class family was described as a family that could not afford more than three servants. What he calls "the learning society" is taking over. In that learning society, Drucker says that schools will change more in the next thirty years than they have since the invention of the printed book. Drucker explains that organizations also will change.[32] One of the organizations that must change the most is the church—not its content or its mission, but its methodology and style.

Back to Basics

Yet, even while we acknowledge the need to change how we "do church" to better fit today's circumstances, it is important to remember how the church came to be where it is today. In some respects, we would do well to revert back to the basics.

In *The Rise of Christianity*, author Rodney Stark provides a detailed account of how the early church grew.[33] He begins by describing his research on why people convert from one religion to another. He says people convert for a very simple reason: the new religion offers them a better way of life. He goes on to show that throughout history, new religions have mainly drawn their converts from the ranks of those who were religiously inactive and discontented.

In summary, Stark shows that Christianity grew by providing new ways of engaging some of the most pressing problems of life in the ancient world, problems the pagan world was failing to address.[34] Christians were authentic people who lived, with integrity, the faith they believed. They not only told their stories, they acted them out. They probably didn't have *WWJD?* wristbands, but they could have worn them, declaring their worldview—that they were directed by the question, "What Would Jesus Do?"

In *The Church in the Postmodern World*, John Phelan summarizes Rodney Stark's observations: "What does all this have to do with today's Christianity and its future? Nearly everything! How are we going to leave the safe confines of our churches and reach this big, bad, postmodern world with the Gospel? In the same way the ancient church did. We need to show the world that the Christian life—following Jesus Christ—is the best, healthiest, most rewarding way to live. . . . We must say that being a Christian is not just true, it is *good*."[35]

Globalization provides challenges to your church. However, the opportunities for changing lives with authentic Christianity are excellent. As you manage your local church, and, if you are open to change, God will use you in a powerful way!

Endnotes

1. Michael A. Hitt, R. Duane Ireland, and Robert E. Hoskisson, *Strategic Management: Competitiveness and Globalization,* 4th ed. (Cincinnati: South-Western College Publishing, 2001), 15.
2. John E. Phelan, Jr., *The Church in the Postmodern World: Understanding the Role of the Body of Christ in the 21st Century* (Fort Washington, PA: Christian Literature Crusade, 1999), 10.
3. Philip Jenkins, *The Next Christendom: The Coming of Global Christianity* (Oxford: Oxford University Press, 2002), 163.
4. Diana L. Eck, *A New Religious America: How a "Christian Country" Has Become the World's Most Religiously Diverse Nation* (New York: HarperCollins Publishers, Inc., 2001), 30.
5. Ibid.
6. Gary McIntosh, *The McIntosh Church Growth Network Newsletter* 13, no. 9 (September 2001): 2.
7. Lyle E. Schaller, "How Does the Culture Impact the Church? The Call to Customize," *Net Results* XXII, no. 11/12 (November/December 2001): 3.
8. Lyle E. Schaller, *The New Context for Ministry: Competing for the Charitable Dollar* (Nashville: Abingdon Press, 2002), 17.
9. David W. Henderson, *Culture Shift: Communicating God's Truth to Our Changing World* (Grand Rapids: Baker Books, 1998), 51.
10. Marshall Shelley, "From the Editor," *Leadership Journal* XXIII, no. II (Spring 2002): 3.
11. Henderson, *Culture Shift,* 140.
12. Ibid.
13. Craig Kennet Miller, *Postmoderns: The Beliefs, Hopes, and Fears of Young Americans* (Nashville: Discipleship Resources, 1996), 170.
14. Michael Pocock and Joseph Henriques, *Cultural Change and Your Church: Helping Your Church Thrive in a Diverse Society* (Grand Rapids: Baker Books, 2002), 38-43.
15. Phelan, 20.

16. Kent R. Hunter, *Discover Your Windows: Lining Up with God's Vision* (Nashville: Abingdon Press, 2002), 25.

17. Darrow Miller, in correspondence with the author.

18. Eddie Gibbs, in correspondence with the author.

19. In correspondence with the author.

20. Ibid.

21. Ibid.

22. Ibid.

23. David Shibley, *Challenging Quotes for World Changers: God's Little Book on the Great Commission* (Green Forest, AR: New Leaf Press, 1995), 12.

24. Gibbs.

25. John Naisbitt, *Megatrends: Ten New Directions Transforming Our Lives* (New York: Warner Books, Inc., 1982).

26. Gibbs.

27. In correspondence with the author.

28. Towns.

29. See Bob Whitesel and Kent R. Hunter, *A House Divided: Bridging the Generation Gaps in Your Church* (Nashville: Abingdon Press, 2000).

30. Bill Gates, *Business @ the Speed of Thought: Using a Digital Nervous System* (New York: Warner Books, 1999), 414.

31. Peter F. Drucker, *Managing for the Future: The 1990s and Beyond* (New York: Truman Talley Books/Dutton, 1992), 331.

32. Ibid, 332-36.

33. Rodney Stark, *The Rise of Christianity: A Sociologist Reconsiders History* (Princeton, NJ: Princeton University Press, 1996), 19-20, 120-21, 161-62.

34. Ibid.

35. Phelan, 35.

5

What Church Leader's Need to Know About . . .

Strategic Planning:
More Than a Process

"If we know where we are and something about how we got there,
we might see where we are trending—and if the outcomes which lie
naturally in our course are unacceptable, to make timely change."

—ABRAHAM LINCOLN[1]

When Worlds Collide:
Strategic Planning in Business and the Church

The word *strategic* comes from the Greek title for the Ten Generals (*strategoi*) of ancient Athens, who were entrusted with planning the growth of Athens. Pericles, a gifted general, recognized that if Greek culture were to retain its dominance, there must be a cultural benchmark representing the pinnacle of Greek influence and power. Athens became that benchmark, through the planning of the *Strategoi*.

Armstrong Chapel United Methodist Church is situated in the wealthy Indian Hill section of Cincinnati, It is anything but a diminutive chapel. Regularly attended by over 400 people, this church was now a mid-sized church[2] with an unwieldy administrative structure, and little idea of where it was headed. Previously the church had been content to trudge along with minuscule growth, fueled by transfer growth. However, a group of younger members became alarmed by the church's attitude toward long-term goals. As a result, they convened a focus group and invited me to assist them in charting their future.

"It's all about having a strategy," began Sue, a pathologist and researcher.

"No offense towards our pastor, but they don't teach strategy in seminary," added Deb, a marketing executive. "And though our pastor has his doctorate, he doesn't know the basics of business planning. But, because he has a lot of power, we can't do anything without him."

"Deb's right. We need a strategy," continued Jill. "It's wrong for us to plod ahead without some strategy. Strategy, that's the key word."

Jill's observations were confirmed by the nodding heads of the assembled group. Around that circle sat lawyers, corporate vice presidents, advertising executives, financial planners, engineers, a lawyer, and banker. In their business lives, they understood the necessity of strategic planning. But in the cloistered walls of theological academia where their pastor was trained, such considerations were rare.

The Church: A Visible and Invisible Organization

In *The Misunderstanding of the Church*, theologian Emil Brunner points out that the church is two manifestations.[3] After the first century, the church grew quickly and needed to be managed. Managing the church became the dominant focus of the church hierarchy until the Reformation. Luther, Calvin, and others stressed the importance of the church as a community of relationships. Brunner calls this network of relationships the "invisible" or "hidden" church. The Reformers attempted to foster a community of renewed spirituality, accompanied by an efficiently run organization founded upon local control.[4] In this respect, Brunner sees the church as two entities: (1) a spiritual community that administers healing, reconciliation, and salvation, and (2) an organizational entity that requires skillful and knowledgeable administration. This dual thrust of the church as a complex network of spiritual and administrative relationships necessitates training leaders in multiple disciplines.

The Strategic Planning Process

Among business students the complexity of the strategic planning process can make the principles cryptic. Terms can be confusing. While "strategic planning" sometimes will be employed to refer to strategy formation, at other junctures the term "strategic management" is preferred. The terms are used interchangeably.[5] The use of dual terminology arises because *strategic management* is preferred by academicians, and *strategic planning* is favored in business. This book is geared toward application in both the business and ecclesial world, we shall use the term *strategic planning*.

The strategic planning process generally is comprised of three stages: strategy formation, strategy implementation, and strategy evaluation. In this chapter, we will examine all three aspects of the process:

1. **Strategy Formation**: We will investigate the *S.W.O.T* of an organization as well as its *core competencies*. We will compare various strategies using tools with cryptic (but soon to be clear) acronyms: IFE, EFE, TOWS, and QSPM.
2. **Strategy Implementation**: We will discuss applying our strategy and attaining goal-ownership though *mission* and *vision* statements.
3. **Strategy Evaluation**: You will learn how to calculate four quantitative tools that can measure church health and growth.

But first, let's look at an overview of the strategic planning process. Figure 5.1 is a scaled-down version of the strategic planning process that I designed to aid learning retention.

Church Health   **Church Growth.**

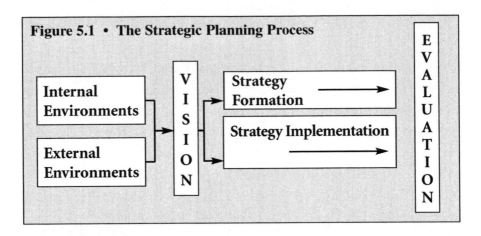

Figure 5.1 • The Strategic Planning Process

Our Strategic Tools

To facilitate the strategic planning process, a plethora of tools is available. However, in the interest of brevity, I will concentrate on several basic tools for strategic planning. Let's begin by explaining how these tools fit into Figure 5.1.

- **Internal Environments**: Kent Miller of the Krannert School of Business at Purdue University stated, "Strategy is a process relating an organization to its environment."[6] Thus, "strengths" and "weaknesses," gleaned from a tool called a SWOT analysis, provide the basis for the understanding of an organization's "internal" environments. You will uncover the things the organization does well—its "core competencies."

- **External Environments**: "Opportunities" and "threats" from our SWOT analysis will provide a basic understanding of the outside forces or "external" forces that affect the organization.

- **Vision and Mission**: You will learn how to create personality, mission, and vision statements based upon our SWOT analysis and our core competencies.

- **Strategy Formation**: You will discover how to create, contrast, and evaluate various strategies for suitability. Using charts to determine an Internal Factor Evaluation (IFE), External Factor Evaluation (EFE), and Quantitative Strategic Planning Matrix (QSPM), you will learn how to contrast and compare strategy options.

- **Strategy Implementation**: You will learn guidelines for fine-tuning strategies, as well as discover how to allow each strategy appropriate time to develop.

- **Church Health**: The term church health is a good corollary to the management term "strategic competitiveness," when strategic competitiveness means a firm can compete in the marketplace. Since strategic competitiveness often feels too ignoble to be applied to the church, the term "church health" becomes an alternative. It describes the process that occurs when a healthy church "competes" against the lure and enticements of secular distractions.

- **Church Growth**: Church growth can be another alternative to a business term Above average returns which describes what happens when investing time, talents and/or resources in a firm results in above average benefits for stakeholders. The goal of Jesus' Great Commission is to "make disciples." Church growth could signify "above average results" in the process of making disciples.[7] Similarly, "average results" in the church context might signify church growth that is only keeping pace with biological growth in the community or biological growth in the church. Above average returns indicates that making disciples is occurring intentionally.

- **Evaluation**: You will investigate how to define and attain measurable goals, allowing you to chart the effectiveness of your strategic processes. You will look at quantitative tools as an aid to measuring the progress of four types of church growth.

Analyze Your "*Internal* Environments"

"No business can do everything… the worst thing to do is a little bit of everything. This makes sure that nothing is being accomplished."

- MANAGEMENT CONSULTANT, PETER DRUCKER[8]

The church appeared healthy and strong. Mt. Zion sat near a busy intersection, on a main artery of a growing Dayton, Ohio suburb. The pastor was a skilled communicator and had overseen the development of a small group network that involved nearly two-thirds of the congregation. An associate pastor had created an advertising strategy, and the church enjoyed an influx of newcomers. But they were not joining the church. "We've got a big front door, and a big back door," confided one layperson.

I was hired to assist in long-range planning and to uncover why the church was not growing proportionally with so many visitors. It became clear that Mt. Zion did a few things well, many things moderately well, and a number of things poorly. Research revealed that some substandard programs along with highly visible programming failures had detracted from what the church did well. The church was headed in too many directions, and many of these directions were neither suitable nor successful.

Newcomers were attracted because of its advertisements for particular ministries. But they found several to be poorly or halfheartedly conducted. The newcomers were inadvertently rebuffed. The inflow of guests was followed by their gradual disappointment and eventual exit. The heart of Mt. Zion's problem was that it had not yet identified its core competencies—the things the church did well—nor had it built its ministry strategy around these core competencies.

Defining Core Competencies

Core competencies are the things an organization does well. Core competencies are characterized by four traits: they are valuable, rare, costly to imitate, and non-substitutable. Another way to say this is that "core competencies distinguish a company competitively and reflect its personality."[9]

Figure 5.2 compares the core competencies of several well-known businesses:[10]

Figure 5.2	
Company:	*Core Competencies:*
Wal-Mart	Lowest prices, large selection
Target:	Low prices, style
Ralph Lauren Clothing	Branding, effective promotion[11]
Gap, Inc.	Forecasting, low price, multi-brand strategy[12]
Sony	Quality, innovation, miniaturization
Sanyo	Innovation, low price

Discovering Your Church's Core Competencies

To uncover a church's core competencies, we must look at the church as it relates to the four criteria that define a core competency.

1. **Valuable**: These are the competencies that make a church valuable to the community and to the church at large. They allow the church to explore and expand opportunities to reach out to the community and to neutralize external threats.

2. **Rare**: Few other groups or secular organizations can offer these core competencies.

3. **Costly to Imitate**. Because a competency may not be financially rewarding, it is difficult for a secular group to imitate the competency. The church does not operate with a for-profit philosophy. The church can offer ministries that are too costly for others.

4. **Non-substitutable**. The core competencies are incapable of being counterfeited or imitated authentically.

What is *worship* as a core competency? Energetic, anointed, and heartfelt worship was a core competency at Mt. Zion. How does their type of worship relate to the criteria of core competencies?

1. **Valuable**: Worship is an expression of gratitude, interaction, and adoration towards God. It meets the human need to be in contact with and express gratitude towards the Supreme Being. This ability to be connected with God is highly "valued" by most people in all cultures. German religious thinker Rudolph Otto describes this as a feeling that "at times comes sweeping like a gentle tide, pervading the mind with a tranquil mood of deepest worship. It may pass into a more set and lasting attitude of the soul, continuing as it were, thrilling vibrant and resonant, until at last it dies away and the soul resumes its 'profane,' non-religious mood of everyday existence."[13] Most who visited Mt. Zion Church would agree that worship was one of its core competencies.

2. **Rare**: Authentic worship, as described by Otto, is rare, considering that much of life consists of what Otto calls the "'profane,' non-religious mood of everyday existence."

3. **Costly to Imitate**. True worship of and interaction with a living God is impossible for secular society to imitate. In true worship, the celebration of the entity (God) takes primacy over musical euphoria; this makes worship costly if not impossible to imitate.

4. **Non-substitutable**. If humankind needs to exalt and interact with God via worship, as the psalmist reminds us in Psalm 100, then true worship is non-substitutable.

Core Competencies at Mt. Zion Church

An analysis of Mt. Zion Church revealed several core competencies. Many of its recently added programs were not in alignment with these core competencies. Much of the new programming had been added because it was popular with other churches.

As a result of our long-range strategy sessions, Mt. Zion soon began to sift through its various programs and eliminate (or give away to other congregations) programs not directly related to its core competencies. This strategy helped the church to focus on what it did well.

Conducting a S.W.O.T. Analysis

S – Strengths

W – Weaknesses

O – Opportunities

T – Threats

The acronym S.W.O.T stands for Strengths, Weaknesses, Opportunities and Threats. S.W.O.T. analysis is a fundamental planning tool that analyzes both the positives (strengths/opportunities) and negatives (weaknesses/threats) of a strategy. S.W.O.T. analysis seeks to create strategies that take advantage of opportunities and strengths, while avoiding weaknesses and threats.

Craig Pifer, of Indiana Wesleyan University, contends that "a S.W.O.T. analysis is not only uncomplicated to apply, but also provides essential insights. And, it is a great discussion starter for planning sessions. In fact, I would say it is the most basic tool for developing an effective plan in business or the church."[15]

Before we look at how S.W.O.T. analysis works, we need to look at the difference between the internal and external factors that affect analysis.

The Difference between Internal and External Factors

Internal factors are programs, strategies, strengths, weaknesses, or any other factor over which the church has direct control. At Mt. Zion, a plan to add more small groups would be an "internal" factor because control, oversight, and management of the small group network would be conducted by forces (leaders and/or policies) that are internal to the organization.

External factors are beyond the control and capability of the church. External factors have an effect on the church, but are beyond their ability to change. An external factor may be a community's changing demographics. Young families move into the area. This is beyond the church's ability to stop or control it. An aging church will have to approach this youthful community influx as an external factor.

In the following discussion, *internal factors* will be addressed under the S and W of the acronym S.W.O.T. stands for the internal "strengths" of an organization and W stands for internal "weaknesses."

<u>S</u>.W.O.T. "Strengths"

As internal factors, strengths are to some degree under the control, influence, and/or oversight of the church. Strengths are the things a church does that are productive, satisfying, and appreciated, and over which the church has control or oversight.

> **Strengths**: The things a church does that are productive, satisfying, and appreciated, and over which the church has control or oversight.

Your church's strengths are an outgrowth of your core competencies. If your church has determined its core competencies, then you can begin to delineate which strengths reflect those core competencies. Ask yourself the following questions to determine your church's "strengths."

1. **Of the ministries your church provides, which ones are most closely connected to your church's core competencies?**
   a. How closely is this ministry connected to the church's core competencies? Rate each ministry from 1 to 5 (with 1 being not closely related, and 5 being closely related).
   b. Take the ministries with the lowest ratings and ask yourself, "Are these ministries the best use of our human, financial, and physical resources?" Try to list alternative, replacement, and/or merger options.
   c. Finally, ask yourself, "What would happen if we ended these ministries?" To maintain health, it is imperative that a church concentrate on its strengths, while eliminating or giving away ministries that do not align with those strengths.
2. **What do the church *and* your community perceive as being your church's strengths?** Be careful not to rely on the perceptions of church attendees. It is important to ask how the community perceives what *you* think you're doing well. The goal is to find the things your community recognizes as strengths. It is helpful to poll community residents.
3. **In which church programs are a significant number of your people involved?** This question will help you determine the ministries whose core strengths are verifiable by the congregation's un-coerced desire to participate.[17] At Mt. Zion, the music ministry attracted a significant number of the church's attendees. Musical programs were some of the most well attended church events. These factors pointed the leaders towards viewing the music ministry as a core competency.

S.W.O.T. "Weaknesses"

Weaknesses are easier to ascertain than strengths. Weaknesses are what a church does *not* do well. The church may fall short in certain areas in comparison to growing churches. The church may simply need to improve certain things in order to compete head-to-head with the lure of secular society. As internal factors, weaknesses are things over which the church has control or oversight.

> **Weaknesses**: These are what a church does *not* do well, either
> in comparison to growing churches, or in its ability to compete
> head-to-head with the lure of secular society. As internal factors,
> weaknesses are things over which the church has control or oversight.

Weaknesses can best be ascertained from two sources: (1) newcomers who have not yet found their niche, and (2) conscientious leaders.

Newcomers are those individuals who have begun attending the church in the last twelve to eighteen months. Once they begin to attend, they will be more aware of your weaknesses as they seek to fit in. While regular attendees might overlook a weakness, or downplay its severity, a newcomer's perception of weakness is magnified due to an eagerness to fit in. The prepared leader will understand that the newcomer's desire to find a niche gives a keener sensitively to the church's shortcomings.

Newcomers who have recently stopped attending the church can be a good source for identifying weaknesses. Convene a focus group of newcomers who have recently left the church. Tell them the purpose is not to persuade them to return, but rather to learn what ministries your church should provide. Always accentuate the positive, the things that "should be done" rather than "things we did wrong."

In addition to newcomers, *conscientious leaders* will have a feel for the church's weaknesses. While many will overlook weaknesses because of the things the church does well, they can still identify areas for improvement. Exercise caution to ensure that critical or easily offended individuals are not given undue influence. Changes evoke tension. Probe the concerns of conscientious and mature Christians.

Analyze Your "*External* Environments"

Continuing Your S.W.O.T. Analysis: *External* Factors

We turn from internal factors to external factors. The things that affect the church but are beyond its ability to change or modify

External factors may be difficult for a congregation to identify. In many churches as they pass 200 in attendance, much of their energy is directed toward internal administration. The church's survival is no longer the primary focus. External forces may go unaddressed and may even be unseen. Therefore, it is advisable to partner with outside specialists to ascertain opportunities.

To better understand the external forces that are coming to bear upon a church, it should consult the Chamber of Commerce, demographers, church growth consultants, planning commissions, business forecasting groups, or other specialists in this field. Businesses and civil governments rely on demographic forecasters to decide everything from where to put a stoplight, to where to build a McDonald's or a Wal-Mart. Businesses know the importance of identifying demographic shifts and trends.

S.W.O.T. "Opportunities"

In a S.W.O.T. analysis, we saw that strengths and weaknesses are internal factors. The external factors in a S.W.O.T. analysis are opportunities and threats. Opportunities are external factors beyond the church's ability to change or modify. They are the events, conditions, or situations in a church's external environment that are well suited to the way it does ministry. If many young families are moving into the community, a church with a strong children's ministry will see this as an "opportunity" for the church.

> **Opportunities**: These are the external factors that are beyond the control of the local church to change or modify. However, they also are the events, conditions, or situations in a church's external environment that are well suited to the way it does ministry.

At Mt. Zion, the community demographics identified an opportunity. Young professionals were moving into the area. Many had children. Young families often show a strong interest in clean and up-to-date facilities for their children. The church saw the changing demographic gave it an opportunity to reach young families. As a result, the church was able to focus on small classes in parenting. They set to work improving the quality and modernization of their children's ministries and facilities.

Another church with a similar opportunity was Eastside Baptist Church in Ft. Smith, Arkansas. Regarded by the community as a church of successful upper-middle-class constituents, the church had an opportunity to reach some of the young people between the ages of twenty and thirty moving into the area. The church knew its image as a successful church of older (and richer) members might put off younger generations. The church implemented come-as-you-are small groups aimed at twenty-something people. By taking note of this opportunity, and building on a core competency of an extensive small group network, Eastside Baptist was able to "grow" with younger generations.

S.W.O.T. "Threats"

Threats are external factors that are beyond the control of the church to change or modify. They are events, conditions, strategies, or situations that are not well suited to the way the church ministers, and should be avoided or minimized.

We don't like to think about threats. But successful people find it energizing to study and address them. Tony was a successful businessman who, at twenty-five, owned a growing electronics store. The retail end of electronics has always been a difficult market. But Tony relished the challenge.

"Each day I can't wait for the newspaper to come out," he confided. "I enjoy seeing what prices our competitors are offering, and then trying to match them. It's a challenge, but usually we can meet and even beat their prices. It's like a game of chess, where each move results in a counter move. I enjoy chess. And usually I win."

Tony's store became somewhat of a legend among small retailers in Minneapolis, as daily he dealt with the threats to his business and overcame them.

> **Threats**: Threats are external factors that are beyond the ability of the church to change or modify. They are events, conditions, strategies, or situations that are *not* well suited to the way the church ministers, and should be avoided or minimized.

Although Tony chose to attack his threats head on, most often we choose to avoid threats. Because threats are external forces, and because we customarily don't like to think about them, outside help is usually advisable. A church growth consultant—what Lyle Schaller calls "an interventionist"[18]—can be beneficial. Church growth consultants identify each component of the S.W.O.T. model and outline the ramifications. A business leader can fulfill this role, provided the leader embraces the same purposes and values as the church. Whosoever serves in this capacity, ascertaining the community factors that will adversely affect a church is difficult and best conducted with the assistance of experts.

Two particular external threats occur with such regularity that they bear further discussion: (1) changes in demographics within a community, and (2) becoming labeled a late mover.

Changing Demographics and Geriatrophy

Changing demographics affect a church when the demographic makeup of the community is changing, but the church is not. C. Peter Wagner, adapting a medical metaphor, labeled this *ethnikitis*.[19]

While at one time ethnikitis was regarded as the number-one killer of churches in America,[20] this distinction may have been replaced by *geriatrophy*. Geriatrophy is "a combination of geriatric, the branch of medicine that deals with the diseases of old age, denoting a wasting away or failure to grow."[21] Geriatrophy occurs when an aging church continues to age, failing to assimilate younger residents.

First Baptist Church of Ferndale was an American Baptist Church in an inner suburb of Detroit. Comprised of members over sixty-five years old, the church hired a consultant to help the congregation identify and respond to changing demographics. The "threat" was an influx of residents under thirty. If the church wanted to remain status quo, it could not avoid this threat without relocating. As a result of the study, the congregation decided to ask a young woman pastor to shepherd the congregation and reach out to younger residents. The external threat was addressed and soon the church was growing,

First Movers, Fast Second Movers, and Late Movers

A second external threat that occurs with great frequency is to be labeled a *late mover*. In the business world, we identify different types of *movers*:

- A *first mover* is an organization that
  1. innovates, taking initial competitive actions to launch a new and desirable idea;
  2. gains competitive advantage as it becomes identified with this new idea.

- A *second mover* is an organization that
  1. responds to the initial competitive action of a first mover by utilizing some parts of the innovative idea and applying them as a response;
  2. gains some competitive advantage, but primarily only over late movers.
  3. Sometimes a company may be a *fast second mover*. It avoids some risk by studying the initial competitive action of the first mover, and then acting quickly.

- A *late mover* is an organization that
  1. responds after some time has elapsed;
  2. is regarded by the community as a poor performer and/or apathetic about the community's needs.

Figure 5.3 compares four types of *first movers* in the corporate world (in the second column from the left), with companies that some business analysis would identify as *fast second movers* (in the third column). Finally (on the right) are businesses that might be identified as *late movers*.

Figure 5.3

	1st Mover:	Fast 2nd Mover:	Late Mover:
Fast Food:	McDonald's	Burger King	Kentucky Fried Chicken
Mega-marketers	Wal-Mart	Target	K-Mart
PDAs	Handspring	Palm (3 Com)	Sony
Computers	Apple	Dell	IBM

Of particular interest in Figure 5.3 is the ability of the *fast second mover* to make strides. The *fast second mover* learns how to employ some new idea after watching how the *first mover* wrestles with it.

What Label Does the Church Wear?

Local churches can suffer from being labeled second movers or even late movers. When Catholic churches began to experiment with folk-rock worship in the early-1960s, many Protestant churches adopted the style. Calvary Chapels began to sprout up across America, addressing the pent-up desire of churchgoers to modernize their worship experience. When small group networks began to sprout up in Korean churches in the early 1970s, American "cell churches" embraced this format and experienced rapid growth.[22] Today most mainline churches include some form of small group network.

A problem may arise when community residents view a church as a *late mover*.

Figure 5.4 shows how some religious organizations might rate on our *First Mover / Fast Second Mover / Late Mover* scale.

Figure 5.4

	1st Mover:	Fast 2nd Mover:	Late Mover:
Radio	Charles E. Fuller	Billy Graham	Mainline churches
TV	Billy Graham	Televangelists	Mainline churches
Modern Music	Catholic Church	Calvary Chapels	Mainline churches
Small Groups	Full Gospel, Korea[23]	Cell churches	Mainline churches
Boomer Min.	Vineyard Fellowship	Some Mainline churches	Most Mainline churches
Gen. X Min.	Harvest Fellowships	Few Mainline churches	Some Mainline churches

Part of the solution is for the church to more quickly distinguish between what is theologically indefensible, and what is a cultural preference. Eddie Gibbs calls this distinguishing between the "medium and the message."[24] The message of the Bible must not be changed; many mediums act as a channel where the message can be adjusted to make the Good News more understandable. Missionaries do this to make the biblical message relevant to new people groups. George Hunter points out in *Celtic Christianity* that it was precisely such adjustments in mediums that allowed St. Patrick to evangelize the Irish. He put the biblical message into story form and used Celtic symbols with which the Irish were familiar.[25]

When musical mediums and other cultural preferences change, and the church has difficulty adjusting appropriately, the church runs the threat of being labeled a *late mover*. Unfortunately, late movers are routinely dismissed by outsiders as irrelevant at worst, and out of touch at best.

Rating Your Internal and External Factors

How to Conduct an Internal Factor Evaluation (IFE)

An Internal Factor Evaluation (IFE) Matrix is good for evaluating the strengths and weaknesses of a church, and how well it is addressing them. The process helps summarize relationships between areas. Professor Fred David tells us, "Intuitive judgments are required in developing an IFE Matrix, so the appearance of a scientific approach should not be interpreted to mean this is an all-powerful exercise."[26]

The process of conducting an IFE involves five stages:

1. **List** all external strengths and weaknesses in the column on the left. Usually this will be from ten to twenty factors.
2. **Assign a weight** for each, ranging from 0.0 (not important) to 1.0 (all important). Each assigned weight indicates the importance of that factor for the general health and growth of the church. Weights can be determined by comparing successful and unsuccessful churches, or by discussing a factor and reaching a group consensus. Factors that have the greatest effect on potential growth or health (whether a strength or weakness) should be

assigned the highest weight. *Note:You must divide up these weights so that the sum of all weights is 1.0.*

3. **Rate** each factor from 1 = major weakness, 2 = a minor weakness, 3 = a minor strength, to 4 = a major strength.

4. **Multiply** the weight by the rating to get the WEIGHTED SCORE (far right column) for each variable.

5. **Sum up** the weighted scores to determine the TOTAL WEIGHTED SCORE for the organization.

Total weighted scores will range from 1.0 to 4.0. An average will be 2.5. Scores below 2.5 will characterize organizations that are weak internally, scores above 2.5 will indicate internal strength.

Let's look at an example of an IFE Matrix that could be developed for Mt. Zion Church.

Figure 5.5 • An IFE Matrix for Mt. Zion Church

KEY INTERNAL FACTORS	Weight	Rating	Weighted Score
Internal Strengths			
1. Strong small-group network	.15	4	.60
2. Strong prayer/healing ministry	.15	3	.45
3. Strong outreach emphasis	.05	3	.15
4. Excellent music ministry	.10	4	.40
5. Quality in lay & professional leadership	.05	3	.15
6. Strong program for teens	.05	4	.20
7. Sr. pastor is a good communicator	.05	3	.15
Internal Weaknesses			
1. Growth has slowed	.10	2	.20
2. Size has stalled around 550	.05	2	.10
3. Boomers and Gen X are underrepresented	.10	1	.10
4. The church facilities are limited	.10	1	.10
5. Church administration is weak	.05	2	.10
TOTAL	1.00		2.70

In Figure 5.5, Mt. Zion Church's major strengths (as indicated by ratings of 4) are: small groups, music ministry, and a teen program. Its major weaknesses are missing generations (Boomers and Gen Xers), along with the church's limited facilities. Although the church faces challenges, the church leadership can clearly see that overall Mt. Zion is strong internally (denoted by a 2.7 total score). Thus, the leaders could decide to investigate building a new facility. Such an aggressive plan usually would not be appropriate if the total internal score were significantly lower than 2.5.

How to Conduct an External Factor Evaluation (EFE) Matrix

An External Factor Evaluation (EFE) Matrix is similar to an EFE, but lists *external* opportunities and threats instead of *internal* strengths and weaknesses. The process of an EFE involves five stages:

1. **List** all external opportunities and threats in the column on the left.
2. **Assign a weight** for each, ranging from 0.0 (not important) to 1.0 (all important). Each assigned weight indicates the importance of that factor among the general church world for health and growth. Weights are determined by comparing successful and unsuccessful churches, or by discussing a factor and reaching a group consensus.
3. **Rate** each factor to indicate how effectively the church is responding to the factor, with: 1 = poor, 2 = average, 3 = above average, and 4 = superior.
4. **Multiply** the weight by the rating to get the WEIGHTED SCORE (far right column) for each variable (*same* process as with IFE).
5. **Sum up** the weighted scores to determine the TOTAL WEIGHTED SCORE for the organization (*same* process as with IFE).

Total weighted scores will range from a low of 1.0, to a high of 4.0. An average will be 2.5. Thus, scores below 2.5 characterize organizations that are poorly addressing external factors. Scores above 2.5 indicate organizations that respond positively to opportunities and threats.

Figure 5.6 is an overview of a possible EFE Matrix.

Figure 5.6 • An IFE Matrix for Mt. Zion Church

KEY EXTERNAL FACTORS	Weight	Rating	Weighted Score
External Opportunities			
1. Younger generations are moving into the area	.15	2	.30
2. Church has a long history in the community	.10	3	.30
3. City road adjacent to church has been widened	.05	3	.15
4. Community growth to the east is unlimited	.10	1	.10
5. County-wide shopping center nearby	.10	1	.10
6. Church is popular with local media	.05	1	.05
External Threats			
1. Church is viewed as a "late mover"	.10	1	.10
2. Building facade looks unkempt and outdated	.05	1	.05
3. Nearby churches have built new facilities	.10	1	.10
4. Growing churches have relocated to the area	.10	1	.10
5. Land for relocation is increasingly expensive	.10	1	.10
TOTAL	1.00		1.45

The EFE Matrix is helpful for gauging how successfully a church addresses external factors. For Mt. Zion Church, the fact that younger generations are moving into the area bears significant weight. Its sum total weight is 1.45 for external factors and 2.70 for internal factors. While Mt. Zion needs to continue to improve its internal factors, it has a far greater need to address its external factors.

Stating the Vision & Mission

Analyzing your church's core competencies and S.W.O.T. will form the foundation for demarcating the church's vision. Once you have researched and codified your core competencies, you then should create and adopt three different statements describing the organization's direction.

These statements become an important precursor to strategy implementation, since they should unify and unite the organization's stakeholders. Each statement should carry some sense of a battle cry, or what Fred R. David calls "a declaration of attitude and outlook."[27] They convey to those who hear them a common rallying call that unifies divergent parts. They declare the "attitude" of the organization, and should pervade the organizational culture. Management researchers Andrew Campbell and Sally Yeung believe that good statements create an "emotional bond" and "sense of mission" in the organization.[28]

Summarized briefly below, the three statements are the personality statement, the vision statement, and the mission statement:

- **A Statement of Ministry** is an extended description of the *personality* of the church. Reaching several paragraphs or pages in length, this description of a church's character and persona is helpful for understanding the style and forms of ministry a church will embrace. It should be based on the organization's core competencies and personality. Kent Hunter's book, *Your Church Has Personality: Find Your Focus – Maximize Your Mission* is an excellent step-by-step guide to designing an effective personality statement.[29]
- **A Vision Statement**: Running from several paragraphs to several pages, a vision statement describes a "vision" of where the organization is headed. George Barna describes the vision statement as "a clear mental image of a preferable future imparted by God, and based on an accurate understanding of God, self, and circumstances."[30] A vision statement answers the question, "Where do we believe God is calling our church to go in the future?"[31]
- **A Mission Statement**: Barna labels a mission statement as "the basic stance of the church and its intentions." Mission statements are broad general statements that many churches could share. Sample phrasings would include, "to evangelize, exalt, edify and equip" or "to know Him and make Him known." Both of these are relatively generic statements. While they reflect the basic theological and/or practical stance of the church, they do not differentiate that stance (as does a vision or personality statement) from other churches.

And now, a final word about statements. A "vision statement" helps to differentiate a church in the eyes of the community, it is imperative that the church craft an accurate and understandable vision statement in order to reach that community. For a guide to creating a vision statement (based on Elmer Towns' early model), see the eight-step process for developing a vision statement and accompanying examples in *A House Divided*.[32]

Strategy Formation

The TOWS Matrix: A Tool to Compare Strategies

The first step in strategy formation is to list suitable strategies. A TOWS matrix provides an important visual tool for comparing and contrasting each strategy. Based on our S.W.O.T. analysis, a TOWS Matrix (for "threats," "opportunities," "weaknesses," and "strengths") allows us to see which strategies address which internal and external factors.

A TOWS matrix is a table of nine cells. The top left cell is blank. Across the rest of the top row, the church's strengths and weakness are listed. Down the left-hand column, opportunities and threats are listed. The middle cells are strategy cells—strategies are listed in cells labeled *SO*, *WO*, *ST*, and *WT*. Strategies that build on internal "strengths" to address external "opportunities" would be listed in cell *SO*.

Let's look at Figure 5.7, a TOWS matrix developed for Mt. Zion Church.

Figure 5.7 • A TOWS Matrix for Mt. Zion Church

	STRENGTHS – S	WEAKNESSES – W
	1. Strong small group network 2. Strong prayer/healing ministry 3. Strong outreach emphasis 4. Excellent music ministry 5. Quality in lay & professional leadership 6. Strong program for teens 7. Sr. pastor is a good communicator	1. Growth has slowed 2. Size has stalled around 550 3. Boomers and Gen X are underrepresented 4. The church facilities are limited 5. Church administration is weak
OPPORTUNITIES – O 1. Younger generations are moving into the area 2. Church has a long history in the community 3. City road adjacent to church has been widened 4. Community growth to the east is unlimited 5. County-wide shopping center nearby 6. Church is popular with local media	**SO STRATEGIES** 1. Create new small groups aimed at attracting younger generations 2. Mobilize prayer for younger generations 3. Use signage & media to acquaint new residents with programming 4. Start a new worship service aimed at younger generations 5. Rent a youth facility near the shopping center 6. Sr. pastor gives short daily message on the radio	**WO STRATEGIES** 1. Attract younger generations with new programming 2. Change the management style of the church to a more effective model even though it has never been employed in the recent history of the church 3. Invite more participation in leadership from Boomers and Gen X 4. Relocate or renovate the church's facilities

THREATS – T	ST STRATEGIES	WT STRATEGIES
1. Church is viewed as a "late mover" 2. Building facade looks unkempt and outdated 3. Nearby churches have built new facilities 4. Growing churches have relocated to the area 5. Land for relocation is increasingly expensive	1. Launch and publicize new small group offerings 2. Have skilled laypeople redesign and beautify the building façade 3. Partner with a nearby growing church in outreach and/or youth activities 4. Have real estate professionals in the church investigate relocation	1. Hire a church growth consultant 2. Publicize innovative programming 3. Update signage/façade to be more attractive to Boomers and Gen X 4. Investigate how nearby churches (of larger size) administrate their church 5. Quickly investigate land for relocation

Brainstorming Suitable Strategies

We must fill in our TOWS matrix with suitable strategies. Two very good primary sources for generating strategies are (1) to brainstorm and (2) to examine what is working elsewhere.

Brainstorming

Brainstorming is a creative problem-solving exercise designed to generate a list of potential strategies. Alex Osborn invented the brainstorming process in 1938 as a way to get employees in his advertising agency to think creatively. Brainstorming is particularly helpful because it guards "against being both critical and creative at one and the same time."[33]

When brainstorming, follow these five rules:[34]

1. There will be no discussion of the ideas until after the brainstorming process.
2. The more options the better.
3. All ideas are welcome.
4. Combinations of options are sought.
5. Proposing or hearing an option does not mean it has to be accepted.

Generally, brainstorming should follow these four steps:[35]

Step 1. The leader describes the problem.

Step 2. As group members share their ideas, clarification is allowed, but no one is allowed to criticize. Thus, everyone withholds judgment until all alternatives have been described.

Step 3. Group members should be as innovative and radical as possible. In addition, proposing an option does not mean it has to be accepted. Group members are also encouraged to piggyback on other participants' suggestions.

Step 4. Finally, only after all alternatives have been proposed do group members debate the merits of each.

What Is Working Elsewhere?

The second primary source for idea generation is to observe what is working in other congregations. But exercise caution with this idea generator. New ideas can be exhilarating, even intoxicating. Infatuation with innovation can impair judgment. One mistakes a growing congregation can make is the injudicious use of an idea simply because it works well elsewhere.[36] A cross-pollination of unsuitable strategies can quickly halt growth.

Use careful analysis to ensure that your church does not naively embrace programming that is successful elsewhere but unsuitable for you. With proper and judicious analysis, programming that is productive elsewhere can serve as a pattern around which to build your unique strategy.

The QSPM: A Tool to Select Strategies

The last step in strategy formation is to rate the suitability of each strategy. There is only one analytical tool for doing this. The "Quantitative Strategic Planning Matrix" or QSPM is an essential tool for assigning a "Total Attractiveness Score" (TAS) to each strategy.

A TAS is a subjective assessment of the "attractiveness" or potential effectiveness of each strategy in addressing strengths, weaknesses, opportunities, and threats. These are the steps involved in finding the "total attractiveness score" (TAS) for each strategy you are considering.

Step 1. Make a list of the church's opportunities, threats, strengths and weaknesses in the left column of the QSPM.

Step 2. Assign a weight to each key factor. Do this just as you did with the

IFE Matrix and EFE Matrix, by assigning a weight for each factor, ranging from 0.0 (not important) to 1.0 (all important). Each assigned weight indicates the importance of that factor for the general health and growth of the church. Again, weights can be determined by comparing successful and unsuccessful churches, or by discussing a factor and reaching a group consensus. Factors that have the greatest effect on potential growth or health (whether a strength, weakness, opportunity, or threat) should be assigned the highest weight. *Note: Divide these weights so that the sum of all weights is 1.0.*

Step 3. Determine the Attractiveness Score (AS) for each key factor. First, ask yourself, "Does this factor affect my opinion of this strategy?" If a particular factor does not affect a strategy, put a dash for the AS score. If a factor does affect a strategy, assign it one of the following "attractiveness scores" (AS):

> 1 = not attractive
> 2 – somewhat attractive
> 3 = reasonably attractive
> 4 = highly attractive

Step 4. Determine the Total Attractiveness Score (TAS) by multiplying the weights (Step 2) by the Attractiveness Scores (Step 3).

Step 5. Compute the Sum Total Attractiveness Score. Add the Total Attractiveness Scores in each column of the QSPM. *Higher scores indicate more attractive strategies.*

At the onset, the QSPM seems complicated. However, it is the only analytical technique designed to determine total attractiveness of a strategy. As such, it becomes crucial in strategy evaluation. Regrettably, strategy evaluation is one of the most overlooked steps in the strategic planning process.

Figure 5.8 for a QSPM for two strategies considered by Mt. Zion Church.

Figure 5.8 • A QSPM for Mt. Zion Church

KEY FACTORS	Weight	Strategy A: Relocate or renovate facilities		Strategy B: Start a new worship service aimed at younger generations	
		AS	TAS	AS	TAS
Strengths					
1. Strong small group network	.15	2	.30	2	.30
Strong prayer/healing ministry	.15	2	.30	2	.30
Strong outreach emphasis	.05	3	.15	4	.20
Excellent music ministry	.10	2	.20	4	.40
Quality in lay & professional leadership	.05	3	.15	4	.20
Strong program for teens	.05	2	.10	2	.10
Sr. pastor is a good communicator	.05	3	.15	4	.20
Weaknesses					
1. Growth has slowed	.10	3	.30	4	.40
Size has stalled around 550	.05	–	–	1	.05
Boomers and Gen X are underrepresented	.10	2	.20	4	.40
The church facilities are limited	.10	4	.40	1	.10
Church administration is weak	.05	1	.05	1	.05
Total	1.0				
Opportunities					
1. Younger generations are moving into the area	.15	4	.60	4	.60
Church has a long history in the community	.10	1	.10	–	–
City road adjacent to church has been widened	.05	1	.05	4	.20
Community growth to the east is unlimited	.10	4	.40	4	.40
County-wide shopping center nearby	.10	1	.10	–	–
Church is popular with local media	.05	3	.30	2	.10
Threats					
1. Church is viewed as a "late mover"	.10	4	.40	4	.40
Building facade looks unkempt and outdated	.05	4	.20	1	.05
Nearby churches have built new facilities	.10	4	.40	1	.10
Growing churches have relocated to the area	.10	4	.40	–	–
Land for relocation is increasingly expensive	.10	1	.10	–	–
Total	1.0				
Sum Total Attractiveness Score			**5.25**		**4.55**

From Figure 5.8, it is seen that the sum total attractiveness score for Strategy A: "Relocate or Renovate Facilities" is 5.25. It compares to a sum total attractiveness score for Strategy B of 4.55. If money and energies are allocated to these projects, Strategy A might receive higher priority.

The QSPM should be applied to all of the strategies charted on the TOWS matrix. The result is a helpful numerical score for each strategy, a score that can assist in prioritization.

Strategy Implementation

Rules for Implementing a Strategy

Strategy implementation involves: (1) development, (2) fine-tuning, and (3) evaluation.

Give a Strategy Time to Develop

While change can come slowly, once change is initiated, churchgoers expect prompt results. "We tried their new ideas," stated a church member, "but it's been a year and we've not seen enough growth. We're not any better now than we were before. We should go back to the way we were doing things." Because so much is riding on a new strategy, congregants expect speedy results.

The best avenue is to exercise caution with strategy selection. Then adopt the business approach and patiently give a strategy time to develop. Research shows new ideas are doomed if implemented too quickly, before members have time to embrace them.[37] Slowly watch progress over 6 to 18 months.

There is a caveat. Allowing a program to continue too long without results is not prudent.[38] After allowing for a period of incubation, use measurable goals to assess growth. The period of incubation varies with each strategy, and is best determined by a group consensus.

Fine-Tune Your Strategy

In addition, a strategy often will need adjustment and fine-tuning to adapt properly to a church's unique personality. Regularly revisit your strategic plan and modify it as it matures. Do not be afraid to use the measurable goals discussed later in this chapter to gauge progress (or lack thereof).

Also be aware that fine-tuning your strategy often will require lengthening the amount of time it needs to develop. For example, let's say that you originally allowed six to eighteen months for strategy development. However, if you make significant adjustments to your strategy, it may require twelve to twenty-four months before you see significant progress.

Strategy Evaluation

Good strategic plans incorporate goals that are readily analyzed. Craig Pifer calls this "the critical component in the implementation of a strategy. Church leaders must ensure they have developed a feedback method to evaluate progress. It must include benchmarks that contain measurable goals."[39]

In Christian circles most goal setting is anecdotal rather than empirical. For the church to be taken seriously by businesspeople or the unchurched, we need to develop measuring tools to gauge progress. Four such tools are summarized below.[40]

Goal Setting: Four Types of Church Growth

While most will be familiar with the more sensational of numerical church growth, counting attendees is only one of the four types of growth advocated in Scripture. Using Acts 2:42-47 as our scriptural base, let's look briefly at each type and how they may be measured.

Growing in Maturity

An outcome of God's plans, as expressed in the book of Acts, is a growing maturity among His followers. Acts 2:42, 43 describes this aspect of growth in the early church: *"They devoted themselves to the apostles' teaching and to the fellowship, to the breaking of bread and to prayer. Everyone was filled with awe, and many wonders and miraculous signs were done by the apostles."*

This "maturation growth" signifies the maturity and spiritual sensitivity emerging in the believers. We see the church's devotion to teaching and fellowship, accompanied by attesting miracles.[41] This signifies a church is maturing in its knowledge, experience, and observance of spiritual disciplines.

One way to gauge such growth is to create a formula for computing a "composite maturation number." This means "maturation growth may be measured by numbering a congregation's 'active learners'[42] who are regularly inculcating biblical lessons. Measuring the number of participants involved in educational and training opportunities can give an idea of the active learners in a congregation. The statistic that totals the people involved in these areas we have labeled the 'composite maturation number' (CMN). The following formula tells how to compute this number for your congregation."[43]

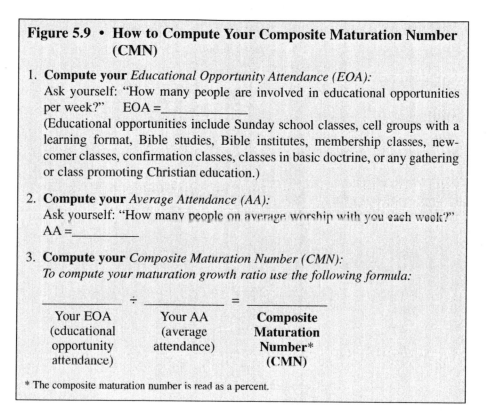

Figure 5.9 • How to Compute Your Composite Maturation Number (CMN)

1. **Compute your** *Educational Opportunity Attendance (EOA):*
   Ask yourself: "How many people are involved in educational opportunities per week?"   EOA =_____
   (Educational opportunities include Sunday school classes, cell groups with a learning format, Bible studies, Bible institutes, membership classes, newcomer classes, confirmation classes, classes in basic doctrine, or any gathering or class promoting Christian education.)

2. **Compute your** *Average Attendance (AA):*
   Ask yourself: "How many people on average worship with you each week?" AA =_____

3. **Compute your** *Composite Maturation Number (CMN):*
   To compute your maturation growth ratio use the following formula:

_____ ÷	_____ =	_____
Your EOA (educational opportunity attendance)	Your AA (average attendance)	**Composite Maturation Number* (CMN)**

   * The composite maturation number is read as a percent.

The Composite Maturation Number shows the percentage of your regular attendees that are involved in the church's educational opportunities.[44] An increasing CMN percentage implies that a growing percentage of the church is encountering discipleship environs.

Growing in Unity

Acts 2:44-47a adds: *"All the believers were together and had everything in common. Selling their possessions and goods, they gave to anyone as he had need. Every day they continued to meet together in the temple courts. They broke bread in their homes and ate together with glad and sincere hearts, praising God . . ."*

This early demonstration of unity and harmony led to selfless acts of inter-reliance. Those to whom God spoke began pooling their money. We know this was not the norm for all New Testament churches. But the unity and interdependence evident in these acts should be a growth goal of all churches.

To measure this growth in unity, there is an available assessment to gauge how pervasive among a congregation are its shared goals, purposes, and vision.[45]

Figure 5.10 • How to Gauge Growth in Unity

Rate each statement from 1 to 5:

1. Indicates <u>strong agreement</u>
2. Indicates <u>moderate agreement</u>
3. Indicates <u>slight agreement</u>
4. Indicates <u>disagreement</u>
5. Indicates <u>you do not know</u>

1. If asked, I could roughly state for visitors and nonmembers our church's *mission* statement.
2. If asked, I could summarize in my own words for visitors and nonmembers our church's *vision* statement.
3. I have a sense of excitement about our church's future.
4. I have a clear understanding of our church's goals.
5. Our church feels like a network of individuals and age groups with the same goals, but with different ways to express those goals.
6. Combined worship services (unity services) are highly valued in our church.
7. Although we are a network of individuals and age groups, we have a unified identity in the community.

If over time this assessment is re-administered and the value of the results decreases (indicating growing consensus and accord), then unity may be increasing.

Growing in Favor

"*. . . Enjoying the favor of all the people*" is how Acts 2:47b describes what has been labeled "growing in favor." Congregational progress should include growth in appreciation and respect among the unchurched. In an earlier analysis of growth, I wrote, "The result can be openness to the Good News. Too often an adversarial role develops between the church and the community. In reality, the role should be one of mutual respect, appreciation, and communication . . . This gratitude then becomes a powerful conduit through which the Good News flows into a community."[46]

Here the measurement is more complex, it involves polling the community and its attitudes about the church. Discovering the community's perception, positive and/or negative, can be a very beneficial undertaking. This requires a great deal of person power to poll a sufficient portion of a community to extract a reliable number. If a church is willing to poll 0.3% (up to 1,000 individuals) or is willing to hire professionals to do this, the church can readily gauge the level of community support.

Figure 5.11 includes questions that can be utilized in a phone survey to gauge growth in community favor.[47]

Figure 5.11 • Community Telephone Survey

Introduction:
"Hello. My name is _____ (name) _____ and I am conducting a short survey for (name of congregation) _____ in ___ (city/town) ___. Would you mind if I asked you a few anonymous and short questions?"
- If the answer is "YES," continue.
- If "NO," say, "Thank you for your consideration.
Good bye."

Open-ended Questions:
Question #1: "Are you aware of _____ (name of congregation) _____ in (city/town) ___?" If *yes*, continue. If *no*, conclude interview by saying, "That concludes our interview. Thank you for your time. Good bye."
Question #2: "How would you describe this church to a friend?"
Question #3: "In general, do you have a positive, negative, or undecided view of this church?"
Question #4: "What advice could you give this church so it could more effectively help people in your age group?"
Question #5: "Are you currently actively involved in a church, synagogue, mosque, or other religious house of worship?"

Conclusion:
"Thank you for your time. Your advice will help _____ (name of congregation) of ___ (city/town) ___ better address the needs of people in our community(ies). Thank you. Good bye."

Growing in Numbers

The first three types of church growth should result in numerical growth. This is reflected in Luke's statement: *"The Lord added to their number daily those who were being saved"* (Acts 2: 47c). While this may be more scrutinized and sensationalized aspects of growth, it is just one portion of the picture.

Some may question the legitimacy of measuring numerical growth. Donald McGavran countered that "the Church is made up of countable people and there is nothing particularly spiritual in not counting them. Men use the numerical approach in all worthwhile human endeavors."[48]

Often in the Bible, numbering through census was conducted for meaningful reasons and with helpful results.

"In *Numbers 1:2 and 26:2* God commands numberings of all Israel along with every segment of each tribe before and after the desert wanderings. In the Gospel accounts we witness accurate countings of Jesus' team of disciples, and in *Luke 10:1-24* we see a company of 72 disciples sent out two by two. In the parable of the lost sheep in *Luke 15:3-7*, only by counting the sheep does the shepherd become aware that one is missing from the fold. If counting those we are entrusted with were odious to Jesus, certainly he would eliminate such imagery from his teaching. And in *Acts 1:15; 2:41; 4:4;* Luke records the growth of the church by a careful record of its numerical increase."[49]

McGavran concludes, "On Biblical grounds one has to affirm that devout use of the numerical approach is in accord with God's wishes. On the practical grounds, it is as necessary in congregations and denominations as honest financial dealing."[50]

To compute numerical growth, it is important to track your growth rate regularly. A table may be used, or the Average Annual Growth Rates (A.A.G.R.) tool can be employed. Employing A.A.G.R.s will ensure that large numbers do not skew your data. Figure 5.12 is an overview of how to compute your congregational A.A.G.R.

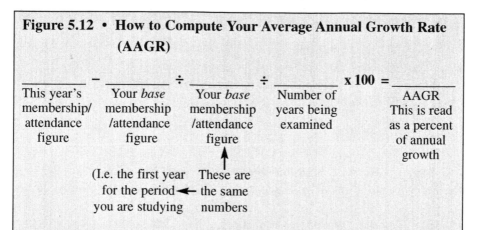

Figure 5.12 • How to Compute Your Average Annual Growth Rate (AAGR)

By using the tools of the strategic planner, the church leader can better ascertain not only the effectiveness of specific strategies, but also perhaps even the elusive presence and direction of the Holy Spirit. Strategic tools must never be used as an end unto themselves, but rather as another tool in our endeavor to effectively present the Good News, and to disciple those who respond.

Endnotes

1. Quoted by Fred R. David, *Strategic Management: Concepts and Cases*, 9th ed. (Upper Saddle River, NJ: Prentice Hall, 2002), 3.

2. Categorizing churches by size can be challenging. However, in the process of analyzing and strategizing, it becomes necessary to define churches by some standard. For many years, Lyle Schaller's definitions were widely accepted [Lyle E. Schaller, *The Multiple Staff and the Larger Church* (Nashville: Abingdon Press, 1980), 27-31]. Schaller's designations are:

    Fellowship Size: 40 or less attendees, where focus is on relationships.

    Small Size: 50-100 attendees, where focus is on the feeling of "one big family."

    Middle Size: 100-175 attendees, where focus is on maintaining adequate ministries.

    Awkward Size: 175-225, where focus shifts toward trying to maintain feeling of smallness as church becomes a "congregation of congregations."

    Large Size: 225-450, where focus is on functioning as a congregation of congregations (i.e., in the business world the analogy is that of a company that has grown into multidivisional structure).

    Huge Size: 450-700, where the focus is on maintaining a burgeoning administrative strategy in a true multidivisional structure.

    A more straightforward size structure has been set forth by Gary McIntosh [*One Size Doesn't Fit All: Bringing Out the Best in Any Size Church* (Grand

Rapids: Fleming H. Revell, 1999), 17-19]. McIntosh views congregations as one of three sizes:

Small Size: 15-200, where focus is the relational base.

Medium Size: 201-400, with focus on programming.

Large Size: 401+, where focus is on the organizational base.

While in my other writings I have used McIntosh's more concise designations, in this book on the management of churches, I will use the more precise terminology of Schaller. For a graph comparing Schaller and McIntosh's terminology, see "Figure 1.7: A Comparison of Two Popular Designations for Congregational Size" in Bob Whitesel and Kent R. Hunter's *A House Divided: Bridging the Generation Gaps in Your Church* (Nashville: Abingdon Press, 2000), 29.

3. Emil Brunner, *The Misunderstanding of the Church*, trans. Harold Knight (London: Lutterworth Press, 1952), 10-19.

4. The idea of local church control—rather than regional and even international control—as the preferred model of the Protestant Reformation is based upon Luther and Calvin's understanding of early church history. In the New Testament, an elder (Greek, *presbyterios*) was a pastor/teacher. Until 200 A.D., a bishop (Greek, *episkopos*) was another primary name for elder. However, after 200 A.D. administrative challenges forced the church to elevate bishops into regional leaders [Thomas H. Greer and Gavin Lewis, *A Brief History of the Western World*, 7th ed. (New York: Harcourt Brace College Publishers, 1997), 152-54]. While this rise of professional managers was a strategic decision, it often removed the strategists from the people they were serving. The necessity to acquaint the local pastor with the basics of planning and administration were ceded to an increasingly detached hierarchy. As a result, local leadership was deprived of management skills. This gulf between regional administrators and local practitioners was further exasperated when Charlemagne (c. 775 A.D.) further politicized the church by appointing political attachés to important church offices because the church was the only institution accepted by all of his subjects. Regrettably, this detachment between strategist and local practitioner endures today.

5. See for example, Fred R. David, *Strategic Management*, 5.

6. Kent Miller, Professor of Strategic Planning, Krannert School of Business, Purdue University, in personal correspondence with the author, December 5, 2002.

7. We will see later in this chapter that "making disciples" is the primary measurable goal of Jesus' Great Commission in Matthew 29:19-20.

8. Quoted by Fred R. David, *Strategic Management*, 3.

9. Michael A. Hitt, R. Duane Ireland, and Robert E. Hoskisson, *Strategic Management: Competitiveness and Globalization*, 4th ed. (Cincinnati: South-Western College Publishing, 2001), 113.

10. Adapted from Michael Hitt, *Strategic Management*, 112-17.

11. Ralph Lauren Clothing has strategically developed an effective marketing strategy by providing clothes with a sense of "history." Today, with many people becoming *nouveau riche* (or simply wanting to look like they are), Ralph Lauren provides upscale clothing that is washed and/or distressed to give the appearance of use and history. Both the Ralph Lauren clothing line and its advertisements exude this sense of history. For those without a long and distinguished family history to draw upon, the Ralph Lauren line offers a classic yet weathered look that can at least make you feel like you summer in the Hamptons, Martha's Vineyard, or the Adirondacks. This attempt to historicize clothing and, conversely, the buyer, is a core competency that few other companies have been able to develop. Of interesting note, clothier Gap Inc. has recently tried to attract the *nouveau riche* on a limited budget with "historized clothing" in its Old Navy line.

12. The multi-brand strategy of Gap Inc. is reflected in its three divisions: Old Navy, Gap Inc., and Banana Republic. While all three divisions seek to be in sync with the latest styles and trends, each division targets a different segment of the market. Old Navy targets the value shopper by offering trendy clothing at a much lower price (with a corresponding lower manufacturing quality). Banana Republic, on the other hand, reflects the upscale division with more expensive items. The original division, Gap Inc., addresses the middle-income segment with moderately priced clothing. However, because the "gap" (pun intended) between the price breaks and styles of Old Navy and the Gap stores is not that significant, Old Navy stores are drawing customers away from the Gap stores. This cannibalization threatens to undermine Gap Inc.'s multi-brand strategy.

13. Rudolf Otto, *The Idea of the Holy: An Inquiry into the Non-Rational Factor in the Idea of the Divine and Its Relation to the Rational*, trans. John W. Harvey, 2nd ed. (New York: Oxford University Press, 1950), 12-13.

14. Bob Whitesel, *Growth by Accident, Death by Planning: How NOT To Kill a Growing Congregation* (Nashville: Abingdon Press, forthcoming). See especially chapter 6, "Missteps with Innovation" and chapter 9, "Missteps with Education."

15. In conversation with the author.

16. See especially the chapter "Identifying the Needs of the Unchurched" in *A House Divided: Bridging the Generation Gaps in Your Church* by Bob Whitesel and Kent R. Hunter (Nashville: Abingdon Press, 2000), 144-60.

17. The term "un-coerced" is employed here because sometimes leaders may use undue pressure to compel participation in certain ministries. This strategy can skew your analysis of strengths and weaknesses, unduly lionizing some programs, while overlooking others. Effective leadership avoids coercion and intimidation, for neither will result in a self-motivated volunteer.

18. Lyle E. Schaller, *The Interventionist* (Nashville: Abingdon Press, 1997), 21. Here Schaller gives an extended rationale for his use of the term *interventionist*, which he summarizes as "a synonym for change agent."

19. C. Peter Wagner, *Your Church Can Be Healthy* (Nashville: Abingdon Press, 1979), 41-43.
20. C. Peter Wagner, *Leading Your Church to Growth: The Secret of Pastor/People Partnerships in Dynamic Church Growth* (Ventura, CA: Regal Books, 1983), 182.
21. Whitesel and Hunter, *A House Divided*, 31-32.
22. Cell churches have at the heart of their experience and structure small groups called "cell groups." Through these cell churches, an alternative format of congregational structure has developed, often eschewing large corporate gatherings and preferring worship in small groups. In cell churches, it is not uncommon for weekly worship celebrations to take place exclusively in small groups, with large gatherings of the entire "cell church" taking place once a month or even less frequently. One of the most prolific and engaging writers of this movement is Joel Comiskey. With C. Peter Wagner, his *Home Cell Group Explosion: How Your Small Group Can Grow and Multiply* (Touch Publications, 2002) serves as a good introduction to the cell church philosophy.
23. An excellent book on the innovative use of small groups within one of the world's largest churches is *Caught in the Web: The Home Cell Unit System at Full Gospel Central Church, Seoul, Korea* by John W. Hurston and Karen L. Hurston (Anaheim, CA: Church Growth International, 1977).
24. Eddie Gibbs, *I Believe in Church Growth* (Grand Rapids: Eerdmans Publishing Co., 1981), 187-233.
25. George G. Hunter III, *The Celtic Way of Evangelism: How Christianity Can Reach the West . . . Again* (Nashville: Abingdon Press, 2000).
26. David, *Strategic Management*, 149.
27. Ibid., 63-64.
28. Andrew Campbell and Sally Yeung, "Creating a Sense of Mission," *Long Range Planning* 24, no. 4 (August 1991): 17.
29. Kent R. Hunter, *Your Church Has Personality: Find Your Focus – Maximize Your Mission* (Corunna, IN: Church Growth Center, 1997).
30. George Barna, *The Power of Vision: How You Can Capture and Apply God's Vision for Your Ministry* (Ventura, CA: Regal Books, 1992), 28, 38-39.
31. Whitesel and Hunter, *A House Divided*, 107-08.
32. Ibid., 108-11. I am highly indebted to Elmer L. Towns' excellent process outlined in *Vision Day: Capturing the Power of Vision* (Lynchburg, VA: Church Growth Institute, 1994), 24-25.
33. A. F. Osborn, *Applied Imagination: Principles and Procedures of Creative Problem Solving* (New York: Scribner Publishers, 1963), 149.
34. Sy Landau, Barbara Landau, and Daryl Landau, *From Conflict to Creativity: How Resolving Workplace Disagreements Can Inspire Innovation and Productivity* (San Francisco: Jossey-Bass, 1991), 128-29.
35. Gareth R. Jones, Jennifer M. George, and Charles W. L. Hill, *Contemporary Management* (Boston: Irwin McGraw-Hill, 2000), 218.

36. Whitesel, *Growth by Accident, Death by Planning*. See especially chapter 6, "Missteps with Innovation," and chapter 9, "Missteps With Education."

37. Whitesel, *Staying Power: Why People Leave the Church Over Change, and What You Can Do About It* (Nashville: Abingdon Press, 2003). In this book, I show how management research into exit behavior demonstrates that divisive groups will form in a congregation if a new idea is pressed too relentlessly and/or too quickly. See the chapter titled "Stage 2: When New Ideas are Introduced," pp. 67-75, to discover how to give new ideas time to germinate and engender broad support before implementation.

38. Whitesel, *Growth by Accident, Death by Planning*. See especially chapter 7, "Missteps with Evaluation."

39. Craig Pifer, in personal correspondence with the author, July 30, 2003.

40. Whitesel and Hunter, *A House Divided*, 202-21.

41. For a look at the more phenomenal aspects of church growth in the book of Acts, see C. Peter Wagner's helpful volumes, *Spreading the Fire: A New Look at Acts – God's Training Manual for Every Christian*, vols. 1 and 2 (Ventura, CA: Regal Books, 1994-1995).

42. "Active learners" is a designation derived from Jesus' Great Commission in Matthew 28:18-20. Here the church is told to *"go and make disciples of all nations, baptizing them in the name of the Father and of the Son and of the Holy Spirit, and teaching them to obey everything I have commanded you."* In *A House Divided*, I wrote, "Within this commission are four verbs, three of which are participles. Participles are helping verbs that modify or further describe another verb. Only one of the verbs in this passage is not a participle, and it is in the imperative and continuing tense. This verb would be the primary verb of the passage that the other three describe. 'Go,' 'baptize' and 'teaching' are the participles in the above passage, and as such must describe further or modify the primary verb. The spelling of the Greek word *matheteusate* tells us that 'make disciples' is the primary verb and that it is an imperative verb in the continuing tense. Being an imperative verb means that 'making disciples' expresses the central command of the Great Commission" (p. 207).

43. Whitesel and Hunter, *A House Divided*, 208-11.

44. While a CMN cannot take into account attendees who seek educational opportunities outside the church, a CMN can project a trend towards or away from discipleship opportunities. As such, it is a valuable indicator of trends.

45. Whitesel and Hunter, *A House Divided*, 204-205..

46. Ibid., 205.

47. Guidelines for convenient times to call, as well as employing appropriate phone etiquette are included in *A House Divided*, 212-15. For additional details on how to conduct a community survey, see chapter 13, "Marketing," in *The Church Leader's MBA*.

48. Donald A. McGavran, *Understanding Church Growth* (Grand Rapids: Wm. B. Eerdmans Publishing Company, 1970), 93.

49. Whitesel and Hunter, *A House Divided*, 206

50. Ibid., 94.

6

Analysis and Decision Making

Effective Ministry Management for the Church

"Speaking the truth in love, we will in all things grow up
into him who is the Head, that is, Christ."

—Ephesians 4:15 NIV

Caught in the Divide

Jim has served for twelve years as the senior pastor of Immanuel Church of Christ in Wisconsin. He recognized signs of division early. Over the years, the division has grown, and the conflict has increased in intensity. Jim became the lightning rod for criticism, slander, complaining, and disagreement. Although the group responsible for this negativity is a minority of the congregation, the volume and frequency of complaints makes Jim feel that half of the worshipping body is involved in the conflict.

Jim is an intelligent, gifted, and fun-loving person. Before the ministry, he was an attorney. Many of his congregants appreciate his quick wit, enthusiasm for life, and desire for effectiveness. They are energized by his vision. Key staff members and a strong core of dedicated leaders share his vision.

The other group continues to vocalize its discontent and foment discord. This group is opposed to nearly everything Jim and his leaders propose. As they have become more opposed to the direction of the church, their attacks have increased. Jim has been criticized for being lazy and unproductive. He also has been identified as an aggressive dictator. After more than a decade, Jim is frustrated, worn-out, and ready to resign. His family has discussed leaving the church, and he has thought privately about leaving the ministry. Jim has come to the conclusion it is time to quit—what else can he do?

Time to Quit, or Time for Analysis?

One of the greatest challenges for pastors is managing emotions. Since faith is located close to the seat of emotions, emotions can cloud the decision process. When that happens, it is hard to see the light at the end of the tunnel. The management lesson? Getting too close to the challenges of ministry makes it difficult to see the forest for the trees. It is typical for pastors and church leaders to digress into "symptom solving" rather than dealing with the "issues behind the issues." As one pastor said, "When you're up to your armpits in alligators, it's hard to think about draining the swamp."

The Apostle Paul was no stranger to challenges. In a letter to the church in Corinth, he lists some of the difficulties he faced. He writes of hard work, imprisonments, being whipped, stoned, shipwrecked, robbers, betrayal from the inside, threats from the outside, going without sleep, being hungry and thirsty, and not having enough food, shelter, or clothing. He writes about being under pressure because of his concern for the churches (2 Corinthians 11:24-29). Paul writes this: *"Do not be anxious about anything, but in everything, by prayer and petition, with thanksgiving, present your requests to God"* (Philippians 4:6). Paul tells them not to worry, but to ask God for what they need—always asking with a thankful heart. In this way, Paul demonstrates how Christian leaders can put perspective on their difficulties.

How Analysis Helps

As the most visible person within the church, the pastor often becomes the lightning rod for challenges and a magnet for complaints. Leaders in every sector of life experience the lightning-rod phenomenon, including CEOs of companies, mayors of cities, and heads of state. At the congregational level, the senior pastor often takes the heat for whatever might be wrong in the congregation.

Analysis Offers Perspective

When Jim backed away from the daily strains of the conflict at his church and allowed himself some perspective, he realized that he was the third pastor who had experienced this kind of turmoil. Since history tends to repeat itself analysis from the historical perspective is part of the diagnostic process.

It became apparent that the church was not really divided in half. It seemed so because the malcontents were louder, more organized, and more energized than everyone else. Looking closer he found that they represented thirty people out of the 200 who worshipped there. Drilling deeper he found that, of the thirty, six really fueled the others. Finally he learned that of the six, one couple led the charge. At the deepest level, Jim discovered that these people were unhappy but with life in general. They were dysfunctional members of society: in their church, their community, and in their extended families.

Analysis Seeks Balance

Analysis objectifies and balances the facts. It helps the pastor, as manager, move from reactive efforts based on emotions, to proactive problem solving. In Jim's case, the analysis of the detractors revealed some demographic commonalities. They were generally an older group, and resisted change. Many other older people were supportive of Jim, but they saw change objectively. The majority of the senior members were focused on the future direction of the church.

The church's direction is often a systemic issue of many of the challenges that surface. At Immanuel, the dissenting group generated conflict because it operated out of a different worldview. This group felt the objective was to provide a place of fellowship where congregants could share God's love with one another. In Immanuel's constitution, the goal was to make disciples of all people. This implied personal growth, fellowship with each other, outreach to others, and impact on the community. It was clear that the dissenting group shared a common worldview based on an unbiblical presupposition: "Since God is love, He has a priority for the comfort of His people." Whenever change is proposed by the leadership, people with the "comfort worldview" will always vote for their comfort. God is much more interested in your character than your comfort. The Scripture is filled with stories of individuals who accomplished much for God, but who abandoned their comfort zones. Jesus Christ is a primary example.

Analysis Examines History

Looking closer helped Jim understand why he was being identified as a dictator. This was a denominational and historical issue. Immanuel was created from a merger between a Congregational church and an Evangelical Reformed church. The Congregational form of government is similar to a pure democracy, everyone votes on everything. The Evangelical Reformed congregation operates from a republic form of government. These are very different approaches to decision making. It was clear that this group of thirty had been influenced, by the Congregational tradition. They saw the leadership exercised by the pastor and other elected leaders in the congregation as dictatorship.[1]

Concepts and Tools for Analysis

Consistent and careful analysis is an important part of effective management for the local church. Theologically, it is a matter of good stewardship. It is using the intelligence and tools God has given for the purpose of objectifying reality, and making clear decisions based on factual evidence. Unfortunately, many churches do not view the gathering of information as an important part of the analytical process. It is the responsibility of the pastor, as manager, to encourage careful analysis whenever possible. Proverbs 18:13 (LB) says: *"What a shame—yes, how stupid!—to decide before knowing the facts!"*

On the other hand, analysis is not the end of the process. Gary McIntosh, leader of the McIntosh Church Growth Network, says this about analysis: "Analysis is not a cure all for everything that makes the church sick. Like the doctor's thermometer, analysis is simply a tool to understand the symptoms. A thermometer never healed anyone, and neither will an analysis heal. What it will do is help church leaders understand the issues so that they can make a proper decision on what prescription to make for the church."[2]

Outside Intervention

One of the most constructive dynamics for analysis is to engage a consultant. These analysts provide a valuable function for congregations. Many churches enlist a consultant routinely. This can be as beneficial to a church as an annual checkup by a physician. The church consultant helps to identify the forest and the trees. This professional is trained to analyze more deeply. In the process, they will report reality and make suggestions. "The intentional interventionist is willing to accept the responsibility to change the course of history. . . . In other words, *interventionist* often is a synonym for change agent. . . . The interventionist comes prepared to offer new options that the client had never considered."[3]

The process of using an objective outsider insulates the pastor and the leadership from negative reaction. When pastors and leaders establish a direction that includes change, a church can become divided. A "we/they" relationship can result. *We*, the congregation, are against *they*, the pastor and leaders—who are suggesting this new direction. However, when a church uses an outside objective consultant, the interventionist becomes the "they" and the united congregation, which often includes the pastor and leaders, becomes the "we."

The Johari Window

What appears to be a local church's activity often is not an accurate picture of what is really going on. Norbert Hahn, a German theologian and pastor of Mt. Hermon Lutheran Church in Concord, North Carolina, says: "Church leaders need to know that a good deal of what drives action (and inaction), in both individuals (including the leaders) and organizations, is either fully unconscious, semi-conscious, or intentionally hidden or disguised."[4] He refers to Freudian principles and the work of the Frankfort School of Social Analytic

Theory, which has focused on invisible instincts, drives, and interests that animate individuals and organizations. Hahn notes, "Someone will 'act out' the unconscious anxieties of the organization—especially in times of change and when long-standing interests feel threatened."[5] This is a part of what is happening at Immanuel Church and underscores the challenges Pastor Jim faces.

The Johari Window can bring about a profound understanding of this phenomenon. The Johari Window is a square diagram with four quadrants designed to explain how people interact.

Figure 6.1 • The Johari Window

I see	You see
We both see	Neither of us sees

Notice that in every discussion, there are four areas of understanding. The upper left-hand quadrant of the Johari Window represents what I see and understand, but it does not include anything that you see. The upper right-hand quadrant includes reality as you understand it, but excludes what I know. The lower left-hand quadrant represents what we both see and understand. This is our common ground of agreement. The lower right-hand quadrant represents what neither of us sees.

The first two quadrants require more information, teaching, and revelation. If I see something that you don't see, I need to help you understand. If you see something that I don't know, you have to help me. In the quadrant where we both see, we have common ground. When we are in the lower right-hand quadrant, neither of us comprehends reality.

While the Johari Windows is a simple paradigm, it is helpful for understanding management dynamics and the challenges your church faces. Hahn points out that there are always land mines buried throughout the landscape of a congregation. This line of thinking underscores the reality that history repeats itself, even in congregations. He also affirms the value of consultants: "Leaders need to be in a continuous process of becoming self-aware through interaction with third parties."[6]

The Church Vitality Profile

Many self-study tools are available to aid in the analysis process for congregations. *The Church Vitality Profile* identifies eight character dimensions that impact congregational effectiveness:[7]

- Spiritual Health
- Environment
- Leadership
- Programming

- Outreach
- Openness to Change
- Attitude
- Assimilation of and Ministry to Inactives

This analytical tool includes questionnaires about these character dimensions for a cross section of the leadership. When the questionnaires are scored, the tabulation can provide a graphic reflection of the church's strengths and weaknesses in each of these areas. This enables the church to prioritize allocations of time, resources, and effort. *The Church Vitality Profile* then provides a profile template on which the congregation can be placed. The purpose is to determine the church's relative potential and probability for growth.

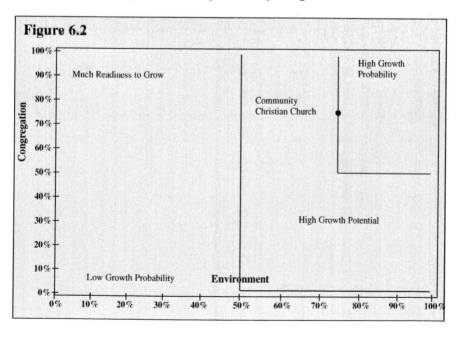

Figure 6.2

When *The Church Vitality Profile* is administered on an annual basis, it provides a benchmark of progress for each of the eight vitality traits, as well as the general growth potential. While this relatively inexpensive resource is a reflective tool only, it can be quite valuable over the course of time.

The Vision Audit

Another excellent analytical tool related to the critical area of congregational vitality is the *Vision Audit* developed by Burt Nanus, Professor of Management at the University of Southern California. Nanus is also Director of Research at USC's Leadership Institute. Designed primarily for secular organizations, the word "church" easily can be substituted for the word "organization." The *Vision Audit* is a simple tool that can help a congregation gauge momentum. It asks these four questions:

1. Does the organization have a clearly stated vision? If so, what is it?
2. If the organization continues on its current path, where will it be heading over the next decade? How good would such a direction be?
3. Do the key people in the organization know where the organization is headed and agree on the direction?
4. Do the structures, processes, personnel, incentives, and information systems support the current direction of the organization?[8]

While vision tends to be ethereal, these questions tie visionary concepts with reality in a way that demonstrates a connection between momentum and performance. The *Vision Audit* is a good analytical tool to use on a yearly basis in a leadership retreat for your church.

Worldview

Another critical area of church behavior and productivity is worldview. This concept is difficult to analyze because, like vision, it is an intangible. At the heart of the challenges that Immanuel Church of Christ faces are two worldview issues that drive the behavior of thirty discontented congregants. Their unbiblical worldviews concern (1) the purpose of the church, and (2) comfort versus change.

Darrow Miller describes worldview in this way: "A worldview is a set of assumptions held consciously or unconsciously in faith about the basic makeup of the world and how the world works."[9] A worldview is much like an iceberg's hidden mass—seven-eighths of the iceberg itself lies below the surface. The behaviors of people within the church represent the tip of the iceberg.

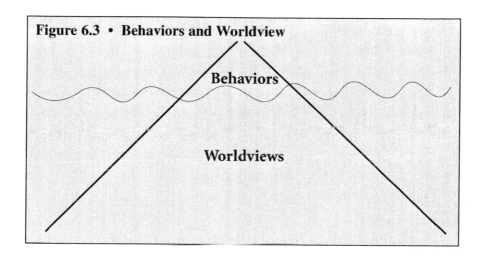

Figure 6.3 • Behaviors and Worldview

Behaviors represent a small part of what takes place within your church. These behaviors are driven by worldviews, which represent the hidden, but largest part of congregational life. Worldviews drive the behavior of people within the congregation.

Most of a pastor's management activities are directed at the behavioral dimension of church life. Jim and the leaders at Immanuel have spent much of the last ten years putting out fires. It was only through the consultant that they began to focus on worldview issues, directing their efforts *away* from "putting out fires" and *toward* "taking the matches away from those who were starting them."

The *Discover Your Windows Questionnaire* is a reflective tool developed to help people understand their worldviews. Used with the book *Discover Your Windows: Lining Up With God's Vision*, church members can be guided toward a biblical worldview in ten key areas that impact the productivity of the church.[10] The ten worldview areas, described as "windows," are based on the assumption that the way you see has enormous impact on how you behave toward your world. The ten windows are:

- Purpose
- Comfort
- Image
- Priorities
- Stewardship

- Financing
- Change
- Leadership
- Teamwork
- Attitude

Discover Your Windows helps the individual identify worldviews in these ten areas and compare them with biblical worldviews. Analytical tools such as outside intervention, the Johari Window, the *Church Vitality Profile*, the *Vision Audit*, and *Discover Your Windows* are helpful not only for church leaders, but for new member or new staff assimilation.

Leadership

Leadership Analysis

Most of those who teach and train Christian leaders recognize that leadership is key to an effective congregation. John C. Maxwell has said, "Everything rises and falls on leadership." Bill Hybels, pastor of Willow Creek Community Church in North Barrington, Illinois, concurs.

Several resources are available today to help congregations analyze leadership qualities and seek the best fit for their leaders. A common analytical tool is a survey of spiritual gifts. Two of the most popular spiritual gifts inventories are the "Wagner-Modified Houts Questionnaire" and the *Spiritual Gifts Discovery Survey and Scoring Sheet*.[11] Another spiritual gifts analysis focuses on "Life Gifts," exploring personality types, values, and passions.[12]

The *Taylor-Johnson Temperament* Analysis® identifies nine prominent character traits that become evident as people relate to one another.[13] Another resource used in churches is the *DiSC Evaluation Instrument*.[14] This identifies a person's type and style, and is helpful in analyzing individuals who work together on a church team. *The Myers-Briggs Type Indicator* is a similar tool that requires training and certification.[15]

Power Centers

We tend to think of power in negative terms. The power of Satan is a spiritual reality, for example. People can be "power hungry," accomplishing their goals at any cost. But power is not necessarily bad. The power of the Holy Spirit clearly was the force behind the Early Church. People who are down and out are often encouraged to seek empowerment.

The pastor and leaders in the congregation should have the ability to understand power in its various manifestations. They should know how to analyze and use power, gently building a supportive power base and mentoring new leaders who share the leadership team's vision.

The pastor and those on the leadership team should know and make use of the power of prayer, Bible study, and personal worship apart from the congregation, as well as continuing education, support groups, and strategic alliances.[17] In *Managing the Congregation*, authors Norman Shawchuck and Roger Heuser write about power as the currency of management: "Management is a special kind of power. Stated another way, power goes with the territory of management. In congregations, managers possess a kind of 'raw' power by reason that they exert tremendous control and influence over the utilization of all of the congregation's human and physical resources. The managers sit 'in the seats of power,' and the pastor-as-manager's seat is the most powerful of all. Yet many pastors are oblivious to the power they possess as managers."[18]

Shawchuck and Heuser also address the use of power and the reluctance that pastors as managers often exhibit in this area.

Many managers and religious organizations express an aversion to the use of power. . . . It is true that persons should not be forced. They should not be seduced. And they should be free to decide for themselves. But in managing paid and volunteer workers, [the unwillingness to use the power of management] may lead to anarchy or, more commonly, systems paralysis. . . . Any organization that succeeds must have managers who understand and use power to free persons to be fully responsible for themselves, and to work with others toward desired and worthy ends.[19]

Lessons for Decision Making

The Danger of Indecision

President Gerald R. Ford said, "Indecision is often worse than the wrong action."[20] "*A double minded man is unstable in all his ways*" (James 1:8 KJV). Immanuel dug a hole because it failed to deal with issues. It failed to confront thirty people who were undermining the congregation. In effect, by default, this group was given the liberty to sabotage the direction of the congregation!

It is difficult for a pastor to make the hard decisions. As manager and leader of the congregation, the pastor frequently finds it challenging to make the tough call. John Maxwell explains:

Many pastors are people pleasers. They feel that it is more important to please people than to lead people. This is a huge mistake. You can't wait for consensus or you will never make a right decision at the right time. The great decisions in life are usually made when you are all alone. They are lonely decisions. You can't wait until everybody agrees. It just never happens. So here is the key principle: You can't lead people if you need people. Learn to unconditionally love people but not need them.[21]

Leadership Discernment

Another key to decision making is to understand when to be involved and when not. Some decisions are more important than others. An important element of management is discernment constantly applied to the relative importance of decisions—made by the thousands every year—in a local church: "The leader/pastor knows that there is a hierarchy of importance regarding decisions and is secure in the ability to distinguish between those decisions that require personal input and those that do not."[22] Know when you should be *involved* in the process, when you should be *in charge* of the process, and when the process can be *delegated*. That summarizes the pivotal management discipline of discernment.

The Strategic Profile

A primary element of good decision-making is to develop an environment that has well-defined parameters that provide focus and boundaries. Warren

Buffett, founder of Berkshire Hathway, Inc., describes it this way: "Berkshire is my painting, so it should look the way I want it to look."[24] In *The Power of Strategic Thinking*, author Michel Robert identifies this as a strategic profile. In church life, the pastor, along with key leadership team members, has the task of developing a strategic profile of what the church would look like if the people in the congregation were submissive to God's will.[25]

What key elements will help you develop this framework for focused decision making? There are three: (1) a philosophy of ministry, (2) a mission statement, and (3) a statement of vision.

The Philosophy of Ministry Statement

The philosophy of ministry is a statement of approximately ten to fifteen paragraphs that defines the answer to the question, "Who are you, as a congregation?"[26] A philosophy of ministry statement can be developed by answering the following questions:

1. What is it that makes your church unique? How is it different from the churches around it? How is it different from churches of similar size within your own denomination or association?
2. What are your priorities? What is it that you do first? Best?
3. How would Christians in your community describe your church? What are you known for?
4. How would you describe this church to an unchurched neighbor who moved in across the street? What aspects of the congregation would you highlight if you were restricted to a five-minute conversation about your church?

This description is similar to the way I might describe my wife. I would describe her attributes. I would likely focus on her strengths and overlook her weaknesses! I would tell you about her interests, how she spends most of her time and finds fulfillment. In a sense, I would describe her personality. Even though you have never met my wife, you would have a picture—a snapshot—of who she is.

Just as every individual person has a personality, so does every congregation. It is formulated by the influences of its history, location, denominational background and theology, polity, key leaders, the spiritual gifts of prominent influencers within the congregation, and many other factors.

Once you have developed a philosophy of ministry statement it should be printed in brochure form. In the context of this discussion, the philosophy of ministry statement is a key tool for decision makers to be "on the same page," regardless of the issue being discussed. Many churches translate their philosophy of ministry into a DVD, which can capture some of the affective enthusiasm that the print medium cannot communicate. Whether in printed form or electronic, the philosophy of ministry should be reviewed regularly and used continually to define the parameters for decision-making.

The Mission Statement

The mission statement also is helpful in defining the boundaries for decision-making. The mission statement for your congregation answers the question, "What do you do?" This is a short statement of no more than four to six sentences that succinctly reflects the congregation's purpose. This, too, should be constantly communicated so that it becomes a platform for the decision-making process.

One of the pastor's management responsibilities is to avoid a subtle or subconscious disregard for the mission statement. Many churches suffer in the decision-making area because people are not clear about the church's purpose. A primary management task of the pastor is to keep this "oral tradition" alive before the congregation. Occasionally, the congregation should take inventory of its stated purpose. Lyle Schaller provides an excellent diagnostic question that should be posed at least annually to the core group of leaders: "If a complete stranger came and identified everything we do under the label of what we call ministry, what would the stranger conclude is the operational definition of our purpose?" Schaller adds, "In other words, let us define our current purpose by what we do, not by what we say."[27]

The Vision Statement

A third key document that sets the guidelines for decision-making is the vision statement. Many have a mission statement, few have a philosophy of ministry. Even fewer have a vision statement. Helen Keller once stated, "The most pathetic person in the world is someone who has sight, but has no vision."[28] George Barna contrasts the vision statement and the mission statement in this way: "The **mission statement** is a definition of the ministry objectives of the church. The **vision statement** is a clarification of the specific direction and activities the church *will* pursue toward making a true ministry impact."[29]

The vision statement answers the question, "Where are you going?" Norbert Hahn emphasizes the value of casting a vision for a new pastor. "It is always advantageous for a leader to start a new position with a vision in hand, to which he or she can ask people to subscribe if they want him or her to be their leader." Hahn says this is similar to marriage vows and can serve as a useful foundation.[30]

Vision casting is a key element of pastoral management and leadership. Many churches need leaders who cast a vision. "One of the most important decisions a leader makes is *how* to 'cast' the vision. Those leaders who have been successful contend that you must take advantage of all opportunities, at all times, to share the vision."[31] The leader must have a personal vision that gives guidance to the congregation and from which the leader draws strength and inspiration when things get tough.[32] Managing the vision includes several vehicles for vision casting: sermons, printed materials, banners, posters, logos, the church sign, a website, the letterhead, teaching, meetings, and coaching of key influencers.

Proper Representation

With key parameters established for decision making through a philosophy of ministry statement, a mission statement, and a vision statement, the behavioral side of decision-making must be considered. The pastor should involve in the decision-making process those who have caught, or who are in the process of catching, the vision. This involves two factors: (1) the pastor should set high expectations when recruiting for leadership positions; and (2) the pastor should carefully monitor the recruitment process. That may sound harsh to those from the paradigm of a congregational form of government. However, no organization made up of human beings is a pure democracy. In our family our children do not get an equal vote on whether or not we make the monthly mortgage payment, or when they should go to school or to the dentist. Likewise, in the church, not every individual, group, or viewpoint must be represented in the decision-making body, or involved in every decision. While it may be contrary to the theological subconscious of many pastors, shutting "trouble makers" out of the decision-making process can reduce wasted time and energy. It is important to add that leaders should always firmly support the vision of the congregation and its biblical foundation, and be accountable to theological integrity.[33]

The Bottom Line

Another key aspect of decision-making is widely known, but almost never discussed. It is the honest admission that the bottom line for decisions is . . . the bottom line: money. In the church every decision ultimately comes down to the "purse strings." Essential to the management process, as it relates directly to decision-making, is the ability to acquire financial knowledge and stewardship skills, and combine them with a strong trust that God will bless faithful ministry. Understanding your congregation's financial history, assets, and potential is a crucial element of pastoral management. The leadership team should consider how the congregation's giving can be increased. In tandem with this principle is a key management maxim that when giving dips, the leadership should not always revert to cutbacks. If we believe that God is the wellspring of boundless resources, then we should not limit the answer to our problems to worldly or secular rescue. This is based on a key theological issue and reflects a primarily Christian worldview: Is God a God of scarcity, or a God of abundance? What does the Bible say?

An Action Focus

Analysis and decision-making are worthless without action. The pastor's management focus must have an action bias. In the New Testament, the *Book of Acts* could be called the *Book of Action*. Disciples are not made by what you know. Disciples are made by what God's people *do*, based on what they know and the decisions they make. It is not enough to be a visionary. You must live out that vision: "Visionary living is more than simply being able to focus on the vision you have received from God. Christian visionaries integrate the elements that make their vision practical. A true visionary believer is one who lives in harmony with his or her mission, vision, values, gifts, and abilities."[34]

In the minutes of every meeting conducted at the church, good ministry management should result in a personal point-of-action list for every person at the meeting. These are specific statements that identify what each person on that committee, board, or ministry team has agreed to accomplish, and include a time frame for when that action is to be accomplished. These points-of-action lists should be appended to the end of the minutes. At the next meeting, one of the first orders of business should be to review the points-of-action lists for each person, holding the relevant people accountable. This helps to develop a framework of action as the purpose for all decisions.

When your congregation hires a consultant, be sure that you partner with an interventionist who requires the congregation to develop action plans for each recommendation. A good action plan will identify an individual responsible for the plan. It also will include steps intended to accomplish the activities that will result in meeting the recommended objective. A good action plan also includes a timetable that will benchmark when certain methodology steps are completed. This presupposes the measurability of completed steps. Each step must require a measurable way of identifying its culmination.

Analysis and decision-making are important parts of ministry management. Without action, however, there are few God-pleasing results. The pastor's responsibility is to manage ministry toward action and accomplishment. In ministry, do not confuse effort with results.

Under God's Direction

The church is a divine creation. Only the presence of God can make it successful. It is also a human organization. It can be crippled by poor management, or invigorated by good management.

In the management process, discipline yourself to stop, step away, and analyze. Ask yourself the question, "What is going on behind the scenes?" Conduct research. Get outside help, if necessary. Identify reality to the best of your ability. Use the information you have gathered for good, prayerful, sound decision making. Manage the decision-making process away from emotional knee-jerk reactions, to intentional, objective conclusions.

Teach people to understand the biblical worldview. Help them to learn that the way they see the world is the way they act, even in the world of the church. Identify and develop the church's philosophy of ministry, mission statement, and statement of vision. Use these as parameters and boundaries for the decision-making process. Help people get on the same page and maximize the mission of your church. Use tools to analyze personality traits, gifts, passions, worldviews, interests, and the corporate health and vitality of your church.

Throughout this process, subordinate your management of ministry to God's direction. Begin each day with this prayer: "God, use me for the work of Your Kingdom today. Direct me according to Your will." Analysis and decision-making must be empowered by the Holy Spirit. Even with the most organized plan, you can become frustrated if you do not commit all of your work to the Lord through prayer. Humble submission in prayer will open the door for the Holy Spirit to give life to your analysis and decision-making, and maximize its impact within your church.[35]

Endnotes

1. For more information concerning church structure as it relates to decision-making, see *Restructuring the Church* (Corunna, IN: Church Doctor Ministries, 2002).
2. In personal correspondence with the author.
3. Lyle E. Schaller, *The Interventionist* (Nashville, TN: Abingdon Press, 1997), 21.
4. Norbert Hahn, in correspondence with the author.
5. Ibid.
6. Ibid.
7. *The Church Vitality Profile* is available from Church Doctor Ministries, www.churchdoctor.org, (800) 626-8515.
8. Burt Nanus, *Visionary Leadership: Creating a Compelling Sense of Direction for Your Organization* (San Francisco: Jossey-Bass Publishers, 1992), 56-57.
9. Darrow L. Miller, *Discipling Nations: The Power of Truth to Transform Cultures* (Seattle: YWAM Publishing, 1998), 36. This is similar to a worldview definition described by James W. Sire, *The Universe Next Door* (Downers Grove, IL: InterVarsity Press, 1976).
10. Kent R. Hunter, *Discover Your Windows Questionnaire* (Corunna, IN: Church

Doctor Ministries, 2003) and *Discover Your Windows: Lining Up With God's Vision* (Nashville, TN: Abingdon Press, 2002).

11. C. Peter Wagner, *Finding Your Spiritual Gifts: Wagner-Modified Houts Questionnaire* (Ventura, CA: Regal Books, 1995) and *Your Spiritual Gifts Can Help Your Church Grow: How to Find Your Gifts and Use Them to Bless Others* (Regal, 1995). Kent R. Hunter, *Spiritual Gifts Discovery Survey and Scoring Sheet* Corunna, IN: Church Doctor Ministries, 1985).

12. Jane A.G. Kise, David Stark, and Sandra Krebs Hirsh, *Life Keys: Discovering Who You Are, Why You're Here, and What You Do Best* (Minneapolis: Bethany House Publishers, 1996). This book includes perforated cards at the back, which help to sort gifts and passions. This organized system can be computerized, allowing you to develop a database to organize gifts and talent-directed ministries with the congregation. Another book based on a Bible study of spiritual gifts is *Gifted for Growth: An Implementation Guide for Mobilizing the Laity* by Kent R. Hunter (Corunna, IN: Church Doctor Ministries, 1985). This book also includes a gifts discovery analytical tool, as well as perforated cards at the back that enable database development.

13. The *Taylor-Johnson Temperament Analysis®* requires certified training before it can be administered. This resource is available from Psychological Publications, Inc., 290 Conejo Ridge Avenue, Suite 100, Thousand Oaks, CA 91361-4928.

14. *DiSC: Dimensions of Behavior* assessment tools are available from the Center for Internal Change and Inscape Publishing, Mt. Prospect, IL.

15. The *Myers-Briggs Type Indicator* (Palo Alto, CA: CPP, Inc. and Davies-Black® Publishing).

16. A good tool to help you understand your conflict management style is the *Conflict Management Survey* by Jay Hall (Waco, TX: Teleometrics International, Inc., 1996).

17. Norbert Hahn.

18. Norman Shawchuck and Roger Heuser, *Managing the Congregation: Building Effective Systems to Serve People* (Nashville, TN: Abingdon Press, 1996), 233.

19. Ibid, 234-35.

20. Quoted in *God's Little Instruction Book for the Workplace* (Colorado Springs: Cook Communications Ministries/Honor Books, 1995).

21. John C. Maxwell, *INJOY Life Club Tape*, vol. 14, no. 2 (Atlanta, GA: INJOY, Inc.).

22. George Barna, *Habits of Highly Effective Churches* (Ventura, CA: Regal Books, 1999), 42.

23. Gary McIntosh, in correspondence with the author.

24. Quoted in "The Warren Buffett You Don't Know," *Business Week*, July 5, 1999.

25. Michel Robert, *The Power of Strategic Thinking: Lock in Markets, Lock Out Competitors* (New York: McGraw-Hill, 2000), 56.

26. *Your Church Has Personality: Find Your Focus—Maximize Your Mission by Kent R. Hunter* provides a step-by-step process for developing a philosophy of

ministry (Corunna, IN: Church Doctor Ministries, 1997). Another resource that deals with this subject is Harold J. Westing, *Create and Celebrate Your Church's Uniqueness: Designing a Church Philosophy of Ministry* (Grand Rapids, MI: Kregel Resources, 1993).

27. Lyle E. Schaller, *44 Questions for Congregational Self-Appraisal* (Nashville, TN: Abingdon Press, 1998), 89-90.

28. As quoted in Jone Johnson Lewis, *Wisdom Quotes: Quotations to Inspire and Challenge*. Located at http://www.wisdomquotes.com, Vision Quotes.

29. George Barna, *The Power of Vision: How You Can Capture and Apply God's Vision for Your Ministry* (Ventura, CA: Regal Books, 1992), 38 (emphasis mine).

30. Norbert Hahn.

31. George Barna, *The Power of Vision*, 143.

32. Norbert Hahn.

33. Ibid.

34. George Barna, *The Power of Vision*, 122.

35. Gary McIntosh.

What Church Leader's Need to Know About . . .

Organizational Behavior

Grasping the Behavior and Personality of a Church

"Even if you are on the right track,
you'll get run over if you just sit there."

—WILL ROGERS, AMERICAN HUMORIST[1]

Growth Inhibitors

"**O**ur consultant told me I was part of the problem," Pastor Bill declared. "And he is right." It was harder for me than it was for Bill to utter that statement. Bill pastored First Baptist, a church that averaged over 200 in weekly Sunday attendance. Although the church had been growing for three of the past five years, it had plateaued during the last two years. Still, the community surrounding the church continued to add new residents. Sensing underlying growth inhibitors, church leaders had hired me to help them develop a strategic plan. My analysis concluded that four key factors were thwarting the church's growth.

First, the church had an inadequate network of small groups. Small groups— whether they are Sunday school classes, task groups, committees, or home Bible study groups—are the interpersonal foundation of a growing church. First Baptist had only seven such groups for 350 members.

Second, the congregation did not have a clear idea of what kind of church it wanted to be. Some wanted the church to become more like the charismatic/Pentecostal church nearby. Others wanted to maintain their Baptist distinctiveness, with an altar call after every service. Others wanted to focus on their music program, which attracted people from across the region. These numerous directions in which the church was headed were laudable, but too diverse for most to ascertain where the church fit. Many people kept from fully committing to First Baptist, fearful that the church might become something unexpected.

A third factor inhibiting First Baptist's growth was the changing median age of the community. Twenty years earlier, the community had primarily consisted of retired blue-collar workers, whose neatly trimmed houses dotted shady, peaceful streets. However, in the last seven years the community had started to experience an influx of Baby Boomers looking for reasonably priced housing and safe streets for their families. The church also was experiencing the entry of Baby Boomers and their families. Pastor Bill had welcomed these families, even as the new attendees began to outnumber the mostly retirement-age members of the congregation. Feeling that they were losing control, the aging members began to subtly resist change. Bill felt caught in the middle, and even had considered leaving.

A fourth key inhibitor was the new size of the congregation. When the number of attendees passed the 200 mark, the church's internal structure began to change. But, the leadership structure did not. Prior to the growth, the church had fewer than 100 in attendance. But now, after three years of growth, two more years of moderate and then low growth; the church had entered a new size structure. Bill and the church leaders continued to administer the church as if were still a church of 100 attendees, relying on a small staff who tried to do most of the labor-intensive tasks themselves. Staff burnout loomed.

From the pulpit, Bill shared with the congregation the growth inhibitors, as well as the action steps the strategy groups had established. There was one more area to address—and this was hard for Bill, for it dealt with a change in his leadership style. "Our consultant told me I was part of the problem," Bill declared. Silence spread across the auditorium. "And he is right," he continued.

"I've been leading this church like it is a church of a hundred, because that's the only size of church I've ever led . . . till now. I'm ready to move forward. But, it's going to require some changes in First Baptist—and in Bill."

It didn't take long for First Baptist to regain its strong growth curve. First Baptist turned a corner and became a vibrant, growing congregation of multiple generations. A name change reflected its vibrant and affable personality. First Baptist Church became known as First Church.

Defining Organizational Behavior

The transition from an aging or declining church to a healthy congregation did not come easily. But it came deliberately, as the leaders incorporated many of the tools listed in this chapter. .

In their seminal text on organizational behavior, Professors Deborah Nelson and James Quick describe organizational behavior as "the study of individual behavior and grow dynamics in organizational settings. It focuses on timeless topics like motivation, leadership, teamwork, . . . exceptional performance, restructuring organizations, . . . [and] what happens when organizations . . . face the pressure to become current, competitive, and agile."[2]

While it is not possible to examine in depth every aspect of organizational behavior, I will focus on four primary principles:

1. *Leadership.* First, we will look at the important role of leadership, and the difference between simply good leaders and great ones. We will see that great leaders customarily are not autocrats, but facilitators and mentors, training others to succeed.
2. *Motivation.* You will learn how to motivate volunteers and staff to achieve top performance. By grasping the future direction of the church, those involved will work together for progress.
3. *Teamwork.* We will see how small groups help build cohesiveness and unity as a congregation grows beyond the "fellowship" atmosphere of a small church. And we will see how these small groups can effectively meet the social as well as the ministry needs of a growing congregation.
4. *Adapting Your Management Structure and Style.* As a congregation grows, its organizational and management structure must also evolve. If

these structures do not evolve, the church will cease to progress, and may even die due to an outdated organizational leadership.

Leadership

Effective leadership is one of the most crucial factors in creating and sustaining organizational growth and health. Resources on this important topic are abundant, readily available, and embrace a surprising number of good ideas. However, for our purposes in this book—which examines what business school instructors wish church leaders knew about management—I will tackle some of the more overlooked yet critical aspects of effective church leadership.

Effective Leaders Learn Fast and Keep on Learning

"Seminary was a great experience. But most of what I learned about managing a church came from the first three churches I almost killed." Bill summed up what he had learned about strategic church management. "Seminary is great for theology, history and the like," Bill continued. "But there ought to be courses that teach pastors how to manage the church. Because without it, you might kill a church first."

Bill sounded a clarion call that echoes continually among church leaders. While the classic disciplines of theology, history, and spiritual formation are adequately addressed in seminary, few schools offer courses that deal with the management and organizational behavior of congregations. Yet, it is this topic that leads most often to pastoral dissatisfaction and turnover.

James Belasco, professor of management at San Diego State University, and Ralph Stayer, CEO of Johnsonville Sausage, put it this way: "Success is a valuable teacher, provided it does not lull us into complacency. Whatever puts us where we are will not take us where we need to go. Circumstances change; leaders must change also, or be left behind. The skills learned to be a good supervisor will not help anyone be a good president. Continued learning is crucial to continued success."[3]

Effective Leaders Are Driven by a Clear Purpose

The Greek sentence construction identifies the imperative verb *"making disciples"* as the goal of this commission. The participles *"going, "baptizing,* and "*teaching*" are part of that disciple-making process. Peter Wagner points out that the *going, baptizing, and teaching* are "never ends in themselves. They all should be used as a part of the process of making disciples."[5]

However, the goal of *making disciples* has to start with the pastor. It is impossible to generate a purpose from the ground up. Selecting an appropriate pastor is critical to the success of discipleship. A church that calls a pastor, or a denomination that appoints a shepherd must carefully screen candidates to ascertain the purpose that drives them, and to ensure that this purpose coincides with God's purpose. Failure to address this stage circumspectly will lead to frequent detours from God's intended course.

Effective Leaders Are Driven by Ethics

The leader of an organization sets the moral and ethical tone for that organization. The Bible warns, "*Whoever can be trusted with very little can also be trusted with much, and whoever is dishonest with very little will also be dishonest with much*" (Luke 16:10). The Bible sets challenging expectations for various leaders in both 1 Timothy 3 and Titus 1, calling them, among other things, to be "*above reproach*" (1 Timothy 3:2), "*not a lover of money*" (verse 3), "*have a good reputation with outsiders*" (verse 7), "*not pursuing dishonest gain*" (verse 8 and Titus 1:7), "*one who loves what is good*" (Titus 1:8).

An example of ethical solidarity with suffering employees is evidenced in Carl Reichardt's leadership of Wells Fargo bank during the bank deregulation crisis. Reichardt stated, "There's too much waste in banking, getting rid of it takes tenacity, not brilliance."[6] Reichardt let his employees know that everyone would suffer as the bank weathered the crisis. He froze executive salaries, closed the executive dining room, and sold the corporate jets. From Reichardt's example of shouldering the pain with his employees, his company emerged from the crisis to become one of the primary banking providers in the twenty-first century.

Motivation for Outstanding Ministry

Motivation for outstanding ministry must pervade the entire organization. It begins when an organization discovers its core competencies and builds mission and vision statements upon those core competencies. A resulting understanding of strengths and weaknesses, combined with a resolute faith in a church's mission and vision drives the organization forward in unity. In his look at "good-to-great" companies, Jim Collins found that "every good-to-great company embraced what we came to call the Stockdale Paradox: You must maintain unwavering faith that you can and will prevail in the end, regardless of individuals. *And, at the same time*, have the discipline to confront the most brutal facts of your current reality, whatever they might be" (italics Collins).[15]

At Every Level

In order for this motivation to pervade the organization, it must be exemplified most clearly at the top. Elmer Towns, dean at Liberty University, has often said about foreign missions that "the light that shines the furthest, shines the brightest at home." The motivation for effective and robust foreign missionary action begins with an even more robust mission program in the home church and its surrounding environs. Leadership, for Towns, must be exemplified and modeled from the source outward.

A leader must transfer the ownership for this outstanding performance from the senior management to every person in the organization. Belasco and Stayer tender an illustration in their article, "Why Empowerment Doesn't Empower: The Bankruptcy of Current Paradigms."[16]

Early in our leadership careers we became grounded in lay involvement. We read a lot about it, and it sounded good. . . . We began by holding church-wide meetings to solicit congregational participation. . . . It rapidly deteriorated, however, into a gripe session. Congregants kept bringing up situations that needed fixing. We made long lists of things to fix and worked hard to fix everything before the next meeting. But this turned out to be a full-time job. We told ourselves, 'You have to demonstrate good faith. It will take time. Eventually they'll run out of things to fix and you can get on with solving the church's real problems.' Fixing their problems, after all, was part of our leadership responsibility. Eighteen months later, we were still receiving long lists to fix at every meeting. We ran out of patience before they ran out of lists. In retrospect, the problem is clear to us. We were owning all the responsibility for fixing the problems."[17]

Eventually, Belasco and Stayer discovered that the missing ingredient was a transfer of ownership for fixing the problems from the leadership to the workers. Leaders must help workers understand that *everyone* should identify *and* fix the problems.

Diffusion Theory

As Belasco and Stayer found out, the process of transferring ownership is challenging and, thus, must be carefully undertaken. To graph this process, let's outline a seven-step process for "trickling down" goals from the leader to the average participant. This outline is an abbreviated form of what is called "diffusion theory" in the management field."[18]

1. *Start by envisioning yourself.* Through prayer, Scripture, research, and input, gain an understanding of where your organization is, and where God intends it to go.
2. *Envision your circle of accountability.* These are trusted friends and colleagues that can provide accountability and perspective. Allow them to further refine the vision/mission.

   (In some church structures, Steps 3 and 4 may be reversed due to the leadership structure.)

3. *Envision the staff.* The staff often will bear the brunt of change and its ramifications. Thus, early in the process, staff members should be informed and asked to tender advice regarding the mission/vision.
4. *Envision the leadership core.* By leadership core, I mean the primary administrative and decision-making council, board, or vestry of the church. Support from this group is vital for successfully trickling-down ownership. This step, along with step 3, must be undertaken deliberately, but judiciously.
5. *Envision the informal leaders.* Every church has "gatekeepers" and opinion makers who need to understand and embrace the mission/vision. Do not

forget these individuals, treating them with the same respect and regard you gave official leaders in steps three and four.

6. *Envision your congregation.* Only now is it time to approach the congregation. Too many leaders fail to transfer ownership because they *start* with step six. From the pulpit or lectern, they will announce some new idea or plan. "It's just a way to gauge response," Bill said about one such public proclamation. However, leaders, both formal and informal, are usually caught off guard by such experimentation.

7. *Envision your community.* Now you can go public. Once the organization has fully accepted ownership for the new idea, change, or mission/vision, only then should the outside community be given a chance to peruse it. This not only preserves unity in the organization, but also promotes a unified manifestation to a observant world all too familiar with our disagreements.

Defining Small Groups and Teams

Small groups by definition are "any group of three to twelve people formally or informally meeting approximately one or more times a month within the church fellowship network. Though they may on occasion be comprised of more than twelve individuals, the cell group's cohesiveness is rarely found in meetings of more than twenty individuals."[19]

The Benefits of Small Groups and Teams
Productivity

The reason we include the term "teams" is because companies have learned that teams are especially helpful in accomplishing work that is complicated, complex, interrelated, or involved more work than one person can handle. When knowledge, skills, talents, and/or abilities are dispersed across many organizational members, teams can help put together a comprehensive strategy to address a need.

This is especially true in volunteer organizations such the church. In these organizations, no one person may have the time (even if this individual has the talents) to accomplish all aspects of a task without burnout coming into play. Thus, teams become the backbone of volunteer organizations, helping to forge a network of people to accomplish a complex task.

Integrated Involvement

Teams and small groups provide a place where people can belong. Peter Wagner labels them "kinship groups," for they foster family-like kinships. Through their involvement in a group, people recognize where they fit into the bigger picture. Often when I ask clients to tell me where they fit in their congregation, they describe the small group or team in which they participate.

If newcomers do not find or become a part of a team or small group, they may feel that their talents remain untapped or unrecognized. If suitable small groups or teams are not available, newcomers may conclude that the church is too big and impersonal (or too small and clannish) to offer such opportunities. In either case, newcomers may seek involvement in a different congregation.

Psychological Intimacy

Psychological "inter-reliance" is a very important by-product of the team and small group environment. It is here that participants can open up without fear of being ostracized or isolated for their feelings and/or beliefs. And it is here that the Holy Spirit seems especially adroit at breaking down barriers, opening up individuals to new ideas, and coalescing participants into a surrogate family. Corporate America has long recognized the social-psychological benefits of groups, and has sought by way of teams to recreate some of this cohesiveness and solidarity. But the church must not abdicate this responsibility to the business realm. The church should be the primary venue for people to develop a psychological intimacy established on an understanding of their Creator and His creation.

Types of *Teams* in the Church

In New Testament times, task-oriented teams were organized when necessary. Acts 6:1-4 shows how the early disciples organized a team of servers:

In those days when the number of disciples was increasing, the Grecian Jews among them complained against the Hebraic Jews because their widows were being overlooked in the daily distribution of food. So the Twelve gathered all the disciples together and said, "It would not be right for us to neglect the ministry of the word of God in order to wait on tables. Brothers, choose seven men from among you who are known to be full of the Spirit and wisdom. We will turn this responsibility over to them and will give our attention to prayer and the ministry of the word."

Since that pattern was first set with the early believers, the church has actively embraced task-oriented teams.

Types of *Small Groups* in the Church

Fellowship-oriented small groups have emerged over the last 500 years. Protestant churches began to use "gender" as a primary way of dividing churches into two subgroups. It is continued today in the Amish/German Baptist traditions: "Men on one side . . . women on the other." In 1872, B. F. Jacobs, a Chicago produce broker, persuaded the Sunday School Union to adopt classes graded for differing "ages. The Sunday school was born. Out of these Sunday schools came a system of age-specific small groups.

From 1935 to 1965, "marital status" was added to "gender" and "age" as a designation for organizing new small groups. This was an era when nearly all adults were married. As a result, "singles groups" now met apart from "married groups."

In the early 1970s, a new subgroup emerged. A culture of never or formerly married individuals gave rise to distinctive subgroups under the "singles" umbrella. Some groups that fell under this heading were Parents Without Partners, Single Mothers, Divorce Recovery Groups, and Widows and Widowers.

In the mid-1970s new groups were organized along "stages of faith development." Groups were now available for new converts, seekers, and/or mature Christians. The current popularity of the "Alpha Course," a user-friendly introduction to Christianity created at Holy Trinity Brompton, an Anglican congregation in London, is an example.

With that in mind, many churches might look like Figure 7.1, composed of a multitude of formal groups/teams (solid lines) and informal groups/teams (dotted lines).

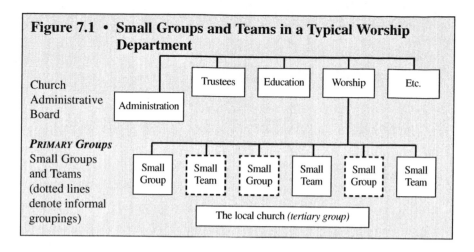

Figure 7.1 • Small Groups and Teams in a Typical Worship Department

How Many Small Groups Are Needed?

Figure 7.2 offers general guidelines for the minimum number of small groups or teams needed to produce a healthy congregation. When a congregation successfully integrates the number of small groups in each category listed below, that congregation will exceed the minimum threshold required to develop healthy interpersonal environments.

Figure 7.2 • Target Goals for Small Groups or Teams in a Congregation

Type of Small Group or Team:	*Percentage of Average Weekly Worship Attendance:*
Adult Sunday School Classes	4% (minimum)
Prayer Groups and Teams	4% (minimum)
Outreach Teams — teams that present the Good News to unchurched and dechurched people; the evangelistic mandate	4% (minimum)
Outreach Teams — teams that meet the physical needs of unchurched and dechurched people; the cultural mandate	4% (minimum)
Worship & Celebration Teams — teams involved in leading worship & the execution of celebration duties	5% (minimum)
Fellowship, Self-Help, Bible Study, and/or Home Groups — non-Sunday Morning	6% (minimum)
Administrative Leadership Team - non-Sunday Morning	8% (minimum)
TOTALS	35% (minimum)

Growth by Accident, Death by Planning: How NOT to Kill a Growing Congregation describes four steps to creating a sufficient number of small groups or teams for churches of any size.[20] Use these steps to ensure that your church has a sufficient number of small groups and teams.

1. Use Figure 7.2 to determine the number of small groups and teams in your church, and the number you need.

2. Create organic groups and teams, using demographic, skill, social, and interest data to create groupings. It is important to create teams around natural and not artificial interests and skills. Many churches simply assign people to a group, often by geographic proximity. At other times, nominating committees assign people to teams (committees) based on their availability, or their lack of a good excuse. However, effectively functioning teams will be based around shared goals, gifts, or needs. *Growth by Accident, Death by Planning* further outlines four sub-steps for creating "organic" groupings based on demographic, skill, social, and interest data.[21]

3. Consider utilizing a staff-level human resource director. Churches are discovering the benefit of designating a "human resource director" to oversee volunteerism, skill development, continuing education, and assigning individuals to an appropriate group or team.

4. Make small groups and teams a key part of your church personality, along with prayer, worship, outreach, and the Word.[22]

Changing Organizational Structure and Management Styles

Another important tool for understanding the strategic future of a congregation is to project how the organizational structure and management styles will evolve as the organization grows. Let's first look at a simple diagram (Figure 7.3) that demonstrates how businesses grow.

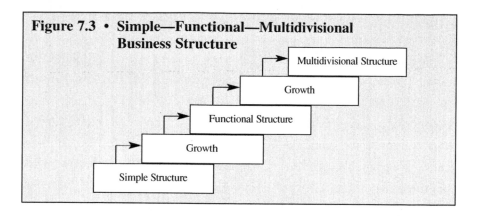

Figure 7.3 • Simple—Functional—Multidivisional Business Structure

In the organizational behavior of the business world, firms grow through these three stages: the simple structure, the functional structure, and the multidivisional structure. Let's look at these stages and how they are paralleled by similar stages of growth in churches.

Simple Structure

The simple structure is the basic structure of a small business or a small church. In the business context, an owner/manager makes all major decisions and monitors all activities. In the church scenario (100 or less attendees), the pastor makes all major decisions and monitors all progress toward goals.

Earlier in this chapter, we illustrated a situation that fits the simple structure scenario. Belasco and Stayer recounted the problem with the "long lists of things to fix," and how the leaders were unable to get past the lists in order to accomplish their vision for the organization. "Eighteen months later, we were still receiving long lists to fix at every meeting. We ran out of patience before they ran out of lists."[23] The organization Belasco and Stayer described had functioned to that point as a simple structure: the leader(s) were expected to make all major decisions and oversee all activities. Even though the organization had grown to the next level, employees still expected the leaders to fix the problems themselves, rather than take goal ownership and join the leaders in solving the problems.

Functional Structure

Functional structure means organizing around an organization's "functions." This often results in the establishment of "departments." A functional structure allows for some autonomy, along with a higher degree of specialization. In business, an accounting department may emerge, research and development may become a separate area, and sales may have its own department. Each department may have its own director, but the organization remains one entity, with departments carrying on specific duties.

In a church, a congregation may develop departments of music, Christian education, youth, missions, outreach, etc. Often, each department has a departmental head that reports to the senior leader. Churches can grow to 500+ within this structure. If they want to grow beyond a single-generational church and reach multiple generations, they must adopt the next structure, the multi-divisional structure.

Multidivisional Structure

In business, the multidivisional structure means the organization literally becomes two or more companies under the same umbrella. An example is General Motors includes divisions such as Chevrolet, Pontiac, and Cadillac. Each division provides the same commodity: a vehicle for transportation. But each division provides this commodity with its own style, image, and corporate culture.

In the same way, churches grow into multidivisional structures when they reach out to multiple generations. Because different generations worship, fellowship, learn, and reach out to their friends using different styles and structures, trying to blend generations can cause undue friction.

Many churches try to thwart this inevitable and healthy multidivisional structure by blending ministry among several generations. Blending church ministries is like the failed missionary strategies of the nineteenth-century Europeans who tried to force Africans to adopt European culture and language in order to convert them to Christianity. These failed efforts are a testimony to danger of confusing culture with theology. While theological consistency is important, the European strategy was not successful because it failed to inculcate its message into the "heart language" and cultural customs of the people.

In contrast, two centuries earlier, Saint Patrick was successful in winning the Celtics to Christianity. He did this by rejecting the strategy Peter Wagner calls "the creator complex, where we try to make over people in our image."[24]

Rather, Professor George Hunter points out that Saint Patrick was successful because he translated the Good News into the symbols, language, stories, customs, and culture of the Celtics.[25] Hunter demonstrates that for older generations to reach younger generations today, older generations must allow indigenous strategies modeled after Patrick's success with the Celtics. Hunter concludes, "The supreme key to reaching the West again is the key that Patrick discovered . . . The gulf between church people and unchurched people is vast, but if we pay the price to understand them, we will usually know what to say and what to do; if they know and feel we understand them, by the tens of millions they will risk opening their heart to God who understands them."[26]

Regardless of changing generational demographics in the community, any church of 100 or more members can grow steadily with multiple sub-congregations if it allows each generation within the church to develop its own style of ministry while maintaining theological consistency.

Figure 7.4 shows how churches grow through simple-functional-multidivisional structures.

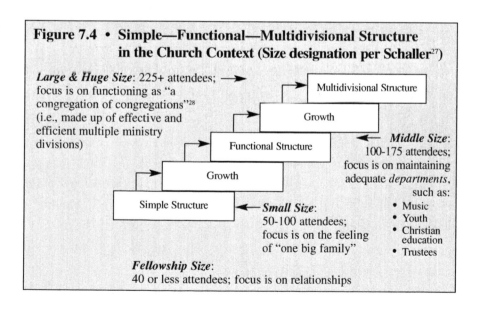

Figure 7.4 • Simple—Functional—Multidivisional Structure in the Church Context (Size designation per Schaller[27])

Large & Huge Size: 225+ attendees; focus is on functioning as "a congregation of congregations"[28] (i.e., made up of effective and efficient multiple ministry divisions)

Multidivisional Structure

Growth

Functional Structure

Growth

Simple Structure

Middle Size: 100-175 attendees; focus is on maintaining adequate *departments*, such as:
• Music
• Youth
• Christian education
• Trustees

Small Size: 50-100 attendees; focus is on the feeling of "one big family"

Fellowship Size: 40 or less attendees; focus is on relationships

In the business and church context, organizations grow through each stage, different management structures and styles of leadership are necessary. If adjustments do not occur, the organization's growth stalls. The church world often refers to the factors that stunt growth as "growth barriers." Business people call these same factors "growth stages" because organizational behavior changes as growth occurs.

Churches tend naturally to divide into sub-congregations based on generational preferences. In Figure 7.1 we described small groups/teams in congregations. That is updated in Figure 7.5, showing how generational sub-congregations emerge once a congregation grows beyond 100 in weekend worship.

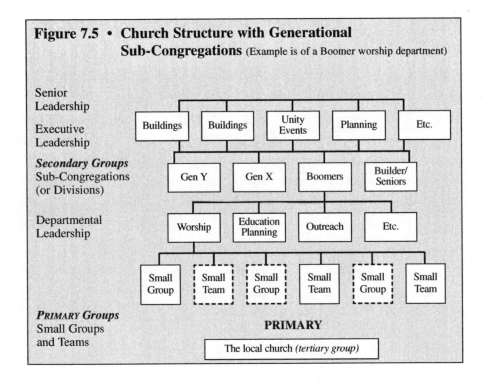

Figure 7.5 • Church Structure with Generational Sub-Congregations (Example is of a Boomer worship department)

Sub-Congregations: The Overlooked Key to Managing the Growing Church

Generational sub-congregations (designated in Figure 7.5) naturally develop as the church passes 100. These sub-congregations can be the key to managing the growing church. Like business divisions in the multidivisional structure (see Figure 7.3), which are given some autonomy and self-rule, these sub-congregations must be granted the same opportunities.

A church comprised of several accepting and mutually beneficial sub-congregations can be called a "multigenerational church." *A House Divided: Bridging the Generation Gaps in Your Church* defines "multigeneration" or "Multi-Gen" in this way:

> The multigenerational church is a holistic congregation with three or more distinct generational sub-congregations peacefully coexisting under one roof, one name, and one leadership core.[30]

Figure 7.6 briefly describes each of these generations and the preferences that can readily polarize sub-congregations.

Figure 7.6 • Generational Differences

Name	Birth Years	Cultural Preferences	Church Preferences
Seniors *Rationale of name*: They are the senior group, the oldest living generation in the church.	Born Before 1926	Cultural preferences mirror the Builders (see below).	Cultural preferences mirror the Builders (see below).
BUILDERS *Rationale of name*: They *built* the Western world into a worldwide military and economic power. Their European heritage means they appreciate fine craftsmanship, seeing it as a reflection of their God-given skills and a vital part of their worship.	Born between 1927-1945	*Perspective on change*: Stability. They want constancy and few changes in a world already beset by the insecurities of old age. *Learning*: Builders prefer the lecture format. *Legacy*: They built the Western world into a safe and secure environment.	*Church size*: 75-300 *Affiliation*: Mainline *Church emphasis*: Need to be heard *Worship style*: Traditional hymns, customary liturgy. *Best worship times*: Sunday morning and evening, Wednesday evening.
Boomers *Rationale of name*: The term *Boomer* was appropriated by media pundits to describe an increase in births after WW II in much the same way that a "boom town" in Old West parlance was a town that sprouted up overnight due to the discovery of gold or silver.	Born between 1946-1964	*Perspective on change*: Experimentation. Boomers like to experiment to find new and more efficient ways of doing things. *Learning*: They prefer the participation format, where questions are encouraged. *Legacy*: Through innovation and creativity, they made the world a better place (however, in the process they did not necessarily make the world a safer place).	*Church size*: 300+ *Affiliation*: Independent *Church emphasis*: Needs of the congregation *Worship style*: Modern (soft rock), with use of choruses. Some, but limited, media usage. *Best worship times*: Sunday morning, and Saturday or Friday evening. Not weeknights.

Figure 7.6 • Generational Differences *continued*

Name	Birth Years	Cultural Preferences	Church Preferences
Generation X Rationale of name: Originally, the "x" was intended to portray a nihilistic bent. However, Gen X tends to be a very religious generation.[31]	Born between: 1965-1983	*Perspective on change*: Radical experiment-ation. Gen. X likes to experiment even more than Boomers, often combining seemingly incompatible concepts. *Learning*: They prefer the Socratic format, where questions and dissent are encouraged. *Legacy*: They saved the world from itself (pollution, terrorism, overpopulation, etc.)	*Church size*: 200-300 *Affiliation*: Mainline, due to the perceived security that mainline affiliation affords. *Church emphasis*: Needs of the community. *Worship style*: Interactive postmodern (edgy rock) with extensive use of media, videos, etc. *Best worship times*: Sunday morning and Friday evening. Not weeknights.
Generation Y *Rationale of name*: While some have tried to call them the "Millennials" because they were raised in a period spanning two millennia, the "Y" designation, (simply meaning they followed the "X" generation) seems to have stuck.	Born between: 1984-2002	Cultural preferences are still developing. *Perspective on change*: Gen Y embraces *electronic* community, living, and communication for better living. *Learning*: They prefer a hyper-Socratic format; active confrontation and discord lead to insight. Also prefer electronic communication in all areas. *Legacy*: Gen Y wants to be the generation that is plugged into all areas of life.	Cultural preferences are still developing. *Church size*: 75-300 *Affiliation*: unknown *Church emphasis*: Gen Y needs to be closely connected to one another, even if not in a close physical proximity. *Worship style*: Postmodern (edgy rock), with even more use of interactive media, videos, etc. *Best worship times*: Sunday morning and Friday evening. Not weeknights.

Managing Sub-Congregations
Managing in the Functional Structure Stage

Approaching church management from an understanding of generational congregations can avoid a myriad of problems. As departments emerge, the leadership must adapt to the changing circumstances. It can evolve in the same way as the sole-proprietor's leadership in the "simple structure" business evolves into a team leadership approach. Like the sole-proprietor establishes department heads to oversee each department, so too must the senior pastor delegate responsibility and authority to department heads. The failure to fully empower and delegate authority is one of the greatest oversights of church leadership.

Managing in the Multidivisional (Sub-Congregation) Stage

When the church reaches the next level (225+ in worship attendance), the church needs to undergo a transformation into the M-form or multidivisional structure. In this structure, each sub-congregation (or division) is more autonomous: "associate pastors" or divisional leaders oversee budgets, outreach, ministry development, worship, discipleship, etc., within their generational age grouping.

Figure 7.5 demonstrates how a church can grow into a healthy and balanced "Multi-Gen" congregation of four divisions.

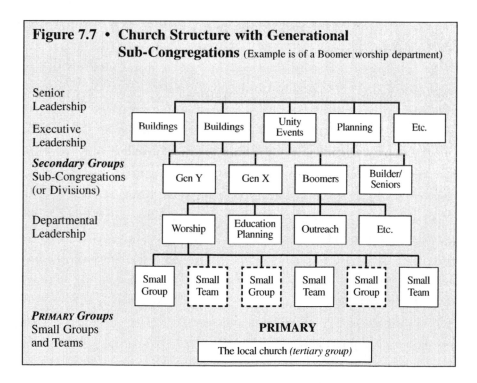

Figure 7.7 • Church Structure with Generational Sub-Congregations (Example is of a Boomer worship department)

Managing the New Small Group Environment

Generations born in and after 1946 appear to prefer the small group environment for developing social, spiritual, and task networks. However, management styles must change to effectively manage this new organizational building block.

In Figure 7.8, Professor Larry Hirschhorn points out some key differences in management style that must be employed in the new small group environment preferred by younger generations.[33]

Figure 7.8	
Old Team Environment (Preferred by Builders and Seniors)	**New Team Environment** (Preferred by Boomers, Gen X and Gen Y)
Members follow orders.	Members exploit team synergies to generate innovation.
Team depends on a supervisor to chart its course.	Teams have considerable authority to chart their own steps.
Members are a team because people conform to direction set by the manager. No one rocks the boat.	Members form a team to collaborate in the face of their emerging right to think for themselves. People both rock the boat and work together.
People cooperate by suppressing their thoughts and feelings. They want to get along.	People cooperate by using their thoughts and feelings. They link up through honest and direct talk.

Figure 7.7 implies that managing in the new small group environment requires a much less autocratic style than it did previously. Thus, those born before 1946 often will feel uncomfortable participating in or managing groups in the new small group environment. As such, leaders born before 1946 must learn to delegate a great degree of authority, as well as grant a lot of leeway for groups to struggle along as they chart their own course.

Just as granting such autonomy to sub-congregations will feel alien to older generations, this autonomy will seem natural to younger generations. Therefore, leaders must be careful to avoid a "disconnect" between older members of the organization and younger members due to different expectations and predilections. The authors of this book believe that diversity is a reflection of God's variety in His creation.

Appreciating the Nexus of Church Behavior and Health

Just as the skilled pastor should have a basic understanding of counseling and psychology, a rudimentary understanding of organizational behavior should also be seen as indispensable. Those shepherds who are bereft of such skills may need to surround themselves with staff and/or lay people qualified in these vital disciplines. A foundational understanding of the behaviors and personalities of organizations must be integrated into leadership strategies to ensure their appropriateness and viability.

Endnotes

1. Quoted by Fred R. David in *Strategic Planning: Concepts and Cases,* 9th ed. (Upper Saddle River, NJ: Prentice-Hall, 2002), 157.
2. Debra L. Nelson and James Campbell Quick, *Organizational Behavior: Foundations, Realities, and Challenges,* 3rd ed. (Cincinnati: South-Western College Publishing, 2000), xxi.
3. James A. Belasco and Ralph C. Stayer, "Why Empowerment Doesn't Empower: The Bankruptcy of Current Paradigms," *Business Horizons* 37, no. 2 (March-April 1994): 29-41.
4. See Rick Warren's seminal volumes: *The Purpose Driven Church* (Grand Rapids: Zondervan, 1995), and *The Purpose Driven Life* (Grand Rapids: Zondervan, 2002).
5. C. Peter Wagner, *Frontiers in Missionary Strategy* (Chicago: Moody Press, 1971), 22.
6. Carl E. Reichardt, "Managing: Carl E. Reichardt, Chairman, Wells Fargo and Co.," *Fortune,* February 27, 1989, 42.
7. Research interview conducted by Jim Collins in *Good to Great: Why Some Companies Make the Leap . . . and Others Don't* (New York: HarperCollins, 2001), 128.
8. Patrick E. Murphy and Georges Enderle, "Managerial Ethical Leadership: Examples Do Matter," *Business Ethics Quarterly* 5 (1995): 117-28.
9. Nelson and Quick, *Organizational Behavior,* 404.
10. Ed. L. Miller, *Questions that Matter: An Invitation to Philosophy,* 4th ed. (New York: McGraw-Hill, 1996), 203-08.
11. Nelson and Quick, *Organizational Behavior,* 404.
12. Bob Whitesel, *Staying Power: Why People Leave the Church Over Change and What You Can Do About It* (Nashville, Abingdon Press, 2003).
13. Quoted in Donald Bloesch, *Freedom for Obedience: Evangelical Ethics in Contemporary Times* (San Francisco: Harper and Row, 1987), 33.
14. Jim Collins, *Good to Great,* 12-13.
15. Ibid., 13.
16. Belasco and Stayer, "Why Empowerment Doesn't Empower."
17. I have modified the original story by changing business terms into church administration terms. Belasco and Stayer's original story described a "company" and its "employees." See the original text for Belasco and Stayer's wording.

18. Bob Whitesel and Kent R. Hunter, *A House Divided: Bridging the Generation Gaps in Your Church* (Nashville: Abingdon Press, 2000), 111-20.

19. Bob Whitesel, *Growth by Accident, Death by Planning: How NOT to Kill a Growing Congregation* (Nashville: Abingdon Press, forthcoming). The designation of these small groups as "cell groups" is somewhat unique to the church environment. From chapter 10: "The 'cell' designation was initially designed to stress this group's ability to divide and multiply as it grows, in much the same manner that a human 'cell' divides and multiplies. I have kept this designation because this diversifying aspect of the small group is important if the group is not to become a closed circle. Small groups should be seen as growing, living organisms that may shed dead elements and add new ones as they thrive. As the larger organism (the church) grows, the division and multiplication of cells into parallel units is important if church growth is to take place logically and coherently."

20. Bob Whitesel, *Growth by Accident, Death by Planning.* To investigate these steps in more detail, see chapter 10.

21. Ibid.

22. To better understand how the axiom "Word – Prayer – Outreach – Worship– Small Groups" provides a necessary foundation for a flourishing church, see Bob Whitesel, *Growth by Accident, Death By Planning*, chapter 10.

23. Belasco and Stayer, "Why Empowerment Doesn't Empower."

24. C. Peter Wagner, *Frontiers in Missionary Strategy.* 97.

25. George G. Hunter III, *The Celtic Way of Evangelism: How Christianity Can Reach the West . . . Again* (Nashville: Abingdon Press, 2000), 47-55.

26. Ibid., 121.

27. Lyle E. Schaller, *The Multiple Staff and the Larger Church* (Nashville: Abingdon Press, 1980), 27-31.

28. George G. Hunter III, *The Contagious Congregation: Frontiers in Evangelism and Church Growth* (Nashville: Abingdon Press, 1979), 63.

29. Bob Whitesel, *Staying Power*, 53-168. Because of the intricacy of this topic, I encourage the reader to read this earlier volume. It describes the polarization process, suggests corrective steps, and includes questions for team discussions.

30. Whitesel and Hunter, *A House Divided*, 83.

31. Ibid., 62-63.

32. The business student will be familiar with Figure 7.5 as the "cost-leadership" structure. In this structure, certain management functions are retained at the executive level to prevent replicating them in each sub-congregation. The financial accountability department, building maintenance department, unity building event planning, and strategic planning are retained at an executive level. Utilizing this process helps to cut costs. Yet, even in this scenario, control over disbursement of funds, program creation, and ministry style are retained in each sub-congregation or division.

33. Larry Hirschhorn, *Managing in the New Team Environment: Skills, Tools and Methods* (Reading, MA: Addison-Wesley Publishing, 1991), 13-14.

8

What Church Leader's Need to Know About . . .

Motivation, Development, and Change

Helping Others See the Future

"For Christ's love compels us . . . And he died for all,
that those who live should no longer live for themselves . . ."

—2 CORINTHIANS 5:14, 15 NIV

Paradigm Shift

Dr. John had served First Baptist for over twelve years. First Baptist is what analysts call a "church of attraction." With 2,500 members in Sunday school and worship, it comprises the largest congregation in the county. Nestled in the center of a medium-sized southern community, it attracts key leaders from the community and appeals to a wide variety of people in the area. Its influence is felt at every level of the social structure throughout the county.

A strong, intelligent leader, a gifted teacher, and a visionary, John effectively led a staff of 20 and guided the deacon board of 40. About a year ago, he launched a fact-finding committee, whose assignment was to analyze the church and assess its future. Behind this effort was his belief that the congregation would experience more growth through outreach. But he felt the church's poor location hindered its future potential to reach lost people for Jesus Christ. With this in mind, he carefully selected the members of the analysis team, specifically including church members who were active in community development and real estate. After several months of solid demographic study, the analysis team brought John its report: the church ought to relocate. This conclusion matched that of an outside consultant who worked independently.

For over 100 years, the church has been located in a neighborhood setting three blocks from the downtown area. For a congregation that had become a church of attraction with regional impact, it was neither visible nor accessible. In the last 40 years, the culture of America had changed, and that had been reflected in the community surrounding the church. The small theater downtown had been abandoned. Grocery stores no longer dotted neighborhood corners. The *neighborhood mentality* of American culture had given way to a *destination mentality*.

People in John's community now shop at the new mall. Located on a major highway, the mall is both visible and accessible. Across from the mall a nationally syndicated theater with eighteen screens provides multiple choices and ample parking. First Baptist fits the paradigm of a regional church of attraction, but it is handcuffed because of its location.

Stepping on Plaid

With the backing of the analysis team and independent consultant, Dr. John's insight and visionary thinking seemed to be right on track. What happened next turned out to be an excruciating but helpful lesson in motivation, development, and change. He brought the analysis team's findings to the deacon board. Speaking from the context of his goal-oriented leadership style (which was not always sensitive and relational), John spoke to the deacons with excitement and visionary challenge. Unfortunately, not all of the forty deacons were prepared for what they were about to hear. Those who were visionaries were excited about his suggestion to relocate the church. Others struggled to process such an enormous paradigm shift in their worldviews.

Some immediately focused on real estate and wondered who would purchase the church's "poorly located" property that was presently worth five to six million dollars. A few focused on a very personal lifelong dream—that their funeral services would someday take place in the building where they worshipped most of their lives.

Although Dr. John asked the deacons to keep the relocation information to themselves, several deacons found the request too unreasonable. For therapeutic reasons, a few deacons felt they had to confide in someone. Some deacons talked to their wives, their wives talked to others, and, within days, most of the people in this large church had learned of the relocation issue. Their responses were varied—excited, threatened, or depressed—depending on their understanding of the issues, their view of the church's mission, and their level of trust in their pastor.

In some ways, First Baptist epitomizes the story of the chameleon who wandered through a fabric store. As it walked across a green swatch of cloth, it turned green. When it walked across red, it turned red. But when it stepped onto a piece of plaid, it blew up!' This is what happened at First Baptist. The church, at least temporarily, blew apart emotionally. What was the result of this explosion? Ultimately, Dr. John learned a valuable lesson in the management discipline of motivation, development, and change.

Initiate Change, Avoid Being Stoned

Two areas seem especially challenging to Christians. Outside consultants who have worked with congregations know these areas well because they *are* the most challenging:

1. Introducing change to a church's customs and habits (particularly worship)
2. Broaching the subject of moving or changing buildings

This challenge is not restricted to First Baptist, or even to the twenty-first century. We can look back to the early church for an example. According to Acts 7, Stephen was stoned to death. While many see his martyrdom as a result of his preaching the Gospel of Jesus Christ, the root cause was connected to some Jews who had stirred up the crowds (see Acts 6:14). They claimed they heard Stephen say that Jesus of Nazareth would tear down the Temple and change all the customs (note the two key factors: building and customs; customs involves and includes, most visibly, worship!)

Dr. John was experiencing a reality of church life that has existed from the beginning: Initiate change and you will find yourself challenged. Initiate change brutally, without proper motivation and development, and you could get stoned to death. This doesn't mean change is evil. In fact, change in the Christian church is one of its foundational principles. However, change brings criticism. As David Hocking said, "The only way I know to avoid criticism is to say nothing, do nothing, and be nothing."[2]

Motivation: From the Inside Out

One of the lessons Dr. John learned was that being a change agent begins as an inside job. That is because *all* leadership development is an inside job. John was right in his assessment of First Baptist. The growth of this church required change. However, a prerequisite for that change was his own growth—growth that had to occur within him. That included his style of leadership. A leader's success is largely determined by the ability to motivate others. Contingent on that is the issue of self-motivation.

Self-Motivation

How are you motivated? What is it that gets you up in the morning, keeps you on task in ministry, and gets you through the challenges? How do you manage your own motivation? The management of self-motivation begins with your call to ministry. It is that divine ingredient, that spiritual spark that occurs when God lays His hand on you and calls you to be a servant and leader of a congregation. Motivation is important. Before his conversion, Paul was arrogant, aggressive, and deviously creative in his persecution of Christians. How did that change after he was converted and called to ministry? He was still quite arrogant, aggressive, and deviously creative—but this time, it was for the cause of Christ. What changed the most when he got the call? His skills, style, and temperament didn't change. But his motivation changed completely. That motivation came from his call to the cause of Christ.[3]

Self-motivation is pivotal because it is the source of motivating others. As John C. Maxwell says, "Motivated people motivate people." Tied closely to your calling is the vision that God has given you for ministry. That vision is the fuel for your motivation. As Maxwell explains further, "Valuable visions give energy. Only he who sees the invisible can do the impossible. Basically, we go where our dreams will take us."[4]

A Balance of Time

Perhaps one of the most profound insights for motivation comes from Dee Hock in his book, *Birth of the Chaordic Age*.[5] Hock is the founder and CEO Emeritus of *Visa* Corporation. He has two ultimate conclusions about management: (1) Management is not about making better people of others. It is about making a better person of yourself. (2) Management is not the key. The key is the task of leadership. Hock draws an amazing conclusion. He says that 50 percent of your efforts should be toward leadership of yourself. Literally, half your efforts should be on self-motivation, ongoing education, honing of skills, and personal growth. He says that the next 25 percent of your effort should be directed toward leading those who have authority over you. In Dr. John's case, that would include, to some extent, the board of deacons. Does that make sense? It eventually did to John! It meant that one-quarter of his time should have been spent influencing those who were above him, who had authority over him.

Hock claims you should spend 20 percent of your time influencing (leading) your peers. Those are people over whom you have no authority and who have no authority over you. They are your associates—other pastors in the area or staff members who work with you on a team level. This represents one-fifth of your time. That leaves 5 percent of your time to spend influencing those over whom you have authority. Dee Hock's point is that you can't really manage those who have authority over you. You can't manage that board of deacons, the elders, the church council, or the church board. You can't really manage the congregation. But you *can* understand them. You can teach, influence, and persuade them. You can motivate them. You can challenge them, forgive them and influence them. You can set an example for them. It means that you can *lead* them. However the balance must be shaped with the investment of half your time (50 percent) in self-leadership and development. This is the core of self-motivation.[6]

Christ, the Source

For pastors, self-motivation should originate in Christ. II Corinthians 5:14-15 says, *"We are ruled [remotivated] by the love of Christ, now that we recognize that one man died for everyone, which means that they all share in his death. He died for all, so that those who live should no longer live for themselves, but only for him who died and was raised to life for their sake"* (TEV). With his focus on motivation, Oswald Chambers wrote, "The great wonder of Jesus Christ's salvation is that He changes our heredity. He does not change human nature—He changes its source, and thereby its motives as well."[7]

Driven to Pray

Personal motivation is also nurtured by a consistent prayer life. The management of your prayer life is essential to your motivation for ministry. Prayer is a disciplined, holy habit. The effort to develop a disciplined prayer life is driven by the presence of Christ on the one hand, and the challenges of ministry on the other. Jim Cymbala reflects, "Prayer cannot truly be taught by principles and seminars and symposiums. It has to be born of a whole environment of felt need. If I say, 'I *ought* to pray,' I will soon run out of motivation and quit; the flesh is too strong. I have to be *driven* to pray."[8]

Motivating Others

When it comes to the fine art of motivating others, different styles are evident. Ken Heer, of the Leadership Development Journey of The Wesleyan Church, suggests that pastors and church leaders should have the freedom to develop a style that is unique to their context and to whom they are. He says, "Church leaders have to be astute at reading their own situation and working within it. . . . Too many pastors listen to others and imitate them rather than being inspired by others and then allowing God to work new principles and practices through them within their setting and situation. How you motivate, develop, and initiate change needs to be appropriate to you and your church. Transformational leadership must work toward its goals with the present local situation in clear focus."[9]

The Law or the Gospel?

When it comes to motivating others there are two basic and opposing motivation starting points. One is the law, and the other is the Gospel. Motivation from the law focuses on fear and retribution: "If you don't share Christ with your neighbor, your neighbor's going to go to hell. Some day, God will look you in the eye and ask you why you didn't share the message of salvation." This type of motivation may inspire or scare people into activity for the short term, it is not a biblically based directive for creating a healthy atmosphere for motivation and change. Dwight L. Moody said, "People have a way of becoming what you encourage them to be, not what you nag them to be."[10]

The Gospel, on the other hand, motivates people by God's love and through His grace: "Isn't it wonderful to know Jesus Christ as your Savior? Isn't it amazing that God would call us to be ambassadors for Christ? What a privilege and what an honor we have! And what an opportunity it is to share this Good News with someone like your neighbor. All heaven rejoices when people repent of their sins and receive Christ. We get to experience that joy and ultimate fulfillment at the highest level when we share the Good News with our neighbor." This is the art of positive leadership. Napoleon was quoted as saying, "Leaders are dealers in hope." It is that positive, hopeful presentation that motivates people and is a key to managing your leadership style of motivation.

Enlarging a Frame of Reference

Church growth advocate Dr. Win Arn provides some outstanding insights on motivation. While conducting research, he asked pastors to identify their greatest growth-restricting obstacles. The most common response that he received from pastors was the challenge to motivate the people in the church to want to grow and be part of the change process. In order to diagram a motivation continuum, Arn developed a scale from low motivation to high motivation.

Duress/ Force	Coercion	Duty	Obiligation	Expectation	Desire	Personal Fulfillment	Love

LOW MOTIVATION---HIGH MOTIVATION

He then asked the question, "Can people move from a sense of duty, for example, to one of self-fulfillment or love?" He answered that question, saying that people surely can move toward the high end of motivation in areas of personal fulfillment and love. How? Arn reported a key part of the answer was that they could do this "by enlarging their frame of reference."[11]

The "ah-ha!" phenomenon can occur when people participate in a mission trip to a different culture. It also happens when church members move out of their comfort zones through a servant activity among the less fortunate.

Another way to enlarge the frame of reference is to ask an "outside expert," like a consultant, to visit your church and dialogue with people, sharing concepts from other churches that can stretch their horizons. This provides a catalytic effect as people are opened up to new paragdigms.

Win Arn tells the story about Bill Hybels, of Willow Creek Community Church near Chicago, wanted to learn more about unchurched people. He wondered if his sermon would speak to the needs of a person who was not involved in a church. Hybels took his sermon notes to a tavern, picked out a person, and watched his behavior. Then he asked himself, "Does this message speak to that man's needs?" This is an important exercise for all Christians interested in enlarging their frame of reference: Meet and spend time with unchurched people. Listen and learn from them. By expanding your frame of reference, you move up the scale of motivation toward the high end.[12]

Change: Always an Imposition

Dr. John learned the hard lesson that change is difficult for people. Change takes you out of your comfort zone. Mark Twain said that the only person who really likes change is a baby with a wet diaper. Your view toward change is directly related to the discomfort you feel at the moment of change. He could have better prepared his church to be more receptive to change. This "environment preparation" might have taken a year or two. He might have begun by raising questions about why the church was stalled in its growth. Through these questions and exploration of various options, he could have raised the congregation's level of discomfort with the status quo. Such preparation would have been essential to enlarging the congregation's frame of reference.

Change Requires Effort

Change is hard. The most common response to the challenges a church faces is to work harder to bring about change. Why? Because effecting change *is* such hard work. Speaking to the business sector about organizations in general, Donald Sull shares business sense that is applicable to the local church as well.

Most leaders today recognize that the future will differ profoundly from the past, and that competitive formulas that led to earlier success can lead to future disaster. History, however, exerts a strong gravitational pull on organizations, particularly successful ones. Faced with dramatic changes in their competitive environment, most . . . respond not by doing things differently, but by doing more of what worked before. When these tried-and-true actions fail to achieve the desired results, most . . . redouble their efforts, and in their haste to dig themselves out of a hole, only dig themselves deeper.[13]

The duplication of old efforts, rather than the development of new initiatives, is evidence that there is a natural, predictable, and expected resistance to change.

Change Requires Leadership

While change is difficult for those who experience it, leading change is even harder. John Maxwell has recently shared an astounding insight. He admits that in all of his years of studying leadership, he always held the bias that leaders resisted change less often than followers do. However, through continued research, he has come to the conclusion that leaders often resist change *to a greater degree* than followers.

So, the first hurdle in leading change is to process the change and accept it yourself. The good news is that, if Maxwell is right, the more difficult stage of the process is finished once you, personally, make the change. As Maxwell reports, this is more than motivation. He calls it "drive." "Drive is more than motivation. It is self-motivation. Success requires that we push ourselves beyond our comfort zone."[14] Ken Heer concurs. Heer makes a great point in noting that people really do not resist change, they resist being changed. There are exceptions. Some people thrive on change. However, they do not represent the majority of people in your church. Leading people through substantial change is hard on the leader.

Church leaders must understand the cost and pitfalls of being a change agent. Often, leaders are in too great a hurry to get from point A to point Z (let alone point A to point B). They read a book or attend a conference and come up with a whole new idea about what their church and its ministry should look like. On the very next Sunday, they announce their new idea to their congregations, then wonder why they experience conflict during the next weeks of trying to implement their idea. It is still *their* idea.[15]

Does this sound like Dr. John at First Baptist Church—and other pastors as well?

Here is a key lesson: Change is a process. It is not an event, a program, a pronouncement, or simply a rewrite of a mission statement. As a process, change takes time. Change *is* hard. It generates conflict. Change needs leadership. But it requires a leader with patience and courage.

Through his research, George Barna has focused on pastors who are visionary leaders. He also has studied pastors of churches who experienced a turnaround in vitality and growth. These pastors were change agents. Barna notes that "these leaders generally had not given prior evidence of being visionary. Although they had exhibited some leadership qualities and had displayed some visionary tendencies, they generally had not distinguished themselves through previous service as visionary leaders."[16] Through his research, Barna discovered that it takes a special kind of person to be a change agent. Barna found that the pastor of a turnaround church is typically a leader who has slowly refined an innate visionary skill. In other words, becoming a skilled change agent is not just part of one's inherited DNA. It includes a process of learning and growth.[17]

Change Requires Pacing

A key insight in managing change is that the leader cannot get too far out in front of the people. Dr. John is a brilliant pastor and a strong leader. His deacon board is a group of intelligent men, who are successful businessmen. But when he brought the bombshell of relocation to them, he was so far ahead that it blew up in his face.

Someone has asked the question, "What is the difference between a leader and a martyr?" The answer is, "A leader is one step ahead of his people. A martyr is ten steps ahead of his people." For several months, Dr. John felt like a martyr. As Maxwell has pointed out, "He who thinks he is leading but has no followers is only taking a walk!"[18] If the goal is to have others follow your vision, you must do the work that is necessary to keep people with you. "Fresh vision usually comes from the leader of the church. With fresh vision comes passion, energy, and enthusiasm."[19] The task of the leader is not only to share the vision, but to share it in such a way that followers catch hold of it. Only then will followers share in the leader's passion, energy, and enthusiasm.

Dr. John made the critical mistake of moving out in pursuit of the vision before others had caught a passion for the vision. Even with his leadership skills, he wasn't leading if many were not following. He needed to cultivate the environment and prepare the ground for the seeds of the new ideas that would eventually relocate the church and change history. He was senior pastor of a great church with wonderful people, but he needed to learn the important lessons of how a pastor manages development and change.

Drive Change through Purpose

The value of articulating what it means to be purpose driven has become a focus of change management. In developing a change climate, this can be a powerful catalyst. When Dr. John dropped the bomb of relocation, he discovered that some people did not see the church from a purpose-driven perspective—as he saw the church. Instead, because he had not properly cultivated the environment in preparation for change, he learned that their focus was centered on other aspects of the church. For many, the perspective was building centered. Others were less tied to the building, but cultivated a program focus. Still others were people centered, identifying the church primarily in terms of its people. This latter group felt it was best to subordinate programs to serve the needs of the people, and to use the building to serve the needs of the program.

Only as people are purpose driven can they subordinate people to the purpose of the church. To be purpose driven means that programs and buildings are significantly subordinated to the purpose of the church. This is essential when significant change takes place.If the people are not subordinated to the purpose of the church, then those who are disrupted by change (and who disrupt others) can set the agenda.

Dr. John learned this in a most dramatic way. The mayor of the city, who was a member of the deacon board, was quoted on the front page of the local newspaper. He said, "People should not worry. There is no way First Baptist Church is going to change locations."

The concept of the purpose-driven church was made popular in the book, *The Purpose Driven Church* by Rick Warren.[20] "Purpose driven" has become standard terminology to describe a congregation that is more tolerant to meaningful change. In *Turnaround Strategies for the Small Church*, Ron Crandall has expanded this concept: "A purpose-driven church: (1) builds morale by reducing the tension of competing claims; (2) reduces frustration because it helps prioritize and clarify what needs to be done; (3) builds cooperation amoung those inside the church and attracts the interest and cooperation of persons and groups outside the church; and (4) assists in regular evaluation of congregational faithfulness and effectiveness."[21]

How do people *primarily* see the church?

Purpose

↑

People

↑

Programs

↑

?

Develop a Biblical Paradigm

The purpose-driven concept goes beyond the development of a vision statement. Vision statements are important, but they do not guarantee a visionary church. A visionary statement is a good first step . . . but only that. The purpose-driven mind-set translates a biblical paradigm for the church, it becomes a part of the congregation's personality. This is fused with the goals, strategies, and cultural climate of everything the church does. It enhances a pastor's ability to strategically lead development and change in a process of constant renewal that is essential for a vital and healthy church.[22]

This process represents a level of integrity and dedication to values. The biblical values provide a healthy context for development and change. Integrity is not just relevant to the church world, but to all organizations. Warren Bennis explains his understanding of integrity. "By integrity, I mean standards of moral and intellectual honesty on which our conduct is based. Without integrity, we betray ourselves and others and cheapen every endeavor. It is the single quality whose absence we feel most sharply on every level of our national life." Bennis then speaks directly to the leader. "But the nation's integrity will be restored only when each of us asserts his or her own integrity. By their very existence, people of integrity lend hope to our innate conviction that we, as a people, can rise above the current moral cynicism and squalor."[23] Integrity is essential for trust, which provides a platform for development and change.

Cultivate a Climate for Change

Developing a positive climate for change is also important. In *Strategies for Change*, Lyle Schaller describes the characteristics of a church with a positive climate for change. As you read through the list, score your church (from your perspective) in each of these areas. Rate each area on a scale from one to ten (one being "weak" and ten being "strong"). Then, ask your leaders do the same. Instead of focusing on who is right or wrong, use the results of the evaluation as a constructive context for discussion, prioritizing, and problem solving. These twelve characteristics of a positive climate for change in a congregation are adapted from Schaller's book:

1. Institutional survival goals are a low prioritiy.
2. People are very open to new ideas and innovation.
3. There is a high tolerance and even affirmation for those people who have "maverick personalities."
4. The congregation generally responds enthusiastically to big challenges.

5. Most of the people actually enjoy surprises.

6. The church is oriented primarily to the future, not the past.

7. Leaders who think outside the box are supported and encouraged.

8. People are comfortable with the fact that we don't do things the way we always did them.

9. Members in the congregation are generally sensitive to the needs of people outside the church.

10. People are at least as comfortable with innovations as they are with traditional activities.

11. When a new proposal is made, people are able to give serious consideration to it without being threatened or feeling challenged about what they have done in the past.

12. The church is able to attract and keep staff who are above average in professional competence.[24]

Adopt a Coaching Style

Coaching works hand in hand with strategies that foster a positive climate for change. It is a key method for pastors who want to encourage strategic development and change. Tom Bandy has provided an excellent resource in *Coaching Change.* "Great coaches never underestimate the importance of morale – *esprit de corps* – or team spirit. Team spirit is a fluid that fills the gaps between plays, innings, quarters, halves, substitutions, and line changes to create a great game. It is the bond that joins a string of tragic or glorious individual efforts into a shared experience. Team spirit inspires self-sacrifice and injects hope in the midst of despair. . . . This context or environment of team spirit is the foundation for leveraging change in the church."[25]

Honor the Context

As you build a climate for change, it is important to honor the context— the environment in which you conduct ministry. The context includes elements over which you have little control. To honor that context, you first have to understand it. Many pastors come into a church and initiate change immediately, without understanding their place in that church's history. The historical context must be honored as much as the environmental context. You can't change history until you join history. This is a strategic lesson that Dr. John learned the hard way at First Baptist Church. He had not done his homework and thus did not realize the depth of the devotion many of the congregants felt for their physical buildings and geographic location.

William Boast supports what he calls contextual thinking.

> In a rapidly changing world, there is no way you can collect enough pertinent data to arrive at a meaningful conclusion in the time necessary to reach the solution. The details are simply not there to give us the answers we need, when we need them. To deal effectively and intelligently with the dynamic world, the individual must carefully assess the context of the problem without fixing on the incomplete set of semi-related details. The 'big picture,' 'wholistic,' and the 'macro-scene,' are all synonyms that describe the context. They describe, if not define, what we mean and what we have to deal with. . . . Management . . . must come to see the context of our world more clearly than we have ever seen it. Our suffering comes from too much attachment to details, lack of vision, and poor context perspective.[26]

This concept of initiating change and honoring the context is biblical. It is exemplified in the biblical dynamic of the Incarnation. C.W. Perry says it simply, "Leadership is accepting people where they are, then taking them somewhere."[27] Jesus did this. God comes to human beings as a human being, to meet people where they are, and takes them somewhere. This ultimate, divine expression of honoring the context is a dramatic model for ministry and a strategic guideline for initiating change.

Understand the Audience

Who is the audience of your change initiation? Dr. John should have asked this question as he diagnosed the context at his church. For many years, students of change in social organizations have followed a template to understand the distribution of people who will respond in different ways to the initiation of change.[28] The model follows a traditional bell curve that demonstrates the behaviors of five groups: Innovators, Early Adopters, Middle Adopters, Late Adopters, and Never Adopters:

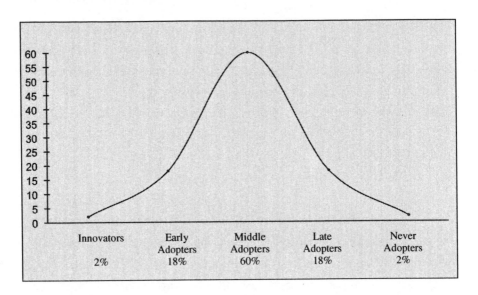

Innovators: Pioneers

The Innovators are those who may be initiating right along with you. They are what has been called "paradigm pioneers," the inventors. They not only accept your ideas about change, but already have thought about change themselves. Even at their most conservative, they find your ideas invigorating and exciting. Unfortunately, Dr. John at First Baptist Church chose only innovators for the analysis team. That is why he and the analysis team were blindsided when some so vehemently opposed their well-intentioned report concerning the demographics of their community—and the future of their church. Innovators represent approximately 2 percent of your congregation.

Early Adopters: Reasoners

Early Adopters make up about 18 percent. They process quickly and are able to receive the concepts of change objectively, without emotional "noise." They rapidly come to the conclusion that "this makes sense," and are "on board" early on.

Middle Adopters: Questioners

Middle Adopters take longer to process change. They require more information. They ask questions and refine the process through their questions. Dr. John should have included some Middle Adopters on his analysis team. They represent approximately 60 percent of the active members of your church. They take longer than the Early Adopters but, in time, they come on board with the proposed change, usually before it is launched.

Late Adopters: Doubting Thomases

Eighteen percent of the congregation are Late Adopters.They usually do not change until they are forced to do so. They do not acquiesce to change until it has occurred and they have no other choice. These are the ones against the proposal to worship in a new time slot—say, half an hour later than the original time. They remain unconvinced even after several weeks. However, after a couple of months, they come to realize the value of the change and ultimately adopt it. This 18 percent are somewhat like the Apostle Thomas—they have to see it to believe it (see John 20:26-29).

Never Adopters: "My Way or No Way!"

The last category are the Never Adopters. Representing 2 percent of your church, they will never grasp the change and will demonstrate this in one of two ways. Either they will resist the change (internal), or they will leave the church (external). You can count on this behavior from the Never Adopters. If you move locations, change leadership style, build new buildings, reinvent the way you make decisions, change a worship service from traditional to contemporary, or cancel the annual church picnic, the Never Adopters will either leave the church, or internally resist the change . . . forever. Remember, the way in which you strategically manage development and change can dramatically impact the percentage of Never Adopters.

As you look at this bell curve, to which category do you think the leaders of great movements belong? Chances are, you are only half right. The leaders of movements include the Innovators *and* the Never Adopters. Their movements differ dramatically, but Innovators and Never Adopters are almost always the leaders of great movements. Innovators are those pioneers who move the church into the next century. Never Adopters are hard-core traditionalists. They lead resistance in churches and denominations. Never Adopters also start what are often called "cults" or "sects."

Introducing Change

Begin Well

How you introduce change is pivotal to success. In 1985, the *Coca-Cola* Company introduced a new formulated brand of their drink, the *New Coke*. Large-scale taste tests demonstrated that the *New Coke* formula overwhelmingly beat old *Coke* 63 percent to 37 percent. Only 10-12 percent of people seemed upset by the new brand.

Unexpectedly, as *New Coke* was introduced, a vocal minority condemned the new product. When the media amplified the story, *New Coke* began to lose ground. The company responded by renaming the old product *Classic Coke*, a tactic that did not work. By 1990, *New Coke* was gone. Why did *New Coke* fail when its taste was actually preferred by 63 percent of the test market? They failed to realize the power that a small group of discontented consumers could have on the opinions of others.

There is a lesson in the *New Coke* example. When introducing new ideas into a church, it is wise to take seriously the influence that a small subset of members can have on others.[29] The importance of this is upheld in studies demonstrating that when pastors are forced out of a church, it is usually, and surprisingly, by fewer than 10 percent of the members. This is exactly what caused a near blowup at First Baptist Church. The key agitators who spread the news that "Dr. John was going to relocate the church" actually amounted to a very small, very upset group. How you introduce change is important!

The Change "Allergy"

Charles Arn, President of Church Growth Incorporated, explains: "People, by nature, resist change. Consequently, *how* you introduce the new idea will greatly affect *whether* it is eventually adopted. Do *not* assume that the idea will be naturally accepted on its obvious merits. It will not. In fact, you are much safer (and more likely to be correct) in assuming that the idea will be resisted. People are allergic to change."[30]

If the church has agreed upon a goal, such as one in a mission statement, and the change introduced can be shown to support that agreed-upon goal, it is much easier for people to accept the change. In his book, *Leading Churches*

Through Change, Douglas Alan Walrath, says that the beginning of the process of change is more important than any other stage.[31] Walrath indicates that it is important to begin well. This is when the tone is set and the direction is made. Unfortunately for Dr. John at First Baptist, this beginning turned out to be so disruptive that it set the change process back for years—or longer. The church will have to redefine and reestablish ground that was lost in the near blowup. What is Dr. John's status today? He is no longer on staff at First Baptist!

Be Transparent

As you initiate change, overemphasize your transparency. Go to great lengths to communicate that you don't know if the change will work. In this way, you model your own tolerance to the discomfort of the unknown. As you do so, people subconsciously say, "If she can put up with it for a while and doesn't know if it's going to work, I guess I can too." At this point you might wonder how Dr. John at First Baptist could have experimented with relocating the church. This is where creative change management is so essential. In this case, John might have employed the services of an outside consultant earlier in the process. Good consultants bring creative ideas. First Baptist could have rented space in an empty store at the mall. They already were considering initiating a contemporary worship service. In order to reduce the "shock" to those who historically gathered in the auditorium for traditional worship (with an orchestra), they could have formed the contemporary service at a satellite location. This would utilize the concept of change by addition, not substitution. It would be treated as an experiment. In this way, the congregation could "test" a different location without relocating.

Be Informed

Proposed change always should be accompanied by abundant, full, repeated, and varied information. All information should be complete. It should be abundant—you cannot overkill information. It should be repeated in different formats, in different ways, and at different times. In *Leading Change*, author John Kotter concurs: "Vision is usually communicated most effectively when many different vehicles are used: Large group meetings, memos, newspapers, posters, informal one-on-one talks. When the same message comes at people from six different directions, it stands a better chance of being heard and remembered, on both intellectual and emotional levels."[32]

When introducing change, it is important to undergo a reality check. Recognize that not everyone will be happy. Some members will leave. But remember, some people will leave even if you don't change—or because you don't change. Change is hard. Expect challenges along the way.

Constant Renewal

A healthy and vital church is a church that is in constant renewal. In his challenging book, *Christian Chaos*, Tom Bandy addresses the issue of leadership and organizational change. He explains the church as a permission-giving organization. This is the posture of a thriving church and is very different from the traditional organizational model. Many churches are set up with boards and committees that see their primary purpose as permission denying rather than permission giving. Constant congregational renewal provides opportunities for old structures to be changed so that innovation can take place.[33]

Focus on the Essentials

One of the key principles for providing constant renewal and openness to change is to teach church members to differentiate between the essentials and the nonessentials. Christianity is comprised of several essentials derived from the truths of Scripture. These are the doctrines or teachings for which Christians will "go to the wall" and die, if necessary, to uphold. These essentials ought to include biblical worldviews about the nature and purpose of the church. They should include the core values without which the church will become anemic.

In order to deliver these essentials, the church in every age has developed a number of nonessential vehicles. While they are useful, these vehicles aren't part of the essentials. They include things like Bach's music, a particular liturgy, pews, language patterns ("thees" and "thous"), architectural forms, and websites. At one point in history, all of these nonessentials proved to be useful vehicles for carrying the essentials of the Christian faith. But they should be considered temporary. Culture changes and nonessentials are not part of the core essence of what might be called "raw Christianity."

Unfortunately, many Christians have no clear distinction between essentials and nonessentials. Consequently, they define Christianity as a mixture of essentials and nonessentials. When that happens, customs, habits, and traditions are perpetuated beyond their usefulness. Many would-be change agents spend enormous volumes of energy trying to hammer away at changing people on the level of their vehicles. Of greater importance is to change their worldview about essentials and nonessentials. This is an important prerequisite for enhancing opportunities for renewal. That this is such a common challenge in churches is even more astounding, since this challenge is as old as the New Testament church. In Acts 15, one of the first and most heated church-wide meetings in history was a debate about whether Gentiles could become Christians without being circumsized and maintaining a kosher kitchen. Could they be real Christians without following all the customs and traditions of the Jewish culture? In a landmark decision, the early church leaders provided an understanding of the essentials and nonessentials of the Christian faith, allowing Gentile Christians access to the Gospel with disregard to cultural baggage that was not in conflict with essential truth. At that precise moment in history, the Christian movement changed from a Jewish sect to a worldwide religion of enormous potential.

Tradition and Traditionalism

Lyle Schaller said that in this world, there are only two constants: Christ and change.[34] Another clear distinction that is basic for the constant renewal of the church is that between tradition and traditionalism. Tradition is the living faith of the dead. Perhaps the best example of tradition in Scripture is Hebrews 11. This is a list of biblical characters who, down through the ages, expressed faith in God. They are all dead, but their expression of faith is like a crowd of believers still cheering us on from the grandstands as we travel the journey of faith. This is tradition at its finest. It is the living faith of the dead. For many of us, it is the memory of our parents, grandparents, former Sunday school teachers, or pastors who have now gone on to glory. Their spiritual witness and testimony live on in our memories and encourage us through difficult times. This is a powerful encouragement for the constant renewal of the church.

Then there is traditionalism. Traditionalism is the dead faith of the living. This is faith in customs, habits, cultural baggage, and vehicles. Traditionalism is reflected in the young woman who said, "We tried that new church not far from our house, but it didn't even seem like church. They didn't have pews." This is making a nonessential into an essential—traditionalism, the dead faith of the living. Jesus reserved His most severe words for those who were rigid, religious traditionalists. When the Pharisees asked, "Why do your disciples break the tradition of the elders?" Jesus replied, "Why do you break the command of God for the sake of your tradition?" (Matthew 15:2, 3 NIV) Fulfilling God's purpose must always take priority over preserving tradition.[35] Traditionalism discourages the continual renewal of the church.

Issues surrounding tradition and traditionalism are, at their center, spiritual issues. Leonard Sweet explained it this way:

> The church builds on tradition; it doesn't live on tradition. Churches that live on tradition die on tradition. There is an old Chinese saying about clinging to tradition just because it is tradition that reminds us of the reason for spiritual practice in the first place: "It's like carrying a raft on your back after you have crossed the river." Tradition is important, but it's not God; it is a route to God. Transition leaders need to be 'turnaround' (that is, *metanoia*) artists. But it is God who effects the turnarounds. Religious leadership is less about turning around or turning ahead and more about turning toward God.[36]

When you cast a vision for change, it is also important to recognize that you choose who you lose. When you say, for example, "We're going east," there will be others who recognize that they are traveling west, and you will inevitably say goodbye to one another. That is a reality of change. Unfortunately, Dr. John did not develop the change process or nurture the motivation. The congregation said goodbye to him. Jesus said that new wine has to go into new wineskins (Matthew 9:17). Change is a part of life in the church. Being a change agent is part of what it means to be an effective pastor.

Endnotes

1. David Bryant, *The Hope at Hand: National and World Revival for the 21st Century* (Grand Rapids, MI: Baker Book House, 1995), 108.

2. David L. Hocking, *Be a Leader People Follow* (Glendale, CA: Regal Books, 1979), 95.

3. Leonard Sweet, *Soul Tsunami: Sink or Swim in New Millennium Culture* (Grand Rapids, MI: Zondervan Publishing House, 1999), 315.

4. John C. Maxwell, "Vision: The Process of Passing It On!" INJOY Life Club Tape Series (Atlanta: INJOY, 1992).

5. Dee Hock, *Birth of the Chaordic Age* (San Francisco: Berrett-Koehler Publishers, Inc., 1999).

6. Ibid., 69-70.

7. Oswald Chambers, *My Utmost for His Highest* (Grand Rapids, MI: Discovery House Publishers, 1992), devotional reading for July 24.

8. Jim Cymbala, *Fresh Wind, Fresh Fire: What Happens When God's Spirit Invades the Hearts of His People* (Grand Rapids, MI: Zondervan Publishing House, 1997), 49.

9. Ken Heer, coordinator of the Leadership Development Journey, The Wesleyan Church, Indianapolis, Indiana, in correspondence with the author.

10. Quoted by Marvin Moss, pastor of King of Kings Lutheran Church, Omaha, Nebraska, September 19, 1993.

11. Win Arn, *The Win Arn Growth Report*, no. 25 (Monrovia, CA: Institute for American Church Growth), 1-2.

12. Ibid.

13. Donald N. Sull, "Management by Commitments," *Leading Change: A Leader to Leader Guide,* ed. Frances Hesselbein and Rob Johnston (San Francisco: Jossey-Bass, 2002), 73.

14. John Maxwell, leadership conference materials.

15. Ken Heer, in correspondence with the author.

16. George Barna, *Turn-Around Churches: How to Overcome Barriers to Growth and Bring New Life to an Established Church* (Ventura, CA: Regal Books, 1993), 71-72.

17. Ibid.

18. John C. Maxwell, "How to Gain Influence," INJOY *Maximum Impact* tape, vol. 1, no. 11, 1997.

19. Ken Heer, in correspondence with the author.

20. Rick Warren, *The Purpose Driven Church: Growth Without Compromising Your Message and Mission* (Grand Rapids, MI: Zondervan Publishing House, 1995).

21. Ron Crandall, *Turnaround Strategies for the Small Church* (Nashville: Abingdon Press, 1995), 116.

22. The concept of infusing visionary ideology into the environment is adapted from concepts described by James C. Collins and Jerry I. Porras in *Built to Last: Successful Habits of Visionary Companies* (New York: HarperCollins Publishers, Inc., 1994), 201-02.

23. Warren Bennis, *Why Leaders Can't Lead: The Unconscious Conspiracy Continues* (San Francisco: Jossey- Bass Publishers, 1989), 117.

24. Adapted from Lyle E. Schaller's *Strategies for Change* (Nashville: Abingdon Press, 1993), 42.

25. Thomas G. Bandy, *Coaching Change: Breaking Down Resistance, Building Up Hope* (Nashville: Abingdon Press, 2000), 127-28.

26. William M. Boast, with Benjamin Martin, *Masters of Change: How Great Leaders in Every Age Thrived in Turbulent Times* (Provo, UT: Executive Excellence Publishing, 1997), 101-02.

27. C.W. Perry, quoted in *Leadership Journal* XVIII, no. II (Spring 1997), 73.

28. I first saw this model explained by Win Arn and Charles Arn of the Institute for American Church Growth in Monrovia, California, and taught by C. Peter Wagner in a doctor of ministry course in church growth at Fuller Theological Seminary in Pasadena, California.

29. Gary McIntosh, *The McIntosh Church Growth Network Newsletter* 12, no. 9 (September 2000): 2.

30. Charles Arn, in correspondence with the author.

31. Douglas Alan Walrath, *Leading Churches Through Change* (Nashville: Abingdon Press, 1979).

32. John P. Kotter, *Leading Change* (Boston: Harvard Business School Press, 1996), 93.

33. Thomas G. Bandy, *Christian Chaos: Revolutionizing the Congregation* (Nashville: Abingdon Press, 1999), 141-42.

34. Quoted in Walt Kallestad, *Entertainment Evangelism: Taking the Church Public* (Nashville: Abingdon Press, 1996), 27

35. Rick Warren, *The Purpose Driven Church*, 237-38.

36. Leonard Sweet, *Soul Tsunami*, 91.

9

What Church Leader's Need to Know About . . .

Finance and Accounting

A Christian Perspective on Handling and Tracking Money

"The simple believeth every word:
but the prudent man looketh well to his going."

—Proverbs 14:15

Feeling the Pinch

After graduating from a small Bible college, Pastor Rod Simon worked as an associate pastor in two different churches before becoming the senior pastor of a small church in the South. Under his leadership, church attendance doubled, causing the church leaders to consider building an addition or searching for a new church building.

Two influential church leaders had different ideas for the church. Both were long-term members who remembered the days when "everybody knew everybody's name." Both also made it a point to thwart Pastor Rod's vision for growth. Sadly, more church members followed these individuals than followed Pastor Rod.

Farther north, another church was experiencing growing pains. One of the larger churches in a medium-sized town in the Midwest, Sunnyside Bible Church had seen its membership grow fivefold under its senior pastor, Wayland Morris. Pastor Morris, however, began to sense God's call to become an evangelist. He tendered his resignation, but agreed to stay on until the church located a replacement.

When it became apparent to Pastor Rod that his church was not interested in pursuing his vision, he began to seek employment with other churches. Almost immediately, he received a call from Sunnyside. When Rod visited the church, the members of the search committee realized that they had found their new pastor. The church unanimously extended a call to Rod, which he graciously accepted.

During Pastor Rod's first year at Sunnyside, he shared his vision with the congregation. Overwhelmingly, the church threw its support behind its new leader. Eventually, the building committee recommended addition and expansion plans that carried a price tag of $5 million. Sunnyside already had an outstanding debt of $500,000, which it had incurred to expand its sanctuary and to purchase new (and badly needed) equipment for its growing television ministry.

Despite his strong sense that God was leading the church to greater heights, Pastor Rod was somewhat overwhelmed by the sheer size of the building program. Never before had he embarked on a building and faith commitment program of such magnitude. In the past, he had entrusted the church finances to a treasurer or someone with a finance background.

Pastor Rod is 35 years old. His wife is pregnant with their third child. He and his wife recently purchased their first home. They also just financed the purchase of a minivan and an SUV. Because his wife is a stay-at-home mom, they are beginning to feel the "pinch."

Pastor Rod has never taken a course in business, finance, or accounting— not during his college years, during the fifteen years he has ministered, or even during the time he studied for his master's degree, which he received two years ago. When he graduated from seminary fifteen years ago, he left with $15,000 in school loans—on which he is still paying. As he assesses his leadership role in piloting Sunnyside Bible Church through an expansive and expensive building program, he cannot help but feel inadequate and ill prepared.

An Overview of Finance and Accounting

Unfortunately, Pastor Rod's story seems to be all too common: little knowledge in the area of personal or church finances coupled with a tenuous personal financial situation and a daunting church financial situation, and you have the potential for a financial meltdown.

This chapter provides a basic knowledge needed to grasp **finance** and **accounting**. The chapter is subdivided into *personal* finances, *personal* accounting, *church* finances, and *church* accounting. Many of the principles that apply to *personal* finances and accounting also apply to *church* finances and accounting. After reading this chapter, pastors should feel more comfortable about all of these areas.

Many use the terms finance and accounting interchangeably. But the two are separate. Finance relates to how you *handle* your money, accounting relates to how you *track* your money. Consider the decision by Pastor Rod to purchase a home. When they shopped for a loan, they gathered information about interest rates, points, and bank charges from five different banks. After comparing Pastor Rod's take-home pay with the various monthly mortgage payments available, they determined how much home they could afford. This process relates to how to *handle* his take-home pay—the **finance** decision. As the Simons began to make monthly payments, they also began to *track* Pastor Rod's take-home pay—the **accounting** decision. Accounting and finance are closely related, but they are not interchangeable.

A pastor would be well served to secure resources that discuss finance and accounting from both a biblical point of view and a secular perspective. Some resources are listed at the end of this chapter. Resources also can be obtained from the library, a bookstore, or the Internet.

Personal Finances

Having read a number of resources about personal finances; taught and counseled individuals with financial problems; taught church members about personal finance from a biblical point of view; and taught college students from a secular point of view, I have both a theoretical and practical perspective. The major topics that should concern pastors are ownership, stewardship, financial planning, taxation, credit, home and vehicle purchases, insurance, investments, retirement planning, and estate planning.

Ownership

In Psalms 24:1, David says, "The earth is the Lord's, and the fullness thereof; the world, and they that dwell therein" (KJV). What David is saying is that everything and everyone belongs to the Lord. Those who realize the importance of this principle are in a position to understand how essential it is to exercise good stewardship over what God has entrusted to them.

Stewardship

Part and parcel with the principle of ownership is the principle of stewardship. Matthew 25:14-30 (The Parable of the Talents), which has multiple meanings (see "Investments" below), also teaches that we are to exercise good stewardship over that which God has entrusted to us. One of the best ways to exercise good stewardship is to establish a budget and stick to it. (We will discuss budgeting in greater depth later).

Financial Planning

Personal financial planning involves managing your money and resources to reach your goals. If your goal is to accumulate a certain amount of money by a certain age, you would decide how much to invest, the rate of return you could expect, and the time needed to meet your goal. You would then choose from among various investment alternatives and translate your plan into action. These steps find support in Proverbs 16:9, which says, "*A man's heart deviseth his way: but the Lord directeth his steps.*" The final step would be to revisit your plan periodically and make any necessary revisions. This is supported in Scripture: "*Be thou diligent to know the state of thy flocks, and look well to thy herds*" (Proverbs 27:23).

Home and Vehicle Purchases

These will be the two largest purchases you will make in your lifetime. For most people, a house and a vehicle are necessities. Given that God has promised to supply our needs (Philippians 4:19 and Matthew 6:25-34), we should focus on exactly what housing and vehicle choices will meet our needs.

Home. Compare the cost of renting versus the cost of owning. You do not build equity when you rent, but you forego the closing costs involved when purchasing a home. With renting you eliminate other costs related to home purchase, such as property taxes, homeowner's insurance, debt, and the costs associated with repairing, maintaining, and remodeling a home. If you purchase a home, you would be wise to ask a trusted individual to recommend a good realtor. (Also true if you are selling a home).

Vehicle. Since a vehicle depreciates quickly suggests that you should not purchase a new car, it may be wiser to purchase a vehicle that is one to three years old. By then, a significant amount of depreciation has occurred. Leasing a vehicle does not allow you to build equity in the vehicle as an asset. (You may think that this is inconsistent with the information above about renting/purchasing a home. The difference is that the costs associated with a home are greater than those associated with a vehicle).

Insurance

Biblically speaking, insurance can be considered part of the way an individual cares for his/her family (1 Timothy 5:8). If you don't understand the different types of insurance, you should consult a qualified insurance agent. According to Proverbs 14:15, seeking such advice is wise: "*The simple believeth every word: but the prudent man looketh well to his going.*" The major forms of insurance are homeowner's, vehicle, life, disability, and health.

Homeowner's. This coverage is for a home, personal property, other structures on the property, and those who may be injured on the property. If you borrow money to purchase your home, the lender will require you to insure it for at least the amount of the loan.

Vehicle. By law, you must insure your vehicle for harm caused to other individuals and their vehicles. Depending on the state personal injury coverage ranges from $10,000 to $50,000. The coverage for property damage ranges from $5,000 to $25,000. Some of the more common optional coverages include medical (cost of medical care for persons in your vehicle); collision (damage to your vehicle); and comprehensive (damage to your vehicle other than through collision). The decision as to what types and how much coverage to purchase boils down to legal requirements and how much you can afford to pay.

Life: Although there are different types of life insurance, the two most common are *term* and *whole life*. (Universal life is a variation of whole life.) For younger people, the cost of term insurance is much lower than whole life, and you can get more coverage. As your age increases, so do the premiums. Some employers offer term insurance, although you can purchase additional coverage if you wish.

Whole life is sold on the premise that the policyholder builds cash value in addition to the coverage. This cash value—similar to a savings account—can be used in later years to pay premiums. The downside with this is that you build cash value more slowly than if you had invested the money elsewhere.

If your budget is limited, term insurance may be the best buy. Many methods are available to help calculate the amount of insurance that you need. The least complicated method is for the insurance to equal eight to ten times the gross salary of the wager earner whose income would need to be replaced.

Disability. This type of insurance provides a stream of income if you become disabled. While disabilities normally include accidents, illnesses, or pregnancy, not all policies are the same. The cost will depend on factors such as the waiting period to collect benefits, and the length of the benefit period. A number of employers provide this benefit, although you can purchase an individual policy.

Health. Medical insurance plans come in a variety of forms, and include common provisions concerning eligibility, deductibles, out-of-pocket limits, co-payments, exclusions, coordination of benefits, and benefit limits. Some employers offer medical insurance plans that vary widely in premiums, deductibles, coverage, and co-payments.

Investments

One of the key themes in Matthew 25:14-30 concerns investing. Establishing investment goals is a major component of financial planning. Safety and risk are the two most important factors affecting your investments. In general, the safer the investment, the less risk, and vice versa. Also, the closer you are to retirement, the less risk you should accept.

Other factors affecting your investment choice include income, growth, and liquidity. *Income* refers to the stream of income that you can expect to receive while you hold the investment. *Growth* refers to the increase in the value. *Liquidity* refers to your ability to convert the investment to cash quickly.

Common types of investments are stocks, corporate bonds, government bonds, mutual funds, certificates of deposit, and money market funds. Each type varies according to safety, risk, income, growth, and liquidity. If you don't understand the various types, you may wish to consider obtaining advice from an investment consultant (Proverbs 14:15).

The concept of compound interest is integral to understanding how wise it is to invest. The concept refers to earning a return on top of a return. For example, if you put $1,000 in a bank account earning 5 percent interest, at the end of the year, you would have $1,050 in your account. At the end of year two, you would have $1,102.50. Your original $1,000 earned 5 percent interest, as did the $50 you earned after year one. Compound interest is a very powerful tool for anyone's investment plan.

Retirement Planning

Contrary to conventional thought, retirement is not biblical. The only passage in the Bible that remotely touches the subject is Numbers 8:24-26, which teaches that the Levitical priests were to serve in the Tabernacle from twenty-five to fifty, after which they were to assist other priests. Nowhere else in the Bible does anyone speak about retirement. Scripturally speaking retirement is better thought of as the end of one phase of life and the beginning of another.

If you are planning to cease working in the future, you may experience a decrease in income. You may have to seek income from another source, such as a different vocation or from your investments. This will involve budgetary considerations and investment planning.

Estate Planning

Estate planning finds plenty of biblical support. In Genesis 25:5 the Bible says that *"Abraham gave all that he had unto Isaac."* In Proverbs 13:22, Solomon describes the wisdom in planning for the orderly succession of one's estate. As you acquire assets (e.g., home, investments, retirement account, cash, vehicle, and other personal property) and responsibilities (e.g., spouse, children), you should consider things such as joint ownership, wills, trusts, estate taxes, and gift taxes. You should seek advice from a competent estate planner (Proverbs 14:15)

Church Finances

The larger churches are more likely to have staff handle its finances. Those with oversight might include a treasurer and a finance committee. For smaller churches, the finances might fall on the shoulders of a bookkeeper or the pastor. It would be wise for a small church to include a treasurer and finance committee. In medium-sized churches, there should be one individual handling the finances on a regular basis, as well as a treasurer and a finance committee. For larger churches, it might be necessary to add a full-time church business administrator, in addition to a bookkeeper, treasurer, and finance committee.

The aforementioned structures provide a system of checks and balances. For instance, the bookkeeper could prepare all checks for bills and payroll, which the treasurer then could sign. If a church business administrator is involved, this individual could cosign the checks with the treasurer.

While these structures may provide some relief to the overworked senior pastor, they also may remove the pastor from the area of church finances. No matter how large the church, the pastor would be wise to learn as much as possible about church finances, and play an active role in the financial decisions.

For a church to prosper materially and spiritually, it must be managed properly. How a pastor manages his personal finances may impact how he assists the church in the management of its finances. A pastor who is responsible in the area of personal finances is more likely to have a positive impact on the finances of the church than a pastor who is irresponsible.

Church finances involve some of the same topics discussed in the section on personal finances: ownership, stewardship, financial planning, taxation, credit, insurance, and investments. Church finances also involve some new topics, among them building projects and technology.

Ownership

Most churches are incorporated, meaning that they have their own identity. Depending on state law, title to church assets can be held by the church's trustees, the church itself, or key church administrators. Church assets include facilities, vehicles, personal property, parsonage, and bank accounts. Biblically speaking, however, God owns everything and everyone (Psalm 24:1). No matter how many assets the church possesses, it must recognize God as the true owner.

Stewardship

Matthew 25:14-30 teaches the principle of stewardship. A church should know that good stewardship of money is a prerequisite to being used by God for greater things (Luke 16:10-12). A church can demonstrate good stewardship is to properly care for its assets. A church can also exhibit good stewardship by establishing a benevolence program to help those in need. Those who qualify include the poor (Deuteronomy 15:7-11); the diligent (2 Thessalonians 3:10); orphans (Psalm 10:14); those with immediate needs (James 2:15-16); and those with legitimate needs (2 Corinthians 8:13).

Financial Planning

Church financial planning involves managing money and resources in an effective and efficient manner to achieve goals. Goals like hiring additional personnel, remodeling facilities, purchasing a van, or building a new sanctuary. Whatever the goal, the church must have the necessary resources. This means that the church must live within its budget and develop a plan to accumulate resources. This plan might include special fund-raising efforts, borrowing, or investment of funds. Given that a number of church projects are short term, a church would be wise to invest its funds in safe, low-risk, liquid investments. If the pastor lacks expertise in this area, he should seek the counsel of others (Proverbs 11:14).

Building Projects, Vehicle Purchases, and Technology

Building projects and vehicle purchases often will be the two largest expenditures a church will make. For most churches, these are legitimate needs. Given that God has promised to supply needs (Philippians 4:19 and Matthew 6:25-34), it is important for the church to focus on exactly what building and vehicle choices will meet its needs. Technology, too, is becoming an ever-increasing component of the church budget.

Building Projects. If the congregation is small, the church should compare the cost of renting a facility versus the cost of purchasing or constructing its own facility. Purchasing an existing facility is a complicated endeavor; constructing a building is an even more complicated one. Compare lenders and builders, seek recommendations from key individuals in the church, and prayerfully consider the decision.

Vehicle. Since a vehicle quickly depreciates the church should avoid purchasing a new vehicle. It would be wise to purchase a vehicle that is one to three years old. Leasing a vehicle is not recommended. There are exceptions. For a church with vibrant ministries and ever-growing transportation needs, leasing a vehicle might be a sound decision. Generally a leased vehicle will require less maintenance than a purchased vehicle because the leased vehicle will be returned to the dealer.

Technology. It is necessary to invest in computers and software, both of which are necessary for accounting purposes and keeping track of members and their contributions. Increasingly, technology has been given a major role in nearly every area of a church's functioning—from sound systems and the audio-visual aspect of worship or church newsletters. Given how rapidly technology changes, current hardware might become obsolete very quickly. Input from an IT specialist may be invaluable in making technology decisions.

Insurance

The major forms of insurance are building, vehicle, life, disability, and health. In many cases, insurance companies issue policies that are standard for every church. The differences usually lie in the deductible amounts, the amount of coverage, the premiums, and the extensiveness of coverage. For additional information, the church should consult a qualified insurance agent (Proverbs 14:15).

Building. Insurance coverage is for the building, personal property, other structures on the property, and those who are injured on church property. How much insurance a church should carry depends upon a variety of factors, including the values of the church assets and the risks to be insured. Concerning liability, more and more churches are requiring criminal background checks for Sunday school workers who deal with young children and nursery workers.

Vehicle. By law, the church must insure any church-owned vehicles for harm caused to other individuals and their vehicles. The decision as to what type and how much coverage to purchase depends on statutory requirements and how much the church can afford to pay.

Life. A church may choose to offer a group-term life insurance benefit to its employees. The cost will depend on the size of the church staff and other factors, but normally is not that high. Coverage may be available through a church's denominational structure.

Disability. A church may choose to offer a disability insurance benefit to its employees. Like group-term life insurance, the cost will depend on the size of the church staff and other factors. The cost is usually not that high. Coverage may be available through a church's denominational structure.

Health. A church may choose to offer a health insurance benefit to its employees. The cost for this type of insurance can be high. The church may consider asking employees to contribute to the plan.

Investments

One of the key themes in Matthew 25:14-30 concerns investing. If the church has excess funds or is saving for a future capital project it may wish to establish investment goals. Safety and risk are the two most important factors. The safer the investment, the lower the risk, and vice versa. The nearer the project is about to commence, the less risk the church should accept.

Church Accounting

Managing church finances depends upon the manner in which the church accounts for its income and expenditures. The most important accounting tools are

1. the profit and loss (P&L) statement,
2. the budget, and
3. the net worth statement.

The P&L states the financial activity for a particular period, which, in most cases is a month, quarter, or year. The budget looks forward to the next year. The net worth statement details the assets, debts, and net worth of the church at a particular point in time. All three provide solid accountability (Romans 14:12).

10

What Church Leader's Need to Know About . . .

Marketing

Outreach and the Ministry

"You can give people responsibility and authority;
but without information they are helpless.
Knowledge is the ultimate power tool."

—BILL GATES[1]

Growth of a Little Country Church

Corinth United Methodist Church sits on a peaceful country road only a few miles from a university town. Less than a mile from the church, new homes are being built to accommodate Gen X and Boomer families moving into the area. However, for most of these new residents, Corinth is invisible.

For many years, Corinth UMC had been in the ideal location. It was across from a small schoolhouse that had been the center of this farming community until 1955. After the school closed and relocated, a four-lane bypass had cut a swath across the adjacent farmland, cutting off Corinth from the nearby town. Although the road on which Corinth sat intersected the bypass, few community residents traveled the country road because it was a dead-end lane.

However, Corinth had an energetic new pastor and a dedicated team of lay leaders. They were of one accord in realizing their future was hampered by their nearly invisible location. Subsequently, a team was launched to map out appropriate programs and a marketing strategy to inform the community of the new ideas emanating down this "dead-end" country road.

They met with me to discuss their choice of a leader for their marketing team. "We've chosen June Mason (a pseudonym)," began Jack. "She's got the best understanding of what needs to be done." June's farm abutted the church property, and she was the matriarch of one of the oldest families in the church. Definitely of the Builder generation, and somewhat refined and retiring, she was not the candidate I envisioned. It seemed to me she might be out of touch with the marketing strategies and outreach ideas this church needed. I was soon convinced otherwise.

"We built the church here in 1937 because we wanted to be across from the school, to minister to families," June said quietly. "We've got to keep that tradition alive. And, the steeple was our advertisement for years," she continued. "We built the prettiest steeple, and lit it too. Some people complained about putting a light on it. But it was to remind the people that there was a church here. . . . But now people can't see it (from the bypass). It's too far away. So, we're going to start ministries that will be what our steeple used to be: a light to tell the community that Christ is here."

Over the next several months, June's team created an amazingly sophisticated strategy of family-oriented programming, advertisements, radio ads, an eye-catching logo, a billboard, directional signage to the church, and even advertisements on placemats in nearby restaurants. The exhaustive nature and creativity of this plan was nothing short of amazing, especially considering that it had been created under the auspices of someone who did not fit my image of the ideal "marketer." I soon learned that June's appearance belied her outgoing and likeable personality. Her deep concern for the church reflected an intuitive understanding of its problems. In addition, she had run a farm for many years. Whether dealing with grain, cattle, or churches, she understood the importance of marketing.

Soon, Corinth was enjoying an influx of newcomers—more in one three-month span than in the previous year. With a newcomer assimilation process in place, Corinth began to add new Sunday school classes and fill its daycare center. This little country church was buzzing with an excitement that amazed visitors. June had led the charge into the world of marketing, a realm where many churches hesitate to go.

Marketing:

Why does the business world feel so compelled to invest in marketing, while the church eschews such endeavors? The reason may be marketing's reputation for abuse. However, in every human realm, including marketing, there is the temptation for manipulation and exploitation. Although marketing can be abused, it must not be shunned because of its potential for misuse. Marketing is a valuable tool for getting across a message. It is another resource the Christian can use to communicate the Good News. Marketing is basically about meeting needs. Viewing marketing through this lens, we identify four components.

The Four Stages of Marketing

Stage 1. Identify the needs of people.

Stage 2. Design something, such as a ministry or program, to meet those needs.

Stage 3. Communicate information about those ministries and services to the people who need them.

Stage 4. Evaluate the satisfaction levels of those who receive the ministry and/or service.

From this four-stage definition, many church leaders will recognize that they are already involved in some marketing. Most churches are engaged in stages one and two. However, because many people regard stage three as suspect, it is the often ignored by the church.

"Outreach" Instead of "Marketing"

Because the term "marketing" has a somewhat callous resonance in church circles, I shall use the term "outreach."[5] By outreach, I mean a strategy that addresses the same four areas or tasks explained above and diagrammed in Figure 10.1.

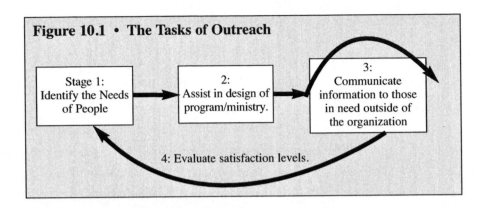

Figure 10.1 • The Tasks of Outreach

Stage 1: Identify the Needs of People → 2: Assist in design of program/ministry. → 3: Communicate information to those in need outside of the organization

4: Evaluate satisfaction levels.

To Whom Are We Reaching Out?

To identify the needs of those to whom we are reaching out, we first must ask the question, "Which people?" In the business realm, this group is often referred to as an organization's target market. This refers to the people the organization is attempting to touch. .

Avoid Outreach Myopia

As a church begins stage one, it should first conduct a self-appraisal to ensure that it is not suffering from outreach myopia. This is the malady that occurs when an organization is too shortsighted to see beyond what it is doing now. AT&T for years saw itself strictly as a telephone company. After deregulation, it had to escape this myopic view and transform itself into a multifaceted communication network. This expanded understanding thwarted myopic tendencies and allowed AT&T to branch out into new and profitable areas, including the Internet, cable TV, and wireless communication.

Outreach myopia arises when a church becomes so consumed with the day-to-day running of the organization that it fails to address or identify the needs of those outside their fellowship. Jesus appears to address this myopia when He urged His disciples to *"open your eyes and look at the fields! They are ripe for harvest. Even now the reaper draws his wages, even now he harvests the crop for eternal life . . ."* (John 4:35, 36 NIV). Jesus' analogy that His disciples must be harvesters harvesting *"a crop for eternal life"* reminded them to see their mission field and its magnitude.

Find Your Mission Field

Finding your mission field requires hard-nosed investigation into two areas: (1) the things that you do well, and (2) the needs of your mission field. What an organization does well can be defined in its core competences. In this book's chapter on strategic planning, we looked at how to define these internal strengths. However, identifying the needs of your mission field involves a five-step process. Let's look at this graphically in Figure 10.2 before we investigate each section individually.

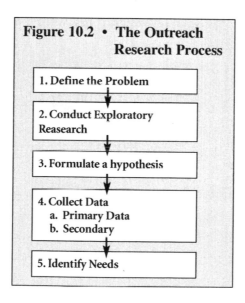

Figure 10.2 • The Outreach Research Process

1. Define the Problem
2. Conduct Exploratory Reasearch
3. Formulate a hypothesis
4. Collect Data
   a. Primary Data
   b. Secondary
5. Identify Needs

1. Define the problem

Defining the problem begins with conducting a strategic analysis of the organization. This includes a S.W.O.T. analysis, which investigates the strengths, weaknesses, opportunities and threats to the organization.

Church illnesses are often referred to as "pathologies."[6] Maladies that affect the "body" of Christ. Common church illnesses include:

- **Geriatrophy**. This is the wasting away of an aging church because it does not have an influx of younger generations. Younger generations often feel the aging congregation does not understand nor reach out to them so they go elsewhere. This weakens the congregation, leading to its demise. *A House Divided: Bridging the Generation Gaps in Your Church* describes a seven-step growth process to facilitate the coexistence of three generations.[7]
- **Ethnikitis**. This church illness is caused by a change in the ethnicity of a neighborhood. It is the second biggest killer of churches in America.[8]
- **People Blindness**. This malady prevents a church from seeing the important cultural differences that exist between groups of people who live in close geographical proximity. These differences tend to create barriers to the acceptance of the church's message.[9]
- **Hyper-cooperativism**. Hyper-cooperativism describes a local church's loss of identity when all or most of its outreach efforts are conjoined with those of other congregations.
- **Koinonitis**. Sometimes called "fellowship inflammation." This describes a church in which spirituality and unity are so high that newcomers and/or unchurched people are hindered in their efforts to be assimilated. If growth does occur, it is "transfer" growth from other churches.
- **St. John's Syndrome**. This illness is congregational "lukewarmness" as Christ warned the Apostle John in Revelation 3:16. It is characterized by an apathetic attitude toward spiritual disciplines and formation. It is often the disease of second generation churches.
- **Sociological Strangulation**. This malady occurs when the facilities/staff are unable to keep up with the influx of people. The famous "80% Rule" is that if in any regular service your worship facility is 80% full, you are entering into sociological strangulation. *"The shoe must never tell the foot how big it is,"* stated Robert Schuller.[11]
- **Cardiac Arrest**. As the name implies, this is a serious church illness. Sometimes, the "heart" of the congregation has been so hurt by some traumatic event that the congregation would rather die than continue on. *Staying Power: Why People Leave the Church Over Change and*

What You Can Do About It examines this serious problem and explains how unity can be preserved.[12]

When Are You Not Ready for Marketing?

Several of the maladies are internal illnesses that must be dealt with before a church can initiate an outreach strategy. Koinonitis, St. John's Syndrome, and Cardiac Arrest must be addressed before a churches reaches beyond its walls. Often it is important to make progress towards internal unity and wholeness than it is to initiate an aggressive outreach strategy.

Don't Market Beyond Your Reach

Defining your problem also means defining the scope of that problem. If your problem is geriatrophy and you need to reach younger generations, determine how far you can expect those generations to travel to your church. Reaching out across a geographic zone may limit your success. Looking at outreach, we identify two limiting factors regarding scope: geographic reach and social reach.

Geographic reach means finding the geographic size of your mission field. this is the size of the area from which they attract existing and potential constituents. To discover your reach, take five steps:

1. Place pins representing existing attendees on a map. Draw a boundary around the area where most of these pins lie. This is your Rough Geographic Boundary (RGB).
2. Look at major transportation arteries that connect your church location with potential constituents. Compute how far along these arteries a person could travel in twelve-and-a-half minutes. (However, if you live in a metropolitan suburb or a rural area, increase this to twenty-two-and-a-half minutes.) In a different color ink, draw a boundary around this area. This is your potential geographic boundary (PGB).
3. Now draw a third boundary (using a third color ink) that roughly falls between the two boundaries. This is your Combined Geographic Boundary (CGB). Most of your outreach should be confined to avenues that target your mission field in your CGB.
4. Recalculate your RGB, PGB and CGB yearly.

Social reach means that a congregation should not attempt to reach out beyond its own social sphere, unless the congregation is willing to undertake radical cultural changes. A congregation of Hispanic Builders/Seniors may successfully reach out to Hispanic Boomers. The only social barrier will be age. However, if that same Hispanic Builder/Senior congregation sought to reach out to Asian American Boomers, the combination of two social barriers (age and ethnicity) might thwart the process.

A more common scenario would be if a predominately Builder/Senior Caucasian church tried to reach out to Boomer Hispanics. The combination of two social barriers means that success would be more tenuous. If a congregation's survival was at stake, such chasms might need to be bridged. Then the church will have to radically subdue its own preferences and even adopt the culture of those they seek. The lesson here is to cross as few social barriers as necessary for survival.

2. Conduct Exploratory Research

The next step in locating your mission field requires researching the problem, both theoretically and practically. In step two, leaders should undertake the following:

1. *Read* books, articles, research internet pages, etc. Do not limit yourself to one source. A Google search with appropriate key terms will bring up a number of articles.

2. *Look for successful examples of organizations that have overcome the problem you are facing.* Business author Jim Collins profiles many organizations which have overcome problems to be successful. Problems besetting your church will be common to the other churches. Overcome any inclination toward competition or envy, and investigate churches that have been successful in overcoming the problem you are encountering. But do not simply accept their explanations. Pastors often attribute growth to the wrong sources.[13] Look closely, and use impartial judgment.

3. *Get outside help*. During this stage, an outside consultant is invaluable. Denominational departments often offer such help. The American Society for Church Growth serves as a clearinghouse for consultants trained in the

mechanisms, procedures, and strategies of church management, growth, and health.[14]

Step three is the most overlooked area in the process of identifying your church's mission field. initial insights gained in steps one and two can be so euphoric leaders will not sit down and codify the problem. It is imperative to know what you are looking for.

3. Formulate Hypthesis

Many churches will discover that they are suffering from unbalanced generational ratios. In the case of Corinth Church, June's marketing strategy team discovered that 70 percent of the congregants were aging Builders/Seniors. However, an investigation of county records revealed that Boomer and Generation X families comprised 72 percent of community residents, and were the area's fastest growing segment. The team discovered that Corinth Church's generational ratios were opposite the community's ratios. The church was suffering from geriatrophy.

Corinth then formulated a hypothesis: "Corinth is dying because we do not have programs and ministries attractive to community residents born after 1945." To test this they advanced to the next step.

4. Collect Data

To confirm the hypothesis, look at primary and secondary data.

b. Secondary Data

Secondary data is published data. The marketing strategy team at Corinth Church investigated governmental, denominational, and business data to understand the new people moving into the area. It became clear that these new people were Boomers and Gen Xers with young children.

Secondary data resources available from county offices, planning commissions, libraries, and the Internet include (but are not limited to) the following:

1. *Monthly Catalog of the United States Government Publications*, published annually

2. *Statistical Abstract of the United States,* published annually[15]
3. *Survey of Current Business,* updated monthly
4. *County and City Data Book,* published every three years on counties and cities with over 25,000 residents

b. Primary Data

Primary data is information collected specifically for the task. This is conducted through "sampling." Sampling requires taking a representative "sample" of an overall population and deducing certain area-wide conclusions. *A House Divided: Bridging the Generation Gaps in Your Church* explains how a church can conduct a simple sampling. These suggestions appear below in abbreviated form.

Focus Groups

As small gatherings of six to twelve individuals, focus groups are designed to bring to the surface feelings that often remain buried in one-on-one interviews. Focus groups help organizations "focus" on information or advice from the group.

One-on-One Interviews

These types of interviews are the best avenues for obtaining detailed information. They also can be intimidating for the interviewee. It is best for a church to approach this carefully.

1. **Door-to-door or street interviews**. These types of interviews are not as well received today as they were in the 1950s and 60s. Today it is best to proceed with caution. If you decide to conduct a door-to-door or street interview, follow the sample guidelines in Figure 10.3 to ensure that you conduct your research effectively and appropriately.
2. **Phone Interviews**. Because of the caveats of door-to-door and street interviews, the telephone interview has become increasingly popular. But in recent times many young adults have dropped their land line in favor of a cell phone. This must be a consideration in conducting phone interviews. Proceed cautiously, using a variation of the sample survey in Figure 10.3.

3. **The number of interviews required**. Demographers have discovered that a random sample of 1,500 people can provide accurate information regarding the larger population as a whole.[17]

The questions in Figure 10.3 can serve as a guide to testing your outreach hypothesis in any of the above types of one-on-one interviews.

Figure 10.3 • Sample Survey Questions

"Hello. My name is _____(name)_____ and I am conducting a short survey for (name of congregation)_____ in ___(city/town)___. Would you mind if I asked you a few anonymous and brief questions?"
  - If "YES," continue.
  - If "NO," conclude by saying, *"Thank you for your consideration. Good bye"* (if via the phone), or *"Have a good day"* (if via personal interview).

Survey Parameters:
"We wish to interview individuals who were born in the years.
    ___(year)___ to ___(year)___.[19] Were you born in or during these years?
  - If "YES," continue.
  - If "NO," conclude by saying, *"Thank you for your time. Good bye/Have a good day."*

Open-ended Questions:
Question #1: *"What do you think a church could do to help people age _____*
    to _____?"
Question #2: *"Why do you think people age _____ to _____ do not attend church services?"*
Question #3: *"What are people your age looking for in a church?"*
Question #4: *"What advice would you give me so that a church could help people age _____ to _____ more effectively?"*
Question #5: *"Are you actively involved in a church, synagogue, mosque, or other religious house of worship at this time?"*
Conclusion:
"Thank you for your time. Your advice will help ____(name of congregation)____ of (city/town)___ better address the needs of people in our community(ies). Thank you. Good bye" (if via the phone), or "Have a good day" (if via personal interview).

---

5. Identify Needs

Finally, your task is to identify the specific needs of your mission field, so that you can select strategies based upon these needs. One of the most productive and easiest to implement is called the debriefing and correlation procedure.

1. Immediately upon completion of the interview, or meeting of the focus group, etc., the leader and moderator should rank the needs they perceived. At that same time, they should write down creative ideas and suggestions generated during the process.
2. After all interviews have been conducted, the leaders/moderators should meet and combine all rankings into a master list, ranking them from most to least prevalent.
3. Gather all leaders/moderators and correlate responses and suggestions gleaned from the interview process. Then proceed to stage 2.

Stage 2: Select Strategies to Meet the Needs of Your Mission Field

We investigated the tools for selecting strategies in this book's chapter on strategic planning. With that in mind, let's look at Figure 10.4 to see how strategies that might meet the needs of those in Corinth's mission field could be graphed.

Figure 10.4[20] • Mission Needs and Strategies	
A List of Needs This list of needs was culled from the data-gathering process.	**Potential Strategies:** Brainstorm to create a list of potential strategies.[21]
Child care for working mothers of preschool children.	Day care provided by the church. Carpooling service for preschoolers in the area. Have the youth group organize child care on Saturday morning, so mothers can grocery shop or spend time with other mothers. Serve a breakfast for mothers with preschool children once a week from 6 to 8 AM. Staff it with stay-at-home mothers or Builder/Seniors.
After-school care for school-age children.	Kid's Club provided by church after school day ends. Join with other community churches to provide after-school recreational activities. Start an after-school choir called "Praise Kids."

Use Figure 10.4 as a basis for the marketing team and the strategic planning team to rate each strategy via the Quantitative Strategic Planning Matrix (QSPM). Then implement each strategy (the most highly rated first), as resources and time allow.

Stage 3: Communicate Information about Appropriate Ministries and Services to Needy People

Outreach Caveats

Employing football terminology, author Herb Miller once urged churches to "throw your message to wider receivers."[22] By this, Miller meant that a church must share its message effectively and widely to those outside its walls. Many churches attempt this, but often fail to witness any response from the community because of one or more of the following caveats:

1. ***Results are expected too quickly.*** Often, a budget committee will allocate money to advertising, and then attempt to judge success or failure within a short span of time. In the marketing realm, years may be required to establish customer loyalty. Thus, marketing is a long and slow endeavor. While evaluation is important, evaluating results of strategies that have been implemented for less than eighteen months to two years can be hasty. Visiting a church (much less joining one) is an important cultural, spiritual, and personal decision. Many times, a great deal of time will elapse before results are identifiable.

2. ***Christians advertise in the wrong places, typically to other Christians.*** Every Easter I am amazed by the sheer number of churches that advertise on the religious page of local newspapers. Nestled among dozens, if not hundreds of similar ads, a small church such as Corinth has little chance of increasing visitor flow. Unfortunately, ads on the church page are predominantly read by other Christians, not by the unchurched people most churches are attempting to reach. Unchurched people most likely decide what they will do this weekend by reading the entertainment page or the sports page. Thus, for the church, these pages (that often cost more) can yield the biggest return on investment, since they reach more unchurched people with their message.

3. ***Christian advertisements often promote the same things as other churches.*** Churches have many differences, but they also have many things in common. Thus, when churches promote their commonality with similar sayings, they can overwhelm and confuse the reader. For example, one church page at Easter was filled with churches offering "a place for your family to grow," "contemporary ministry for today's families," and "family friendly and Christ centered." These descriptors were all variations of a fundamental desire to welcome people into fellowship and discipleship. Now, there is nothing wrong with this objective, for we have seen that discipleship is the goal of the Great Commission (Matthew 28:19-20). However, when many churches side-by-side promote this same objective, it can confuse the potential guest. The reader might feel that every church is the same. As church leaders, we know that this is not the case. Therefore, describe your core competencies in your advertisements, so potential attendees will know your strengths and personality.

Employ the Right Advertisement

Marketing students are familiar with the three types of advertisements and the appropriate times to employ them. However, in the religious world, these three types are largely unknown. Here is a brief overview of each, and a graphical representation in Figure 10.5 of their appropriate use.

1. ***Informative Advertisements.*** These advertisements provide basic information, and announce availability. The ads may give directions to a church or tell about a new worship service or ministry. However, due to their informative nature, they are short lived. As the new ministry, worship service, etc. continues, interested parties will become informed. Thus, the informative ad will lose its value.

    Churches overuse informative ads. These ads almost exclusively describe service times, directions, etc. However, in doing so, they neglect to convey their core competencies. In the marketing world, informative advertising is employed only at the inauguration of a product or service. That should be the same strategy a church uses.

2. ***Persuasive advertisements.*** These advertisements plainly describe the core competencies of a church and, as a result, what the church offers. They explain the benefits of specific programming in more detail than an informative ad. This is often the missing element in church advertising. Congregational leaders know the rationale and benefits of a new program, but sometimes overlook the receivers' corresponding lack of knowledge. Churches must use persuasive advertising to explain how programs and ministries meet the specific needs of the people in their mission field.

3. ***Reminder advertisements.*** These ads reinforce previous promotional activity. They are usually short, concise, and designed to remind the receiver of the persuasive advertisements they follow.[23] Many churches err by employing reminder ads before they have established their core competencies in persuasive ads.

Figure 10.5 shows how informative, persuasive, and reminder ads are utilized at different stages in the life of a church or program/ministry.[24]

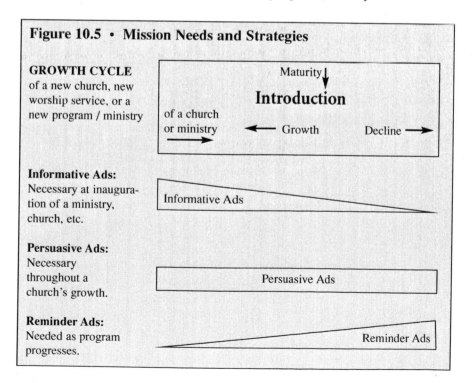

Figure 10.5 • Mission Needs and Strategies

GROWTH CYCLE of a new church, new worship service, or a new program / ministry

Introduction of a church or ministry → ← Growth   Maturity↓   Decline →

Informative Ads: Necessary at inauguration of a ministry, church, etc.

Informative Ads

Persuasive Ads: Necessary throughout a church's growth.

Persuasive Ads

Reminder Ads: Needed as program progresses.

Reminder Ads

Advertising Media Alternatives

The types and effectiveness of various advertising media are staggering. To help the reader consider the options and their suitability, Figure 10.6 compares various forms of media. The "% of total budget" indicates how much money churches spend in each category.

Figure 10.6 • The Church and the Media[25]

Media Type	% of total budget[26]	Advantages for churches	Disadvantages for churches
BROADCAST			
Network television	17	Mass coverage, repetition, flexibility, prestige	High cost, temporary message, public distrust; may be reaching a larger geographical segment than the church's mission field
Cable television	8	Same strengths as network TV; less market coverage since every viewer must also be a cable subscriber	Same disadvantages as network TV; however, ads are more targeted to specific viewer segments
Radio	8	Immediacy, low cost, flexibility, targeted audience, mobility	Short life span; highly fragmented audience due to differences in musical tastes
PRINT			
Newspapers	19	Tailored to individual communities; ability to refer back to ads	Short life span; papers are read quickly
Direct mail	19	Selectivity, intense coverage, flexibility, opportunity to convey compete information, personalization	High cost, consumer resistance, dependence on an effective mailing list
Magazines	5	Selectivity, quality image production, long life, prestige	Lack of flexibility
Billboards	2	Quick, visual communication of simple ideas; link to local congregation with directions; repetition	Each exposure is brief; environmental concerns
ELECTRONIC			
Internet	3	Two-way communications, flexibility, fuller information, links to more information	Poor image reproduction; difficult to measure effectiveness

The Broadcast Media: Network Television, Cable Television, Radio

Traditionally one of the costliest endeavors, the rise of local cable outlets has opened the door for the church on a budget to advertise. Radio stations are also effective, offering relatively low-cost advertising outlets. Here are some guidelines to keep in mind when using the broadcast media.

1. *Oversee quality in your advertisements.* Local cable channels and radio stations are often looking to fill space. Thus, they may be less judicious on what they allow to be aired. Radio stations often find it difficult to fill required public service announcement postings, or Sunday morning time slots. Because these media outlets often lower their expectations, the church must take it upon itself to ensure a high level of quality that honors God and the church's constituents.

   Today, a number of organizations and denominations offer churches professionally rendered advertisements for print, electronic, and broadcast media. If they can be personalized as well as correlated with a church's core competencies, these prefabricated advertisements can help to increase quality.

2. *Advertise in the right places.* With radio, do not advertise on Sunday mornings because the primary listening audience is Christian (unless this is your mission field). Instead, advertise during drive time, lunch, and other times when the station's demographics indicate a significant listenership.

   Remember that radio listeners are highly segregated by musical style. Investigate various stations and the ages, preferences, and socioeconomics of their listeners to decide which station will best help you to reach your mission field.

3. *Broadcast media is especially effective with persuasive and high quality advertisements.* Earlier we saw the need for persuasive advertisements; however, be careful not to appear unreasonable or obsessive. Well meaning, but overly ardent Christians have made many listeners wary of Christian advertisements. For that reason, professionally created ads, although expensive, are more effective. On some occasions, the church might want to advertise against its stereotype. For instance, Vineyard

Fellowship of Dayton, Ohio, understands that many unchurched people are turned off by churches insinuating they are better than other churches. Thus, Vineyard Fellowship advertises its church with the byline, "a pretty good church." Their refusal to compete with their ecclesial neighbors has made them stand out.

The Print Media: Newspapers, Direct Mail, Magazines, and Billboards

If handled appropriately, the print media continues to be a good place for the church to advertise. Here are some guidelines.

1. *Advertise in the right places.* As noted earlier, churches should avoid running print ads in religious sections of the paper or religious magazines, instead concentrating on areas the unchurched would be more likely to peruse. With direct mail, ensure that you have an effective mailing list, and that you are targeting the right mission field (i.e., be sure you are not targeting people too far away to attend, or of the wrong generation).

2. *Write your own stories for newspapers, magazines, etc.* Smaller community newspapers are often looking for information to fill their pages. When they cannot find enough, they will print space-filling trivia. Whenever a reader sees an abundance of these space fillers, it should be a signal that this newspaper is searching for content. Because journalists at smaller newspapers are not readily available to write stories, a church should pen its own stories. If a local church writes an engaging story and attaches attractive pictures; the local newspaper may gladly print your self-created story. Five to six column inches of a story may translate into several hundred dollars of advertisement. However, professionalism is important. Look in your church for school teachers, journalists, part-time writers, etc. to entrust with this duty.

3. *Use billboards for impact, and to display directions to the church.* Corinth Church's location on an out-of-sight rural lane meant the church had to increase its presence on the nearby bypass. A billboard would be an excellent advertising alternative (and cheaper than relocating the facilities to a more visible site). In addition, the billboard would offer directions to the church.

Electronic Media: The Internet

At one time, the telephone was the greatest communication tool at the consumer's fingertips. The appeal to "let your fingers do the walking" though the phone directory reminded people that it was easier to find out about an organization from their phone directory, than it was to visit the organization in person. As a result, churches advertised heavily in phone directories. Today, we might say instead, "Forget your fingers, and let your browser do the surfing." A survey by the Online Publisher's Association discovered that 57 percent of people today prefer to find information over the Internet.[27]

The Internet contains more information than any phone directory imaginable. As computers become faster and more convenient, searching for information on the Internet will become the norm. Today, churches must offer a professional, uncomplicated, but extensive website. Also, with social networking and text messaging, the church must be prepared for Facebook and Twitter to communicate.

Miscellaneous Media: Posters, Flyers

Probably the least effective advertising avenue for the church is the use of flyers, handouts, and posters. Because of a growing appreciation for keeping the environment unspoiled and clean, distributing flyers or posting posters has steadily lost effectiveness. These can be appropriate avenues at private events, such as church gatherings, where distribution and posting is controlled. But for public spaces and events, the other advertising avenues mentioned above are preferred.

Becoming a Learning Organization

In the business realm, effective organizations are often praised for becoming "learning organizations." Noel Tichy, Professor of Organizational Behavior and Human Resource Management at the University of Michigan Business School, and researcher Eli Cohen describe a learning organization as those who "in order to succeed in a highly competitive global marketplace . . . need to be able to change quickly; (thus) their people must be able to acquire and assimilate new knowledge and skills rapidly."[28]

Moving Toward a *Teaching Organization*

In their investigation of successful companies, Tichy and Cohen found that being a learning organization was not enough. In order for a company to thrive, it also had to become a "teaching organization."

In the church context, where teaching biblical truths is a central task, the idea of the church as a "teaching organization" can be confusing. Therefore, let's differentiate what is meant in the business world by a "learning organization" and a "teaching organization" Figure 10.7 offers a comparison.

Figure 10.7 • Comparing Learning and Teaching Organizations	
The *Learning* Organization	The *Teaching* Organization Adopts all of the learning organization's characteristics, but adds these:
1. Insists that leaders become learners; encourages leaders to see learning as a responsibility	8. Insists that leaders become teachers; encourages leaders to see teaching as a responsibility
2. Studies the marketplace	9. Studies training principles
3. Changes quickly to reach a changing market	10. Adapts new teaching skills, tools, and procedures to reach a changing work-force
4. Encourages people to acquire and assimilate new knowledge	11. Encourages people to pass knowledge on to others
5. Encourages people to acquire and assimilate new skills	12. Encourages people to pass skills on to others
6. Helps leaders and workers *understand* the ideas and concepts that drive the company	13. Helps leaders and workers *master* the ideas and concepts that drive the company
7. Focuses on developing strategies	14. Focuses on developing leaders

Thus, it can be seen that the "teaching organization" goes beyond learning, embracing as a core competency the ability to pass skills and knowledge on to others. Tichy and Cohen put it well: "In teaching organizations, leaders see it as their responsibility to teach. They do that because they understand that it's the best, if not the only, way to develop throughout a company people who can come up with and carry out smart ideas about the business . . . A teaching organization's insistence that its leaders teach creates better leaders, because teaching requires people to develop mastery of ideas and concepts."[29]

A teaching organization is often characterized by the following:

1. *Leaders are committed teachers.* Larry Bossidy, who transformed AlliedSignal in the 1990s, is an example of a committed teacher. Bossidy didn't slash and downsize AlliedSignal on its way to success. Rather, Bossidy spent hundreds of hours teaching senior leaders about strategy, goals, and inculcating an atmosphere of "teaching." The remarkable turn-around of AlliedSignal in only five years is a tribute to Bossidy's success as a committed teacher.

2. *Leaders are models.* The late Robert Goizueta, CEO of Coca-Cola, was a quiet engineer with a thick accent. His success at Coca-Cola and its battles with rival PepsiCo are legendary. Goizueta frequently recounted to his employees his personal experiences with his family's business in Cuba, drew on the wisdom of Spanish poets, and often quoted his grandfather. He served as a model of teaching in a humble self-effacing manner.

3. *Leaders are coaches.* AlliedSignal's Larry Bossidy wrote personal letters to each manger after meetings, encouraging and guiding them in their performance. He took it as his personal responsibility to let mangers know that he was there to laud good performance and diplomatically redirect poor performance.

4. *Leaders identify workers' goals and help them develop a "leadership pipeline" toward their dream career.* GE develops a career map for each employee called a "leadership pipeline." Regularly consulted by managers, this visual graph details the jobs an employee has held and the positions that employee wants to hold in the future. The leadership pipeline helps managers to identify the goals and aspirations of workers and assist them in fulfilling their dreams.

5. *Leaders ensure that teaching becomes a core competency of the organization.* GE, under Jack Welch's legendary leadership, inculcated its teaching orientation with the Six Sigma approach.[30] By developing six memorable traits, Welch ensured that employees would be embraced, and that a far-flung GE organization could see itself as one large but unified organization.

When a congregation becomes a teaching organization, and not just merely a learning organization, its leaders will more readily embrace the important principles of outreach and marketing. As a result, marketing and outreach will inherit their rightful meanings as the methods through which the Church presents Jesus' Good News.

Endnotes

1. Quoted in Louis E. Boone and David L. Kurtz, *Contemporary Marketing*, 11th ed. (Mason, OH: South-Western Publishing), 2004, 194.
2. Ibid.
3. Ibid.
4. Often, the four stages of marketing are addressed by several disciplines concurrently. In the business world, the marketing department may work with executive management to establish strategic goals. Thus, stages are often a combined effort of several disciplines. This is why we address stages two and four in the earlier chapter on strategic planning.
5. The business world also has begun to embrace *outreach* as an alternative term for marketing. In many universities, such as The Pennsylvania State University, the marketing department is now the "Dept. of Outreach and Cooperative Extension." See the letter from Dr. Craig D. Weidemann, Vice President for Outreach and Cooperative Extension, The Pennsylvania State University, www.outreach.psu.edu.
6. An expanded discourse on church pathology is found in C. Peter Wagner's *Your Church Can Be Healthy* (Nashville: Abingdon Publishers, 1979).
7. Bob Whitesel and Kent R. Hunter, *A House Divided: Bridging the Generation Gaps in Your Church* (Nashville: Abingdon Press, 2000).
8. C. Peter Wagner, "Principles and Procedures of Church Growth: American Church Growth," quotation from a lectureship given at Fuller Theological Seminary, Pasadena, California; January 31-February 11, 1983.
9. Ibid.
10. C. Peter Wagner, *Frontiers in Missionary Strategy* (Chicago: Moody Press, 1971), 139-60. See especially the chapter titled "Evangelism In-Depth a Decade Later."
11. As quoted by C. Peter Wagner, "Principles and Procedures."
12. Bob Whitesel, *Staying Power: Why People Leave the Church Over Change and What You Can Do About It* (Nashville, Abingdon Press, 2003).
13. Lyle Schaller, *Growth by Accident, Death by Planning: How NOT to Kill a Growing Congregation* (Nashville: Abingdon Press, forthcoming).
14. The American Society for Church Growth website is www.ascg.org.
15. This is available on the Web at www.census.gov/prod/www/stastical-abstract-us.html
16. Whitesel and Hunter, *A House Divided*, 144-60.
17. David G. Myers, *Exploring Psychology* (New York: Worth Publishers, 1990), 13.
18. Adapted from Whitesel and Hunter, *A House Divided*, 156-58.
19. For Generation X, birth years are 1965 to 1983; for Boomers, 1946 to 1964; and for

Builders, 1945 and before. Birth years are easier to use than specific ages, since the latter will keep changing. However, it is helpful to utilize the exact ages in the remainder of this survey.

20. From Whitesel and Hunter, *A House Divided*, 160. Used by permission.
21. For brainstorming principles and guidelines, see Bob Whitesel, *Growth by Accident, Death by Planning*.
22. Herb Miller, *How to Build a Magnetic Church* (Nashville: Abingdon Press, 1987), 15.
23. *Reminder advertisements* were employed in the 1970s by Campus Crusade for Christ in conjunction with an outreach campaign called "I found it." After laying the groundwork by training thousands of Christians in how to share their faith, Campus Crusade gave these trained workers buttons that said, "I found it." Finally, after the workers had worn the buttons for months, Campus Crusade launched a media campaign showing a young person wearing the "I found it" button. The billboards and TV ads served as "reminder advertisements" to support the young person's one-on-one testimony of faith.
24. Adapted from Boone and Kurtz, *Contemporary Marketing*, 534.
25. Adapted from "Advertising Boom in U.S. Ended in '01," *Advertising Age* (May 13, 2002): 24.
26. The reader will notice that an estimated 20 percent of total expenditures are not spent on these avenues, but rather on miscellaneous media such as phone directories, transit (bus, subway, train) displays, posters, exhibits, etc.
27. Scott Hays, "Has Online Advertising Finally Grown Up? *Advertising* (April 1, 2002): C-1.
28. Noel M. Tichy and Eli Cohen, "The Teaching Organization," *Training and Development* 52, no. 7 (July 1998): 27.
29. Ibid., 28.
30. GE explains Six Sigma on the GE website at www.ge.com/sixsigma as follows:

"GE began moving towards a focus on quality in the late '80s. Work-Out®, the start of our journey, opened our culture to ideas from everyone, everywhere, decimated the bureaucracy and made boundaryless behavior a reflexive, natural part of our culture, thereby creating the learning environment that led to Six Sigma. Now, Six Sigma, in turn, is embedding quality thinking — process thinking — across every level and in every operation of our Company around the globe. . . . First, what it is not. It is not a secret society, a slogan or a cliché. Six Sigma is a highly disciplined process that helps us focus on developing and delivering near-perfect products and services. Why 'Sigma'? The word is a statistical term that measures how far a given process deviates from perfection. The central idea behind Six Sigma is that if you can measure how many 'defects' you have in a process, you can systematically figure out how to eliminate them and get as close to 'zero defects' as possible. Six Sigma has changed the DNA of GE — it is now the way we work — in everything we do and in every product we design."

11

What Church Leader's Need to Know About . . .

Spiritual and Personal Development

Striving for Balance in Your Life

"Each one should use whatever gift he has received to serve others,
faithfully administering God's grace in its various forms."

—1 PETER 4:10

A Case of Intuitive Misgivings

Gerry's first assignment after seminary was to serve as associate pastor of St. John Lutheran Church in Memphis, Tennessee. Less than four years later, the senior pastor shared with Gerry that he had decided to accept a position at a larger church in southern California. During his four years as associate, Jerry had benefited greatly from the senior pastor's wisdom and experience. He also appreciated the shield the senior pastor provided, insulating Gerry from many of the difficult and emotional challenges of congregational life.

Gerry's emotions were mixed. On the one hand, he felt a genuine sense of loss. As the senior pastor's departure date approached, Gerry experienced anxiety at the impending separation. He even went through a time of mourning after the senior pastor left. On the other hand, he couldn't help but wonder what would follow. Would the congregation consider him a suitable replacement for the senior pastor?

The congregation also was in shock. Some congregants realized that a window of opportunity might open for the senior pastor and his family when their oldest daughter finished high school. But few thought the family actually would leave. The senior pastor had served St. John for six years. Many congregants felt that the church was just beginning to gain momentum—in another five or six years, the gifted senior pastor could have taken the church to another level. The congregation, too, went through a time of mourning. Emotions ranged from joy at the senior pastor's bright future, to personal hurt—even a sense of betrayal—at losing their well-loved leader.

The church appointed a search committee to hire another pastor. In the meantime, a part-time retired minister was hired to help with time-consuming duties such as visiting those who were hospitalized or homebound. Although Gerry's ministerial load increased, he knew the congregation eventually would attract another full-time pastor. That light at the end of the tunnel gave him increased energy through the transition. He still wondered whether or not he would be considered for the senior pastor position. Had he been called for that role? Did he even have the gifts and experience necessary to meet the challenge?

In reality, Gerry's gifts were stronger in a support role. His limited experience could prove detrimental, especially in light of some of the challenges St. John would face over the next five to ten years. Gerry was not the logical choice, but he was a convenient choice. Like many congregations that gravitate toward what is easiest, Gerry got the call. Like many associates who feel trapped between emotions of flattery and hesitation, Gerry gravitated toward taking the call. Against some intuitive misgivings, he accepted the position of senior pastor for St. John Lutheran Church.

Fast Forward Twelve Months

The church labored to attract an associate. Many of those the search committee called or interviewed had reservations about serving under a young, relatively inexperienced senior pastor. At the end of six months, an associate pastor was hired. He needed another two months to make the transition to St. John's. The new associate pastor was a graduate student assigned by the seminary. Although he was a good man, his experience and aptitude were inferior to Gerry's—even when Gerry was at that same point in life. During the first two to three years Gerry was nearly overwhelmed with the time required to nurture the new associate pastor. In fact, the commitment he expended seemed to outweigh the help he received from the associate pastor. At the end of his first year in the senior pastor position, Gerry was barely keeping his head above water. The "honeymoon phase" was over. He knew the congregation was comparing his performance to that of the former pastor. It was evident that Gerry wasn't filling the shoes of his predecessor. He wasn't measuring up. Everyone knew it, including Gerry.

Meanwhile, Gerry's burdens at home increased. His wife began struggling with health issues. Their five children needed more of his time, especially wheelchair-bound James. Gerry was learning that the senior pastor's position demanded more time, energy, and experience than he ever had realized.

In an effort to meet the demands of his everyday schedule, Gerry started skipping his day off—once in a while at first, then every week. He shortened his scheduled vacation, and took work along. Gerry became erratic in his daily Bible study. He neglected it altogether on some days. Soon, he was missing several days in a row. Time away from personal Bible study represented larger gaps in his spiritual life. His prayer life dramatically diminished. He just didn't seem to have the time or energy. He had too much on his mind.

Gerry began feeling distant from God. Sometimes, he even felt angry at God for the pressure and stress of his workload. He began to ask this question, "Just what does it mean to be a faithful servant?"

Averting Spiritual Crisis

Gerry is not the first pastor to feel overworked and overwhelmed. Fortunately, many excellent management practices and leadership skills can help pastors focus and become more effective. This book is filled with them. It's all about working smarter, not harder, right?

No, it's not *just* about working smarter or harder. At the center of everything in which you are involved is your spiritual life as a pastor. At the epicenter of Gerry's challenges is a spiritual dynamic. This is not just true for pastors. It is true for all Christians. When the spiritual dynamic is neglected, spiritual crisis can result. Bill Hybels talks about this common reality and the motivation necessary to reverse the course. In explaining fractured relationships, he says this:

> Believers in Christ sometimes come to the same point in their relationships with God. 'Choked by life's worries, riches, and pleasures' (Luke 8:14), they realize they are no longer growing and maturing. Their walk with Jesus has slowed to a crawl or stopped altogether. If this has happened to you, one day you may have to say, 'That's it! I am not going to go through the motions of being a Christian any more. I am not going to put my Christian life on autopilot, go through the meaningless prayers, and page through a Bible that I don't let saturate my life. I'm not going to play halfway games anymore. I'm going to pay whatever price it takes for an authentic walk with Jesus.'[1]

Understand God's Will for You

Pastors experience spiritual crisis at one time or another. How did ministry begin to go south for Gerry? It may have begun with a crisis of clarity about the call to ministry. Pastoring is not just a job. There is no ladder to climb. Ministry is a personal call from God to you—the unique person He has created—to do what uniquely suits you. Gerry didn't follow the Spirit's promptings as he wrestled with the senior pastor position. The result? Gerry got in over his head. However, that isn't his primary problem—it is only a symptom of something greater.

Personal management from the perspective of spiritual and personal development begins with how you understand God's call and God's will in your life. Henry Blackaby has given this concept prominence. He says, "Don't ask God to bless what you are doing, but ask God to lead you to do what He is blessing."[2] For some, this is a 180-degree reversal in respect to God's will.

Have you ever taken a position or assignment in ministry and prayed with intensity, asking God to bless that decision? How much better would it be to discover what God is doing and focus on how you might fit into the middle of it? This is a starting point for spiritual management in your personal life. It was the point at which Gerry started down a path that he now regrets taking. This regret also spilled over into the people at St. John Lutheran Church in Memphis, who became increasingly uncomfortable with Gerry's lack of productivity. Tragically, the people at St. John had no clue how this began. When focusing on the area of ministry management, incorporate this prayer into your daily devotional life: "Dear Lord, I want to be in Your will, not in Your way."

Understand Who You Are

To avert a spiritual crisis, understand who you are and who you are not. It is important to learn all you can about yourself. In the process, recognize that your self-esteem is not based, as the world would tell you, on your productivity and accomplishment. According to the biblical perspective, you are a person with unique gifts, talents, passions, abilities, and styles. God has given you a personality that is unique in all creation. He also has given you a certain level of energy. The great truth about ministry is that there are endless ways to serve God in this world. All of them are equally honorable and important. Your main tasks in life are to find your niche in the worldwide Body of Christ, to remain sensitive to the Holy Spirit's promptings, and to be responsive in obedience to God's call.[3]

Understand the Importance of Humility

To avert spiritual crisis, commit to humility. Humility provides a servant attitude that empowers you to serve within your abilities. It provides strength to resist temptations for worldly position, honor, titles, or offices. Ministry is about none of these things. It *is* about finding your niche, within your abilities. When that happens, you experience fulfillment at the highest level known to humankind. Despite his intuitive reservations, Gerry succumbed to the temptation of a position beyond his capabilities. His church's seemingly supportive stance in hiring him as the senior pastor was nothing more than the easy way out.

Understand the Need for Discipline

If you cannot discipline your life, spiritual crisis will loom. Remain committed to your personal spiritual development. Gerry stopped taking his day off, a practice that eroded his balance. This not only disrupted relationships in his family, but it also interfered with his personal Bible study. Scripture is spiritual food; it is milk and meat. Gerry was starving himself spiritually. His personal prayer time also began to disintegrate. The enemy strategically uses pressures and temptations to undermine spiritual disciplines. As a pastor, you are a strategic person in your congregation. So why wouldn't the enemy develop a strategic attack on a strategic person like you or Gerry?

Understand the Vision

Proverbs 29:18 says, *"Where there is no vision, the people perish"* (KJV). The NIV puts it this way, *"Where there is no revelation, the people cast off restraint."* Gerry lost sight of the vision inherent in his call. When people fail to receive input from God (revelation), they cast off restraint. That means that they give up the ability to say "no." Without discernment and input according to God's will, the tendency is to say "yes" to everything. Gerry said "yes" to the position, "yes" to training the associate, "yes" to all the duties that his predecessor had fulfilled. Without divine guidance, he said "yes" to everything because he had lost the restraint to say "no" to anything. Common with pastors, this propensity often comes disguised as being a "faithful servant." However, when you say "yes" to everything, your life becomes so overfull that you function poorly. The proper stewardship of time, energy, and ministry is compromised. Subconsciously, you subtly say "no" to those areas that are most important. In Gerry's situation, those important areas included his wife, his children, his health, balance, rest, Bible study, prayer life, and—ultimately—his attitude before God. He became angry and unproductive, literally a roadblock to his congregation. It's amazing how quickly a ministry can become such a mess!

Managing Your Personal Spiritual Life

Recognize the Built-In Difficulty

Pastoral ministry is one of the toughest career choices in our culture. Why is ministry so challenging? The following six reasons underscore some of the difficult aspects of a career in ministry:

1. As a pastor, you lead a nonprofit, volunteer organization. Your nonprofit relies on donations to support the work of the church and your salary. A volunteer organization must motivate people by means other than financial reward. Further, it is more difficult to remove "difficult" people from a volunteer organization. You can't fire that argumentative elder. This in itself makes ministry a difficult task.

2. Religious organizations are complex and challenging to manage. We saw in an earlier chapter that religion is near the seat of emotions. Dysfunctional and irrational people are drawn to the church—and they should be, by God's design. They bring their dysfunction with them, often superimposing it on the church or injecting it into the ministry. Further, since religion *is* so closely tied to the emotional part of human life, any change or challenge can cause otherwise calm people to come unglued. Thus, they may exhibit hostility, supercharged emotions, and behavior that is inappropriate, even to their own code of Christian conduct.

3. It's time of great change—and the changes are taking place more rapidly than ever before. People who experience change in every area of their lives look to the church as the one stable area that should not change. Unfortunately, if the church does not change, it soon becomes irrelevant. The pastor has two career choices: (1) resist change and watch the church decline into mediocrity and irrelevance, or (2) make changes, recognizing that this invites negative reaction from many who look to the church for stability. While "*Jesus Christ is the same yesterday and today and forever*" (Hebrews 13:8 NIV), people often confuse the structural, nonessential aspects of the church with its unchanging spiritual truths. Even when those structural aspects are changed to enhance the effectiveness of the church, people may exhibit hostility.

4. In the West, the culture has become highly secularized—entering what many are calling a post-Christian era. This makes ministry at least twice as hard as it was forty years ago. To say it another way, the staff required for a church forty years ago should probably be twice that size today, given the stresses and challenges of ministry. Of course, that requires additional financial support, which most churches find difficult to swallow.

5. Being an unchurched culture means established churches now find themselves on a mission field. However, most do not realize that the stresses on pastors who serve in this new mission field are many of the same stresses experienced by missionaries who serve in faraway places. Historically, Christians recognize the stresses inherent in the overseas mission field and provide routine furloughs for their overseas missionaries. Yet, it is unusual for an established church in the West to provide its pastor (read "missionary") in this post-Christian era the opportunity for furlough.

6. Colleges and seminaries have done little to equip pastors for this rapidly changing world. For example, pastors are given little training in how to minister in a cross-cultural setting—even if the other "culture" consists of postmodern members of the secular society.

Share these realities with the leadership of your church. Broaden their sphere of understanding about how the world has changed and how you as a pastor (and they as leaders) must adapt to these changes.

Depend on God

While you should learn all you can from other disciplines, don't forget the spiritual dimension of your own personal care. Make it a high priority to take care of yourself. As Elmer Towns and Warren Bird make clear, "Church leaders, while continuing to find valid help from secular management insights, are rediscovering the uniqueness of a church's spiritual resources in eternal mission."[4]

Paul Sorensen is the assistant pastor at Community Church of Joy in Glendale, Arizona. He also is president of the Joy Leadership Center, and COO of the Joy Company. He shares this insight:

Outstanding management begins at the center, with a vibrant spiritual connection with Jesus Christ. From the source of grace and truth, we are able to lead and manage with grace and truth. We minister out of who we are more than what we say. Although we can put on a good front for a time, if we aren't living in that vibrant connection with Jesus, eventually those we serve will not sense the life flowing through us. On the other hand, even it we don't manage perfectly, if our faith is alive, people will sense God's presence through us.[5]

Sorensen shares, "Christ-centered management is a radical dependence upon the Holy Spirit for all we do. At Community Church of Joy, when we face a major obstacle, we try to think clearly, but more importantly, we pray earnestly."[6]

Practice Biblical Qualities

Dr. Bill Bright, Founder of Campus Crusade for Christ, was always quick to share these five insights when he was asked what top things church leaders should know about spiritual and personal development:

1. Make sure you know who God is. His attributes.
2. Love the Lord your God with all your heart, soul, mind, and strength.
3. Seek first the Kingdom of God.
4. Trust and obey the Lord.
5. Teach others the same.[7]

Ray Ellis is the senior pastor of Willow Vale Community Church in San Jose, California, and a renowned leader in the Church Growth Movement. Regarding spiritual and personal development, he says this: "Christian leaders need to practice biblical qualities as outlined in Timothy and Titus. Churches get into trouble when the leaders in the church tolerate known sin. Before a person is given a position of authority to lead in the local church, he/she should meet the spiritual qualities outlined in 1 Timothy 3 and Titus 2."[8]

Be a Servant Leader

Another dimension of personal spiritual management is related to servant leadership. A style of ministry born out of humility and commitment, servant leadership is more interested in others than self. "God blesses the church when leaders model the 'one another's' of Scripture. When the 'one another's' of Scripture are practiced, the Holy Spirit blesses and gives spiritual health to the congregation. Every Christian leader is called to help each other become successful in ministry and not allow the spirit of competition to become a part of the leadership team."[9] Servant leadership looks out for others.

Study the Bible

When Gerry got away from Bible study—during busy times at St. John Church—his spiritual life began to unravel. Frequently, pastors are involved in Bible study . . . of sorts. All too often, this is academic or "professional Bible study"—study that is required to prepare for a class or a sermon message. While that is important, it is not a substitute for personal Bible study that intimately appropriates spiritual truth to personal life. As D.L. Moody once said, "The purpose of the Bible is not to change your doctrine. It is to change your life." The work of the Holy Spirit and the power of God's Word help the pastor, like anyone else, mature in the faith. This saying captures the essence of intimate Bible study:

If you have the Spirit without the Word, you blow up.
If you have the Word without the Spirit, you dry up.
If you have the Word and the Spirit, you grow up.[10]

Ground Yourself in Prayer

Prayer goes hand in hand with personal Bible study. Martin Luther, the leader of the Protestant Reformation, placed great emphasis on prayer. He said, "It takes three things to be a minister: Prayer, sweat, and study." In this generation, David Yonggi Cho, pastor of the Yoido Full Gospel Church in Seoul, Korea (the largest church in the history of Christendom), identifies prayer as the single most important factor in the growth and spirituality of that church. It is the norm for many South Korean pastors to spend at least an hour in prayer at the beginning of each day. Paul Sorensen summarizes: "Prayer helps us tap into the creative mind of God. Learning to listen can enrich our creative and breakthrough thinking."[11]

When Gerry's spiritual life unraveled, his prayer life became erratic as well. Most pastors who have experienced a spiritual crisis say their disintegrating prayer life was a key part or symbol of their spiritual disintegration. Ray Ellis makes the point clear: "Everything church leaders do should be grounded in prayer. Church leaders tend to talk a lot about prayer, but few really spend time praying."[12]

A structure for prayer is helpful. One method is to find a prayer partner. By teaming up with a prayer partner, you will hold one another accountable. Some churches schedule prayer breakfasts on a regular basis. Some ministry staffs schedule monthly prayer time when they share their vision and specific goals in ministry as prayer requests. Some churches have prayer services or regular nights of prayer. In South Korea and other places around the world, it is customary for churches to have an all-night prayer meeting. Many churches have an annual spiritual emphasis, which includes forty days and nights of fasting and prayer.

These are all ways to enhance your personal prayer life, as well as the prayer environment within the congregation. In *Fasting for Spiritual Breakthrough*, author Elmer Towns develops numerous strategies for fasting and prayer. Towns says, "When you take control of your physical appetite, you develop strength to take control of your emotional appetite."[13]

Grow Through Desert Times

The subject of "desert times" at first does not appear to be all that positive. However, desert times occur frequently enough that ministers can learn to see them as one dimension of God's plan for strengthening and growing key leaders for ministry. If you have pastored for a reasonable length of time and experienced a tough, dry period, you may have thought of giving up. But seen from a biblical perspective, these difficult times—desert times—may be part of God's training ground for maturing faith, developing leadership, and building character. Perhaps God allows these difficult times as a part of His overall plan to galvanize you for more productive ministry.

In describing the call to ministry, Oswald Chambers said: "This call has nothing to do with personal sanctification, but with being made broken bread and poured-out wine. Yet God can never make us into wine if we object to the fingers He chooses to use to crush us. If we are ever going to be made into wine, we will have to be crushed ? you cannot drink grapes. Grapes become wine only when they have been squeezed."[14]

Most Christians who have influence in wider circles have stories of their own desert struggles. For example, Dave Dravecky is a major-league baseball player who struggled with cancer, made a comeback, then eventually lost his arm. In the process, his Christian faith blossomed and his testimony became powerful. Dravecky says of his desert time, "I have learned that the wilderness is part of the landscape of faith. It is every bit as essential as the mountaintop. On the mountaintop, we are overwhelmed by God's presence. In the wilderness, we are overwhelmed by God's absence. Both places should bring us to our knees—the one in utter awe, the other in utter dependence."[15]

The desert time, or wilderness experience, shows a different side of God. It is the side that demonstrates that your comfort, as a pastor, is not at the top of God's agenda. In fact, you may remember the words of Jesus: "*If they persecuted me, they will persecute you also*" (John 15:20 NIV). The evidence is quite clear that from the beginning the followers of Jesus have identified suffering as part of the "job description." My friend Jerry Mitchell says, "God is more concerned with your holiness than your happiness." In difficult times, develop an attitude that will change your focus from "Poor me, why am I in this mess?" to "I wonder what God is going to improve in my life through this difficult and uncomfortable experience?"

Adopt the Multiplication Model

Another dimension of personal spiritual management is to follow the Ephesians 4 model of ministry. Ephesians 4:11-16 clearly shifts the dynamic of the growth of God's Kingdom from addition (the pastor does all the work) to multiplication (the pastor equips God's people for the work of ministry). While this is a clear biblical principle and a prominently recaptured theological point of the Protestant Reformation, it is woefully neglected in most churches today. For example, most pastors call on those in the hospital in order to minister to them. However, it is rare for pastors to take someone with them, demonstrating the high priority for equipping others (discipling) to minister. The "addition model" is in direct contrast to the model of Jesus Christ and His followers in the New Testament. It is also in direct contrast to Ephesians 4, Matthew 28:19-20 (the Great Commission), and the whole dynamic of how the Kingdom of God is to grow through the multiplication of ministry. Addition instead of multiplication ignores the structure of the church as it is defined through the spiritual gifts given to all members of the body of Christ (see Romans 12, 1 Corinthians 12, Ephesians 4, and 1 Peter 4:10).

Multiplication is not only about the growth dynamic from a biblical perspective, but also provides incredible pastoral value for personal spiritual management. When people are equipped for ministry, Kingdom work belongs to the church and does not fall solely on the shoulders of the pastor. This has a tremendous, far-reaching impact, and helps to relieve the pressure on the pastor. Gerry felt overwhelmed at St. John Lutheran Church because he stepped into the footsteps of senior pastor who perhaps had done too much in the first place. The situation would have been vastly different if the Body of Christ had been in the role of minister and the pastor in the role of equipper for the work of ministry. "God's design is to manage and lead in teams. We can learn to depend upon one another's different perspectives and gifts."[16]

Develop an Outward Focus

As his position crumbled, Gerry was focused internally. He was consumed by maintenance issues that crowded the agenda at St. John. Maintaining the church is important. So is ministering to those who are members of the church. While these are a vital part of the ministry call, ministry without an outward focus lacks the opportunity for the reenergizing aspects of the Great Commission. Reaching out—conquering new ground, so to speak—and seeing new people come to Christ has an invigorating personal and spiritual impact. "Church leaders should have an outward focus. Commitment by church leaders to the 'Great Commission' of making more and better disciples keeps the local church as an outreach mission station."[17] A pastor should know how to lead another person to Christ and regularly practice lifestyle evangelism. An outward focus has an invigorating and energizing effect on the pastor's personal and spiritual vitality.

Balance Your Life

Practice Strategic Withdrawal

Someone said, "If your output exceeds your intake, then your upkeep becomes your downfall." This very clearly expresses the importance of balance in Christian ministry.[18] As part of balancing your ministry life, develop the discipline of strategic withdrawal. This is not the same as isolation. In withdrawing from the crowds on a regular basis, Jesus practiced strategic withdrawal. He went to be alone. He also went to be with His close friends. He got away from the pressures of ministry. He shared, prayed, relaxed, pondered, meditated, fellowshipped, and partied. For balance in life, you should do the same.

In *Leadership Lessons of Jesus*, authors Bob Briner and Ray Pritchard concur with this concept. "In both business and church life, I have seen worthwhile efforts end in futility because leaders were unwilling to strategically withdraw or take a tactical time-out, typically because of their excessive zeal or shortsightedness. . . . A wise leader picks his or her spots, retreating when necessary to accomplish the most good."[19]

Associate

Find a peer group that feels safe, a group of people you enjoy being with and with whom you can experience fellowship Bible study. Spiritually, this may be where you will learn and grow the most. This is true for all adults, not just pastors. Knute Larson says, "Adults can get Bible teaching from sermons, tapes, the radio, home Bible studies, and Sunday school. Yet, in surveys all over the country about why adults come to Sunday school, the number one reason is fellowship. Relationships. Getting to know others."[20] Your peer group may consist of other pastors, or other professionals. If confidence is a concern, you may also need to find a peer group entirely outside your congregation and, perhaps, even outside your community.

Make sure you have a healthy amount of family time and other extended relationships through friends not connected with the business of church. Spend time with your family—when church activities are not on the agenda and church business is not part of the discussion. Among other relationships, find those people with whom you have common interests beyond your career.

Develop Prayer Fitness

Ensure that you have disciplined, organized, personal growth time. This is time devoted to Scripture and prayer for personal application. Bill Hybels calls this prayer fitness. "Developing prayer fitness is like developing physical fitness: you need a pattern to avoid becoming imbalanced. Without a routine, you will probably fall into the 'Please God' trap: 'Please God, give me. Please God, help me. Please God, cover me. Please God, arrange this.'"[21]

Earlier, we suggested that to ground yourself in prayer, you might want to team up with a safe outside accountability prayer partner. This is a person who loves you for who you are and cares enough about you to practice tough love and accountability. Generally, your prayer partner should be of the same sex, someone with a similar lifestyle and who is not a member of your church or family. In his book *Partners in Prayer*, John C. Maxwell explains how to establish a prayer partner ministry in a church. He underscores that for a prayer partner ministry to develop properly, there is one relationship that first needs to be established—"a partnership between the pastor and a committed lay person who will become the pastor's personal intercessor and accountability partner."[22]

Strive for Physical Fitness

It may be that pastors, as a whole, are the most physically unfit people in society. The sedentary demands of study, counseling, and planning can rob shepherds of opportunities for exercise and fitness. Find whatever exercise works for you, to the extent that it works for you. Find exercise that is enjoyable as well as beneficial. Exercise with others, if necessary, to help maintain the discipline of exercising. Exercise while you're accomplishing something else, if that helps you to persevere. For example, you can walk and listen to spiritual CDs. Or you can walk and hunt. If you ride an exercise bike, you can do so while watching television or a DVD. You can read while walking on a treadmill. Combine exercise with something that benefits you in another way and the time will become more valuable, more enjoyable, and more likely to inspire you to continue.

Learn the signs of stress and depression, two of the most common problems that pastors experience. Then learn how to manage these challenges. Understand what works for you to remove the stress and to manage depression.

Improve Yourself

The concluding chapters of this book will focus on lifelong learning—a habit all pastors should cultivate. Consistently participate in continuing education. Some forms of continuing education, like reading, are informal. Balance these informal forms with formal continuing education that is intentional and directed. Consider taking classes at an educational institution, or attend conferences or retreats. It is especially helpful for a pastor to attend a conference with other pastors at least once a year, particularly if yours is a growing church.

Develop a personal mission statement. This statement is basically a description in response to the question: "Why was I born?" or "Why do I get up in the morning?" Your mission statement should be part of the guiding direction for everything you do in ministry. It will also help you decline invitations in areas that are not a part of why God put you on this earth. You should revisit this mission statement at least once a year.

A Delicate, But Rewarding Balance

Spiritual and personal development is about honoring the vessel God has given you. Although humility and altruism are considered laudable in our ecclesial world, these qualities need not displace personal growth. Church leaders who balance their lives between these two realms will usually find a spiritual and physical verve that will be rewarding and long-lived.

Endnotes

1. Bill Hybels, *Too Busy Not to Pray: Slowing Down to Be with God* (Downers Grove, IL: InterVarsity Press, 1988), 101.
2. Henry Blackaby, *Experiencing God* (Nashville, TN: Broadman & Holman, 1994).
3. Church Doctor Ministries provides a service called "Personal Career Consultation." This personal coaching service helps church workers develop their profile and find their niche in Christian ministry. Go to www.churchdoctor.org.
4. Elmer Towns and Warren Bird, *Into the Future: Turning Today's Church Trends Into Tomorrow's Opportunities* (Grand Rapids, MI: Fleming H. Revell, 2000), 189.
5. Paul Sorensen, in correspondence with the author.
6. Ibid.

7. Bill Bright, in correspondence with the author.
8. Ray Ellis, from a presentation at the 1999 American Society for Church Growth. Used by permission.
9. Ibid.
10. *Leadership Journal*, vol. V, no. I (Winter 1984): 22.
11. Paul Sorenson.
12. Ray Ellis, in correspondence with the author.
13. Elmer L. Towns, *Fasting for Spiritual Breakthrough: A Guide to Nine Biblical Fasts* (Ventura, CA: Regal Books, 1996), 31.
14. Oswald Chambers, *My Utmost for His Highest* (Grand Rapids, MI: Discovery House Publishers, 1992), September 30 devotional reading.
15. Dave Dravecky, as quoted by John C. Maxwell, "Paul, A Leader Who Lasted," INJOY Life Club Tape, vol. 13, no. 10 (1997).
16. Paul Sorensen.
17. Ray Ellis.
18. Walter A. Hendrichsen, *Disciples Are Made—Not Born* (Wheaton, IL: Victor Books, 1979), 106.
19. Bob Briner and Ray Pritchard, *Leadership Lessons of Jesus: A Timeless Model for Today's Leaders* (Nashville, TN: Broadman & Holman, 1997), 70-71.
20. Knute Larson, *The ABF Book: Adult Bible Fellowships—Effective Adult Sunday School Classes for Growing Churches* (Akron, OH: Chapel Press, 1997), 10.
21. Bill Hybels, 50.
22. John C. Maxwell, *Partners in Prayer: Support and Strengthen Your Pastor and Church Leaders* (Nashville, TN: Thomas Nelson, Inc., 1996), 113.

12

What Church Leader's Need to Know About . . .

Lifelong Learning, Part 1

Cultivating God's Call to Learn

"Do your best to present yourself to God as one approved, a workman
who does not need to be ashamed and who correctly handles the word of truth."

—2 TIMOTHY 2:15

Line-Item Veto

L arry is an active layman at Paddington Pike Church in Cincinnati. Started in the 1960s, the church has been a stable and solid institution. However, while the church appears to be healthy, the figures show that membership has been slipping by one or two percent annually for the last sixteen years. Paddington Pike is Larry's childhood church. When he returned from college with an MBA, he chose his home church rather than join one of the many vigorous suburban churches in the area.

Larry is a senior manager in a large corporation's home office in Cincinnati. At last night's church board meeting, he proposed adding a new item to the church budget: $2,400 for "Ministerial Continuing Education." Immediately, Blanche and Edwin "came up for air" and pronounced the line item extravagant.

Larry argued that the church's responsibility was to do everything it could to help the pastoral staff stay current professionally. He explained, "My corporation spends more than this per year on some entry-level employees!" Eventually, the board agreed to add the item, but they pared the amount to $400. Larry pleaded, "That would barely pay for one seminar a year for just one of our ministers—we have to do better than that!" In the end, Blanche's retort seemed to represent the rest of the board: "The church is different from your company. We don't need to be sending our ministers off to get new ideas all the time. In the church we deal with unchanging truths from an unchanging Bible."

Should ministers, like managers and other professionals, be encouraged to continue educating themselves? Should they consider themselves lifelong learners? Or is Blanche right? Does the fact that the church deals with unchanging truths mean that all a minister needs to know can be found in the Bible? Certainly the church deals with unchanging truths, not the least of which is that the foundation of faith is found in the Bible. However, there is much to learn about leading an effective church besides basic Bible knowledge. Even Jesus taught through parables on issues outside the strict interpretation of the Torah, and Paul quoted from the Greek classics. Likewise, ministers need a broad base of knowledge and experience in helping and equipping others to find God's truth for life.

Lifelong Learning: The Need

In arguing at church board meetings to do something new, pastors are known to quote a familiar saying: "If we keep on doing what we've always done, we'll keep on getting what we've always got." The idea is that if we don't change, "we'll keep on getting what we've always got." False. The truth is that if we keep on doing what we've always done, we'll not even get what we've always got. Why? Because the environment changes. Ministers are charged with leading their churches to reach and serve people in a new generation by passing on the faith to future generations. While the faith does not change, people do change.

The invention of the printing press meant that people would be able to own their own Bibles—even their own hymnbooks—and the church changed accordingly. "Doing what we always did" would no longer get the church "what they always got." People change. Culture changes. The neighborhood in which a church is located changes. Musical styles change, technology changes, architecture changes. Even the color of carpeting communicates different messages as expectations for interior design change. The minister may deal with unchanging truths, but he or she must do so in a rapidly changing culture.

Defining Lifelong Learning: A Model

In *The Three Boxes of Life,* author Richard Bolles argues that most Americans live as if there were only three stages in life: (1) learning and formal education; (2) toil and labor, in which learning is no longer important; and (3) retirement and a self-indulgent stage of leisure and recreation.[1] Increasingly, that has become an obsolete idea for most professionals and organizational leaders. Because of the rapid rate at which the world around us is changing, learning is a never-ending necessity. Figure 12.1 below illustrates two approaches to learning:

Figure 12.1 • Two Approaches to Learning

Static World Approach

Acquire knowledge & skills . . . . Practice profession

Changing World Approach

Acquire basic knowledge + ... Practice profession and
lifelong learning skills   constantly learn

The Static World Approach

This model illustrates two ways of thinking about preparation for a profession. The upper continuum (Static World Approach) assumes that you go to school to get "all the knowledge you'll ever need" for a lifetime of professional practice, then you practice your profession based on that initial training. This approach assumes a static world approach. For example, a physician with a static world approach would assume that no new medical discoveries or new treatments will occur over the course of that doctor's lifetime. Thus, over the next fifty years, the physician would use the same methods and prescribe the same treatments he or she had learned in medical school.

The Changing World Approach

The lower continuum is based on different assumptions. The Changing World Approach assumes that you go to school to acquire the basic knowledge for a profession *plus* the skills for lifelong learning. This approach considers college or professional graduate training to be "initial" by nature, ideally teaching students how to continue learning through life. In this model, the professional practices the discipline of lifelong learning throughout life, and adjusts and adapts initial learning to reflect the following attributes:

1. Curiosity and desire for more knowledge (which adds excitement to life)
2. Openness to new ideas (especially when the old ways do not work)
3. Awareness that every new situation is an opportunity for learning (rather than fearing the unknown)
4. Capacity for self-monitoring and reflection (thinking about how you are learning; seeking to improve the process)
5. Taking responsibility for autonomous learning (actively seeking learning opportunities)
6. Ability to develop broad strategies for learning (knowing your best learning style, but adapting for other delivery systems, methods, and subject areas)
7. Confidence and perseverance while pursuing a learning task (tenacity while learning stretches your comfort zone)
8. Ability and willingness to compensate for cognitive and learning deficiencies (seeking others for help; developing the ability to locate, evaluate, and use information from new sources; e.g., the Internet)[2]

The Changing World Approach with its extraordinary emphasis on lifelong learning is the way of all professions, including ministry, in today's environment. The Changing World Approach also affects the initial training of ministers. If the world were static, ministerial education as it exists today in many institutions might be able to equip a minister in the content and methodology for a life of ministerial service. The world is not static, however, so it is impossible to achieve this goal. Therefore, initial ministerial preparation in a changing world tends to tilt more toward the unchanging basics—theology, church history, and biblical studies—rather than toward practical programming that will change in less than a decade. Ironically, the more the world changes, the more ministerial education should be tilting toward the unchanging basics. For example, the programming courses that seem most relevant today will be the first to become irrelevant.

In a changing world, ministerial education not only must provide ministers with the basics, it also must equip ministers with skills for lifelong learning, enabling them to keep learning through their ministerial lifetimes. However, if you did not develop lifelong learning skills in the past, you can develop them now by putting into practice any or all of the eight attributes listed above.

Lifelong Learning: Focus on Content

As is true of most professions today, the ministry is a complex one. A manufacturing company may face changes in markets, new equipment, price structures, or fresh competition—this drives the business person to keep abreast of trends and changes in the business environment. But the ministry may be even more complex because it involves intricate relationships, life change, and the supernatural. What "content areas" are of particular concern to ministers as they seek to stay abreast of changes in their working environments?

New Program Methods

Some criticize ministers for their preoccupation with new methods, but ministers have no choice. There was a day when ten-day revivals, tent meetings, and cottage prayer meetings were the newest and most effective methods to accomplish the church's purpose. But these methods have been replaced by newer methods that accomplish the same goals. If a minister does not stay informed on the best methods applicable to that minister's church, the church will be stuck in the past and find itself ministering only to a dying generation.

Technological Changes

While we readily admit the importance of technology to such professions as medicine or business, we might be tempted to see the church as an ageless institution that is impervious to technology. Not so. The Christian Church has often been an early adopter of technology: using the "codex"—hand-copied books of the New Testament—in place of scrolls, as well as capitalizing on the invention of the printing press for Bibles and hymnbooks. When television became dominant, Christians were there. When projection was developed, many churches were as quick to install PowerPoint as they were to adopt hymnals centuries before. When the Internet emerged and E-mail became a major means of communicating, ministers were quick to find ways to advertise and communicate through the Internet. As electronic biblical and theological resources became available, ministers began to use them in sermon preparation. All of this occurs because ministers find it necessary to be lifelong learners. A minister today who is not technologically developing must be as rare as a minister without an automobile. As technology continues to develop, ministers will have to stay informed on technology's continuing application to worship, communication, and personal study.

Shifting Culture

International businesses and missionary organizations have much to teach ministers about ministry as it relates to culture. They approach their work cross-culturally, studying the culture to determine how to approach people based on this knowledge. The competent global worker does not assume "my way" is the right way, but allows for methods to develop in the culture's context. Yet, what is true in Uganda, Sierra Leone, and the Philippians is also true in Michigan, Arizona, and Ontario. All ministry is intercultural and all ministers must learn to communicate cross-culturally as they lead the church to reach the unchurched. Therefore, ministers must be lifelong students of culture.

The Latest Christian Trends

Ministers must stay abreast of the latest trends in Christendom. These trends are not always wholesome or even accurate, but the minister at minimum must be aware of them. For example, when many Christians were reading *The Prayer of Jabez* or *The Purpose Driven Life*, a minister could not dismiss these books as irrelevant to the church. Even if the minister sought to refute them, it would be best for the minister to read them first. Christian publishing has gone mainstream and now produces best-sellers along with the secular press. A minister who is not informed about what Christians everywhere are reading is like a doctor who is totally ignorant of the Atkins Diet. Like the secular press, the popular Christian press is capable of producing fad books with glaring errors and omissions. To prevent his church members from being led astray, the minister must be able to identify and explain these errors and omissions.

Lifelong learning is more complicated for the minister than for the average businessperson. The latter may be able to survive in a particular field by staying abreast of whatever learning opportunities the businessperson's boss suggests. But the minister often has more than a hundred "bosses" in the church, each suggesting books that the minister "must read." To work through that stack, a minister must be a lifelong reader with wisdom and discernment.

New Developments in the Discipline of Ministry

A minister's lifelong learning is not limited to methodology. Even the foundational educational emphases for ministers—theology, biblical studies, history, practical ministry—are experiencing new developments. Developments in the practical fields are most obvious, of course. These include new methods of counseling, church planting, church development, small groups, and worship. However, even the traditionally static fields of theology, history, and Bible exegesis experience change in technique, focus, and understanding.

For instance, a minister who last studied the role of women in the church when he was in college in 1975 has missed major subsequent contributions to scholarship on this topic. Likewise, a minister might sit in a Sunday school class today and hear a lay person raise discussion of open theism. If that minister closed off basic learning in theology in 1980, he will be ill equipped to help the lay person. Worse, if the minister does not even know what open theism is, he will appear ignorant in his own field—like a dentist who has never heard of a root canal. Ministers must be lifelong students in practical ministry, as well as in the more static disciplines of theology, Bible, and church history.

Lifelong Learning: Accessing the Methods

The first part of this chapter has established the breadth and depth of learning a minister must continue to acquire even after completing initial training. So, once ministers have finished college or seminary, where do they get additional learning to carry them through the rest of their lives? What are their venues of lifelong learning?

Reading

A minister's primary access to lifelong learning is reading. Effective ministers spend from five to ten hours a week reading current magazines, books, and Internet columns. While a few ministers might claim to have *not* read a whole book since seminary, they are so rare as to be dismissed completely. For ministers even to survive—let alone thrive—in today's world, they must be avid readers. On this point most ministers are examples for their laity—a practice which dates back to Martin and Katharina Luther, who taught many to read in their community. It is not uncommon for a minister to have processed the equivalent of fifty books a year—an average of a book every week. While they may not have *studied* these works, many ministers have mastered them enough to speak intelligently about their content.

Learning groups

Perhaps the greatest tip for facilitating a minister's lifelong learning is to establish a learning group—a group of ministers who meet regularly to learn together. Most ministers on the cutting edge of learning belong to such groups.

Learning groups are gatherings intentionally designed to help participants learn. Adults learn best when they discuss and process the content in groups.[3] Ministers who are effective leaders are involved in a learning group—no matter what they may actually call it.

Degree programs and Online Courses

Single online courses are being offered everywhere today, but they are only one entry point to lifelong learning. Ministers also are rushing to enroll in both online and onsite degree programs. They do so in spite of the fact that few denominations require it, and many local churches do not financially support it. Ministers are so intent on lifelong learning that they will pay tuition out of their own pockets. This trend says something very positive about ministers (and something not so positive about churches and denominations that don't support it). Some ministers have not been able to acquire advanced degrees because of their pastoral schedules. It is difficult for ministers to be away from their churches when they are supposed to be on call locally much of the time. However, online education has remedied that problem. We are now seeing ministers join an even greater stampede to formal degree programs, including the MA, M.Div, and D.Min programs, along with other degree programs related to ministry, such as leadership and counseling degrees.

Ministers will always gain immediate problem-solving and idea/program learning from reading and attending seminars. Increasingly, they also want to put a solid foundation under these temporary ideas with courses and degree programs in theology, church history and Bible exegesis. This is not because these fields have changed substantially (although some have), but because the minister has changed as a person and now sees the relevance of these foundational studies more than before. These ministers now know that a novel approach to a Christmas show that attracts seekers to their church might work a decade, but a deeper understanding of the Incarnation will last a lifetime.

Lifelong Learning: Three Tips for Ministers

We have noted that many ministers provide a wonderful example of a profession bent on lifelong learning. While that learning in recent years may have been tilted more toward programming that is practical (and often temporary), this is now in a stage of correction as ministers revisit the deeper foundational studies in online and onsite formats. Ministers have hungry minds—even for areas outside their direct discipline. For example, this book offers no quick program to build church attendance. It offers very little that you can work into next week's sermon. But you are reading it anyway. Why? Probably because you already are a lifelong learner—enough of a lifelong learner to read a book relating the MBA curriculum to the ministry. So, what ideas might you continue (or initiate) to ensure that you will continue to be a lifelong learner? Consider these three:

1. **Establish reading goals**. Write down your goals and surprise yourself at how much you already have read. Then expand your reading. Learn to speed-read if you have not yet developed that skill. For further tips

and a resource list on how to read more quickly, visit this website: http://www.indwes.edu/tuesday/speed.htm

2. **Start a learning group.** You are probably already involved in one, but it may not be intentional. Make it more intentional. Establish a policy of "learning accountability" in your group—each of you *formally* reporting what you learn from conventions, seminars, and books. Even if you do this somewhat with your online friends, make your efforts intentional and learn from one another. God often teaches us the best things through others.

3. **Get your church to financially support lifelong learning.** It isn't selfish to get the church to do the right thing. If you don't have a board member like Larry in your church to suggest the line item, cultivate one or do it yourself. Get your board to support lifelong learning for its ministers— present and future. If a worldly corporation can wholeheartedly support its employees' learning, how much more important is it for a church to encourage and support its minister's learning? Not to do so is unacceptable—in fact, it is *wrong*. Be more insistent—it is the right thing for the church, for you, for other staff members, and for your successors. Perhaps suggest multiple lines in the church's budget instead of one—a line for periodical subscriptions, another for seminars and conventions, and a third line for credit-bearing courses and degree programs.

Modeling Lifelong Learning

When ministers practice the discipline of lifelong learning, they often do so at great personal expense and with little financial or career rewards. Why? Perhaps because ministers know that if they become lifelong learners and model continuous learning for their members, then the church will be the influential organization it is intended to be in the world. Peter Senge calls this indicative of a "learning organization."[4] Leaders of learning organizations model learning by regenerating themselves and providing ways for members at every level of the organizations to grow personally and professionally. According to Senge, "It is no longer sufficient to have one person learning for the organization. Organizations that excel will tap into people's commitment and capacity to learn at *all* levels in an organization."[5]

Ministers also understand that the church is a dynamic organism under the direction of the Holy Spirit. The church may stand for static truth, but it is constantly under the leadership of the Holy Spirit to learn new ways to accomplish old and enduring purposes. When ministers continue to learn, they model what they want their churches to be—learning organizations that are not static but dynamic, influential organizations. That is important because ministers come and go. They too some day will join the ranks of other ministers who have passed from the scene. Ministers who have practiced lifelong learning and influenced their churches to be lifelong learning organizations will not have their life's learning interred with their bones. Those ministers will leave behind lifelong learning churches. And that is a worthy goal, for the church is never ending.

Endnotes

1. Richard Nelson Bolles, *The Three Boxes of Life and How to Get Out of Them* (Berkeley: Ten Speed Press, 1978, 2003).
2. Adapted from R. Keith Iddings, *Ten Across Workbook* (Marion, IN: Indiana Wesleyan University, 1995), 19-20.
3. Malcolm S. Knowles, *Andragogy in Action: Applying Modern Principles of Adult Learning* (San Francisco: Jossey-Bass, 1985).
4. Peter Senge, *The Fifth Discipline: The Art and Practice of the Learning Organization* (New York: Currency/Doubleday, 1990).
5. Ibid., 4).

What Church Leader's Need to Know About . . .

Lifelong Learning, Part 2

Learning on the Edge of the Wave:
A Blueprint for a Church Leader's Learning

"Leaders are more powerful role models when they
learn than when they teach."

—ROSABETH MOSS KANTOR[1]

Reading a Church

Pastors are tied down. Oddly enough, most congregations expect their pastors to be there on Sundays. I felt trapped in the job. Unless I used my vacation Sundays, I couldn't visit my colleagues on Sunday to see how they did things. It never crossed my mind to ask for "learning days," and my congregational leaders never offered them. I felt handicapped because I couldn't learn from practical exposure to my peers, especially in the early years of my career when I really needed that kind of learning.

Several years later, I spent a year visiting dozens of churches on behalf of a missionary ministry. Virtually every week of that year I was in at least one if not several new churches. It was a fantastic learning opportunity. By the time the year was half gone, I could read a church pretty well. By the time the weekend was over, after spending time in the facilities, visiting with the pastor, making small talk with the congregation, I felt that I had a pretty accurate sense of that church's current direction.

Organizations that are alive, healthy, and growing qualitatively and quantitatively have a distinctive imprint. They have an esprit de corps, a sense of inner vitality. You can read it in the faces, the words, and the actions of the people who comprise the organization. You can see the mark of this vitality in the physical facilities. You can observe the impact the organization has on its community.

The Power of Leaders Who Learn

At the heart of a healthy organization is a set of leaders who are always learning. There's always a wave to ride in organizational life and health organizations have leaders who are learning on the edge of the wave. That's because life is not static. Life in this world is about change. Organizations that aren't changing on the basis of what they are learning are on the way to becoming irrelevant. The church is no different.

Healthy church organizations come in all shapes and sizes, and represent the full spectrum of theological and ecclesiastical traditions. Willingness to change on the basis of astute learning is what enables churches of different kinds to thrive in a cultural setting that has proven unfriendly to church life.

If you want to lead a church organization to excellence, you will have to be a lifelong learner. Great leaders are great learners, always curious, always looking for insights and ideas to test and put into practice. Good leaders learn for the sake of their organizations because they know that learning is infectious. Chip and Bilijack Bell say this of learning leaders: "Great . . . leaders nurture the spirit of curiosity and are perpetual hunters of insight. They're continually and noticeably on the prowl for new wisdom. They look around the corners of opportunity, feel the power of discovery, and keep an ear to the ground for fresh understanding. They learn all the time. And they learn out loud."[2]

Learning How to Learn Again

Several years ago, I had the privilege of helping to create a customized Masters of Science in Management program for a group of executives in the

Chrysler Corporation. I was fascinated with the perspective and the experience of these corporate warriors. To provide them with a program that was relevant, I knew I would have to learn as much as I could about them and their world. I spent a year sitting in their corporate and private meetings, going to lunch, listening to their conversations, interviewing them, reading their documents, and talking to their employees. I wanted to learn what they knew, see the world through their eyes, experience their challenges, and understand where they felt vulnerable and needy.

Some of the most fascinating aspects emerged when they told me about their experiences in the 1970s, when the company found itself unable to compete with the new Japanese imports that were beginning to flood the American market. Chrysler had been complacent for many years. Almost without warning, the world changed. The oil embargo of 1973 created an instant demand for fuel-efficient cars. American carmakers could not meet this demand. But the Japanese car makers had these products and began flooding the American market. Their cars were more efficient and of a higher quality as well. Chrysler was completely unprepared to compete. Overnight, Chrysler became irrelevant. They desperately needed to learn how to make new products, in a vastly changed environment. The executives I worked with told me that the only hope for Chrysler lay in their ability to learn about themselves, learn about what they public wanted, and learn how to create new processes that would yield new products that the public wanted.

At a moment of supreme challenge the future of their company depended on their willingness and ability to learn.

Clearly, the church is not a car company. It doesn't offer products for sale to the public. But it does serve people, and it exists in a social environment that is ever changing. So there are lessons here for the church and its leaders. One denominational leader said, "A church does not grow past its pastor. The pastor is the lid. If the pastor will grow in leadership, then the ministry can grow."[3] At the heart of your organization's health lies your willingness to keep on learning.

Becoming a Free-Agent Learner

Most leaders accept some responsibility to continue learning as they move through their careers. But pastors need to work harder than most professionals to continue the learning process. Thankfully in recent years congregations have begun to allow pastors to invest in professional development processes, and to take much-needed sabbaticals. The realities of current society are forcing high-impact pastors to adopt a new approach to their continuing professional learning. Human development researchers tell us that high-potential, high-impact leaders are coming to think of themselves as "free-agent learners." Real learning that transforms people, systems, and organizations interrupts the descent of churches into irrelevance.

Rose Opengart and Darren Short recently conducted a multi-organization international study to document this phenomenon in eleven organizations in the United States, Britain, and Brazil. About this new way of thinking about learning they say: "There is evidence that a new career model is operating in the workforce (Kanter 1995), or at least it is in the USA. According to that model, employees' attitudes towards careers are changing, with a greater emphasis being placed on self-managed careers and maintaining long-term employability, most likely by several organizations."[4]

Then and Now

In the past, employees could complete their careers in one organization. Today, they are fortunate if they are able to complete a career in a single industry. In the past, employees didn't need to learn new knowledge, skills, and dispositions to ensure the success of their organizations and their own place within them. Today, the effectiveness of any person's knowledge base is often measured in months. In the past, an entry-level degree was good for a career. Today, even graduate degrees must be supplemented with regular formal and informal learning to keep current. In the past, the penalty for not keeping up was little prospect of personal promotion. Today, the penalty for not keeping up is putting the future of the organization at risk.

Whereas leaders once could afford to slide along, investing a minimum of effort in personal learning, today, we must maintain our employability by continually adding to our portfolio of skills and assets. Today, high-impact, high-potential leaders must think of themselves as highly skilled free-agents whose effectiveness comes from their ability to be of continuing value over the life of their careers.

Free-Agent Learners in Ministry Organizations

The global realities behind the shift to "free-agent learning" may not have hit some ministry organizations, but they are changing the rules for those organizations most vulnerable to changing expectations and support patterns. Many ministry organizations have been losing their support bases. It is important to note that many analysts trace this erosion of support to a decline in the relevancy of many mission organizations to the changed realities of globalization. James Engle and William Dyrness offer this penetrating analysis:

The North American missions movement is facing realities amazingly similar to those confronting American industry for nearly twenty years. Almost overnight a more nimble and highly competitive Japanese industrial juggernaut almost overwhelmed its sluggish counterparts worldwide. An all-new information-oriented approach to production, marketing and management suddenly was forced upon enterprises that somehow had ignored the unmistakable signs of change on the horizon. Few industries were left untouched by an immediate imperative to adapt and change or die! Fortunately, corporate boards and management saw the handwriting on the wall and responded with a startling degree of courage and brilliance.

Similarly ominous signs have been on the world missions horizon for more than two decades, but it seems to take much longer for churches and Christian organizations to recognize realities. And when the light finally dawns, the response all too often is to bury our heads in the sand, trusting that God somehow will make things right.

The time has passed for that kind of sluggish stewardship.[5]

A careful perusal of the ministry landscape shows that what has been said here about mission organizations is true of all kinds of ministry organizations today. Here's the change tsunami that hit Chrysler, for which they were unprepared.

The context in which they were working changed. This changed people's desires, perceptions, and pursuits. This, in turn, made the structure, function, and offerings of the organization somewhat "out of phase" with what people were experiencing and needing.

Perceptive and forward thinking leaders catch these change signals early. They force themselves to keep learning, and they create learning organizations. This pattern of change that demands learning leaders is as true for ministry organizations as it is for any other kind of organization today.

The point is to understand the importance of continued learning in order to understand the realities in which our ministry organizations work and to determine how best to pursue our mission in the face of change.

Metamorphosis

It is difficult to watch how often ministry leaders respond to the erosion of their support bases and changed priorities among their constituents with bewilderment, confusion, and pain.

When this happens, the best of them pass through a kind of metamorphosis. They begin to think in terms of learning what the world is like today and how the timeless truth of the Gospel must be communicated in this world. They stop being employees of ministry organizations and become free agent adventurers, thirsty to know more, to understand more deeply, in order to lead more appropriately. That is the power of lifelong professional learning. It is not an exercise undertaken to comply with a church hierarchy or to satisfy curiosity. It is a life or death enterprise that has the power to give birth to new imagination and transformed careers.

Before we outline the practical steps involved in planning and implementing your learning programs, let's review some key points:

- Leaders are most effective when they are learning and setting an example of learning for their organizations.
- Church leaders are the "lid" on their organizations. The more they learn and grow, the greater the potential they create for their organizations.
- High-impact organizational leaders are adopting a "free-agent learner" approach.
- Leaders who are not learners lead their organizations into irrelevance!

How to Structure Learning

To plan and implement an effective personal program of professional learning, it is important to structure your learning. Two foundational practices are invaluable for this purpose. The first is to create "your learning archive." The second is to conduct an annual personal learning strategy planning session.

My Learning Archive

One practical first step in creating a personal learning plan is to create a "learning archive" and put it someplace in your office where it is conveniently located and visible. Throughout the year, you will collect scraps of paper, printouts from the Web, newspaper or journal articles—all kinds of reminders of ideas, books, people, and suggestions that struck your interest during the course of the year. Sometimes you will write down things that cause you to feel vulnerable, areas where you feel incompetent or in need of better preparation, frustrations that come with your job, or insights and even corrections that people have offered throughout the year. Leaders cannot get through a year without receiving lots of feedback—some of it well-meaning, all of it helpful in one way or another.

Throw all of these scraps into your learning archive. This treasure trove of substance will be useful in helping you to structure your learning. Your archive will fit your personality and the way you work. The point is to quickly and easily capture the ideas for growth that cross your path during the year.

My Learning Strategy Planning Session

The second step in creating a plan for personal learning is to schedule regular dedicated time to conduct your own learning strategy planning session.

Remember that "strategic planning" is about what you should do. "Tactical planning" is about how to get it done.

For learning to pay dividends, you must incorporate strategic planning. Set aside a period of dedicated time at least once a year to take stock of yourself. This works best if you are able to take several days of concentrated, uninterrupted time. You should have access to records of the past year, to your personal mission statement and strategic priorities, and to the critical reporting that helps you track the performance of your organization. And bring your "learning archive."

The point of this learning strategy planning session is to figure out what you need to learn, how you will learn it, and how you will assess the impact of your learning.

With this preparation – assembling your treasure trove of ideas, and setting aside dedicated time to plan – the next step will be to target specific learning needs and implement learning plans.

In the next section we'll talk about how to use a well-known learning design process that will help us give structure to our professional learning plans. Though it isn't necessary to rigorously follow every step of this design process, using a structured approach can pay great dividends in achieving real results for learning needs.

The design process is called the ADDIE system, and it can form the basis for your personalized learning program. Using a careful set of thought processes like this has paid great dividends for many of us through the years.

Using the ADDIE Learning Design Process

ADDIE is an acronym that stands for a proven process that professional educators and trainers use to structure learning programs. The process has five simple but comprehensive steps.

- Analysis
- Design
- Development
- Implementation
- Evaluation

Analysis

Unfortunately, our personal and organizational learning agendas are all too often driven by personal interests, or by "what's hot" in organizational circles. This leaves the fruit of our learning labor too open to chance. There is no guarantee that we will learn what we need to learn in order to keep our organization relevant and healthy. We need a better plan than this. This is where the first step of careful analysis pays off.

The first step in the process is to answer this question: What do I need to learn?

The answer to this question can be cognitive – I may need to learn new information in order to enrich or redirect various aspects of my ministry.

The answer can be skill-based – I may need to learn a new technique, or a new set of skills, in order to take my ministry abilities to a new level. This can range from technical presentation skills, to new pastoral counseling techniques.

The answer can be affective, having to do with your emotional disposition – I may need to learn a new appreciation for some aspect of ministry.

All of these are learning needs, and they are identified through a process of analysis. What do we analyze in this step?

Here we gather the information and the requirements you will need to understand yourself, your organization, the people who are served by your organization, the outcomes you desire for your organization, and any reporting data that will help you understand your current situation.

The analysis phase will show you what knowledge, skills, or tasks need to be learned, by whom, and under what conditions in order to achieve the strategic priorities you have set for yourself and your organization. The analysis phase should compare the required state of knowledge with your existing knowledge in order to yield a "gap analysis" that clearly shows what you must learn in order to be successful in achieving your desired outcomes.

The analysis process works like this.

1. What are my (our) desired *personal and organizational outcomes*?
2. What *knowledge, skills, and dispositions* do I need (do we need) in order to be able to achieve these desired outcomes?
3. What is my (our) *current state of achievement* relative to the required knowledge, skills, and dispositions? In this step, you may wish to use a skills inventory such as that developed by Administrators of Volunteer Resources British Columbia.[vi] See Appendix A.
4. The gap between the required and the current state of achievement is called a *"gap analysis."* This shows you where you are deficient and in need of learning. If there is no gap between your current state and the level required to achieve your desired outcomes, then you don't have a learning problem in that area. You need to focus your attention elsewhere.

Here are some practical things to look at as you conduct this analysis:

- Gather and reflect on the information that you have available about your organization, the context in which it is situated, the people with whom you work, the challenges you are facing, the constraints with which you are working. Most of us work in organizations that can provide us with a fair bit of reporting data that help us to create a picture of where things stand. This shouldn't be so detailed that you lose the picture of the "forest" by focusing too much on individual "trees." Instead, as you think through what the information is telling you, you will begin to identify areas where you will want to know more.

- Make as accurate a description as you can of your current strengths, and then focus on what you need to lean in order to extend those strengths, and apply them to the situation in which you find yourself. Here's where you may wish to rely on material drawn from your learning archive. During the year, did you make notes concerning any areas of vulnerability or frustration? Did any others offer you perspective on yourself? Now is the time to review these as dispassionately as possible.

- Keep your statement of personal and organizational outcomes handy and refer to it throughout this process.

- Here's another technique that can help your analysis. Pull out your job description. If you don't have one, write one for yourself. Be as concrete as you can. Good job descriptions include a list of tasks that must be performed by the person who holds that job. Complete a "task inventory"; that is, look at each task and ask yourself whether and how it is relevant to the achievement of your desired outcomes. Are all the required tasks there in your job description?

- Now study the performance measures tied to each task in your inventory. Do you know how well you need to perform each task in order to achieve your desired outcomes?

- Next, specifically determine the knowledge, skills, and dispositions you need to have in order to achieve the required level of performance on each of your tasks. Did you find any holes? Or, to look at it another way, are there any areas of personal strength that you can further enhance?

- If so, you have just created a gap analysis. This gap analysis is one of your most important insights because it clearly shows you the potential areas on which to focus your learning efforts. You've found some potential keys to boost your level of success and, therefore, that of your organization.

Finally, to complete your analysis, determine the constraints (such as time, cost, and access) that will help to determine what settings and methods will be available to you as you design and implement your learning program.

Design

With the insights driven by analysis in hand, you are ready to design the learning that will close the gap between where you are and where you need to be. The analysis phase exposed the gap between the actual and desired that must be closed. In the design phase, you will identify the content necessary to close the gap.

When you've completed the Design step in this process you will have identified one or more "learning experiences" that you will use to close the gap between where you now stand and where you want to arrive. These may be formal learning events such as taking a course or getting a new certificate or degree. Or they may be less formal like a personalized reading program, or a set of personal interviews with mentors.

Here's how to proceed.

1. Use your gap analysis to *identify the information, skill, or personal disposition* that you need to acquire in order to close the gap between the actual and desired performance levels. Do you need to learn how to converse in Spanish in order to begin establishing contacts with new members of your community? Do you need to learn better exegetical skills in order to prepare richer sermons? Do you need to gain a better appreciation for others experiences and skills in order to make delegation a more functional part of your leadership approach?

2. Once you have identified target areas for learning, it will be helpful to state the *outcomes* you hope to achieve. This may sound daunting, but it is simple and easy to do. Here's how:

- Ask yourself what specific *change* in knowledge, skill, or disposition you wish to produce with the learning experience. An example might be, "In six months I will be able to greet people and make introductions in Spanish." Write down that change in simple and straightforward language using as few words as possible—don't be long and windy with this. Write it more than once until you've got a nice, concise statement that anyone would understand.

- Now ask yourself if there's any way you would be able to *measure* whether or not you achieved the outcome. If not, then write it again so that you can easily tell if you achieve the outcome. For example, if you write, "When I'm done with this learning experience, I will be able to use multimedia communication methods," your statement is too vague and broad. A better outcome statement is this one: "When I'm done with this learning experience, I will be able to create and deliver a PowerPoint presentation with embedded graphics, audio clips, and video clips."

3. While you're in this frame of mind, it's a good time to write down *the way you will measure the impact* of the learning experience. Ideally, you want to measure two things. First you want to measure how well you achieve the learning outcome. Second, and more important in the big scheme of things, you want to measure how you change (or your organization changes) because of your learning. In the instructional design business, we call this an assessment plan. That may sound pretentious and it probably is, but again, it's a simple process.

- Ask, yourself, "What will I measure in order to know that I've learned what I said I wanted to learn?" Also ask yourself, "How will I know if my behavior has changed, or if my organization is different because I have learned this stuff?"

- Write down a realistic way of measuring these outcomes in simple and straightforward language. Again, if you have to use a lot of words, and if your statement is vague and hard to understand, you're not there yet. Write it again.

Once you've completed the design phase, you will have identified at least one content area upon which you will focus your learning for the next six or twelve months. You will have a concrete and specific set of outcomes that you wish to achieve for yourself and your organization. And you'll have a set of measurements that you will use to determine if the learning is meeting your expectations. Now you're ready to develop the learning experience.

Develop

The third step in the process is pretty straightforward. In the Develop phase of the process you account for all the concrete steps you will need in order to put your learning plan into action. Well intentioned plans often go awry because we didn't adequately understand the time, energy, and other resources that the plan would require.

This is the stage at which we count the cost.

- How much time will I need to find in my schedule to commit to this learning plan? What will I change about my schedule in order to make this time?
- Will there be a financial requirement in order to put my plan in action? If so, how will I acquire these resources, or how will I reallocate current resources for this purpose?
- Where will I pursue my learning? Often, it is helpful to choose a location that becomes your personal learning space. This may be as formal as an educational institution. Or it may be as informal as the local coffee shop that becomes your personal reading place.

In the Development phase you are answering the question, "How will I accomplish this learning?" What are the practical necessities that I will have to insure in order for my learning plan to bear fruit?

Implement and Evaluate

The last two stages of the ADDIE learning structure are to Implement your learning plan and Evaluate its impact. This is where you "do" the learning and where you measure the things you said you'd measure to decide how successful your learning has been.

During the Design phase you built into your plan a set of measurements to see how well your learning would pay off. The Evaluation phase is where you compare your desired outcomes with the outcomes you have actually achieved. Sometimes this takes time. It isn't always possible to see the results of your learning plan in the short run. So be sure to give yourself adequate time to evaluate the way your learning plan adds richness to your professional life.

A final element is very important – Celebration!

It is important to recognize your achievements. Sometimes others will recognize the result of your learning plan. If part of your plan is to obtain a new degree, graduation day will give you a built-in day of celebration. But many of our learning goals don't have such formal points at which to celebrate new achievements. Make them anyway, and include the people who are most important to you. Let them help you share in the moments when you recognize the ways in which you and your organization have grown because you committed yourself to learning and you achieved your goal.

Review of Key Elements

Douglas Ready, Jay Conger, and Linda Hill studied the way that "high potential employees" emerge and grow in their organizational settings. These are the employees that emerge as the ones most likely to advance the organization, carrying it forward into a bright future.

High potential leaders, they found, have three important elements. First, they "deliver strong results" with credibility. Second, they "master new types of expertise." Third, they recognize that behavior counts."

Ready, Conger and Hill wanted to go further. They asked what "x factors" cause high potential leaders to emerge within their organizations. They found that high potential leaders exhibit four "x factors."

A Drive to Excel – "High potentials aren't just high achievers. They are driven to succeed. Good, even very good, isn't good enough. Not by any stretch. They are more than willing to go that extra mile and realize they may have to make sacrifices . . . in order to advance."

A Catalytic Learning Capability – "The high potentials we have come across possess what we call a 'catalytic learning capability.' They have the capacity to scan for new ideas, the cognitive capability to absorb them, and the common sense to translate that new learning into productive ideas for their customers and their organizations."

An Enterprising Spirit – "High potentials are always searching for productive ways to blaze new paths. They are explorers . . . ."

Dynamic Sensors – "High potentials possess what we call 'dynamic sensors,' which enable them to skirt [the] risks . . . . They have a feel for timing, an ability to quickly read situations, and a nose for opportunity."

Just as business organizations need high potential leaders to advance and to remain healthy, ministry organizations also need these kinds of leaders. For ministry organizations, the fundamental motivations may be different. But we, too, are driven to give our very best service for the mission to which we are called.

What is striking here is that the ability to learn lies at the heart of high potential, high impact leadership.

So let's review what we've discovered in this chapter.

1. Leaders are at their best when they are learning.
2. Organizations that do not learn are on their way to irrelevance.
3. High-impact leaders become free-agent learners.
4. Lay the structural foundations of your learning by creating a "learning archive" and by conducting an annual "learning strategy planning session."
5. Employ the ADDIE process to target what you need to learn. Then, plan how you will accomplish the learning and assess its effectiveness.

   - In the analysis phase, you gather information and perform a "gap analysis" to discover where to focus your learning efforts.
   - In the design phase, you target the content you wish to learn, establish outcomes, and come up with ways to measure the impact of your learning.

- In the development phase, you put together the nuts and bolts of your learning experience.
- In the implementation and evaluation phases, you "do" the learning and determine the actual impact of the learning.

Cultivating a Zeal for Excellence

In a recent article about the power of learning in organizational settings, Chip and Bilijack Bell tell the following story. It is an inspiring reminder of the power of learning to transform the situations in which we live and generate an exciting future for ourselves and those we serve.

She was one of the most focused children in her neighborhood. You were never able to get past her on a walk without a barrage of intriguing questions. She played piano at age three, read fluently at five. Wise beyond her years, yet innocent, she was the darling of every adult in her Birmingham, Alabama, neighborhood. Some of her classmates viewed her maturity, perfectionism, and dainty manners as prissy; others knew they were witnessing the emergence of an intellectual powerhouse destined for greatness.

"I had parents who gave me every conceivable opportunity," she would tell a *Vogue* interviewer. "They also believed in achievement." Her innocent but probing questions of guests were met with warmth and affirmation, never disdain. She went to grown-up plays and concerts her friends thought were boring. She started college at 15, becoming a distinguished scholar, an award-winning author and professor at Stanford, an accomplished athlete and pianist – and, ultimately, the National Security Advisor to the President of the United States. When Condoleezza Rice speaks of her roots, it's always with allegiance to the support and encouragement of her parents, John and Angelena Rice, in nurturing her curiosity and cultivating her zeal for excellence. Curious people come from atmospheres that are quick to champion and slow to chastise. Their inquiring minds are celebrated not just by ovations, but also by opportunities to apply their insatiable interest in stimulating ways.[1]

Here's to your learning adventure.

May you always see the possible.

May you be intrigued by the yet-to-come.

May you be captivated by the dream that waits to be spoken—the dream that will spur you to action and inspire the people you lead.

May you learn to see, to be, and then to do.

Endnotes

1. Rosabeth Moss Kantor quote. I found this online at a fishing website. As quoted by Chip R. Bell, My Tackle Box, at http://www.chipbell.com/tackle.htm.
2. Chip R. Bell and Bilijack R. Bell, "Great Training Leaders Learn Out Loud, *T&D*, vol. 57, no. 9 (September 2003: 1.
3. Ron F. McManus, "Spiritual Leadership Series (Part 3): Learning to Lead," *Enrichment Journal* (Springfield, MO: General Council of Assemblies of God, 2003), 2.

About the Authors

President, Dr. Mark A. Smith
Ohio Christian University

Dr. Mark Smith is President of Ohio Christian University. Prior to coming to Ohio Christian University, Dr. Smith served as Vice President for Adult and Graduate Studies from 2001 through 2005 at Indiana Wesleyan University. Prior to that, he was Dean at Indiana Wesleyan University.

Dr. Smith has a Bachelor of Arts degree from Hobe Sound College and a Master's Degree in college teaching from Northeastern State University.

He attended Kansas University's Graduate School. He graduated from West Virginia University with a Doctor of Education degree. Dr. Smith was elected and served on Marion City Council, in Indiana, and was appointed by the Bush Administration for a 3 year term to An Education Board which focused on Excellence in Education. Dr. Smith completed Harvard University's Institute of Educational Management for Executive Management.

He has published scores of articles for professional and church organizations.

He has also published a book; *Leading Change in Your World* which he coauthored with Larry Lindsay--the third edition will be printed in 2007.

Dr. Smith has been married to his wife, Debbie, for 20 years and they have two children. Douglas is 13 years old and Micah is four.

Dr. David Wright, PhD
Provost
Indiana Wesleyan University

David Wright serves as Provost and Chief Academic Officer at Indiana Wesleyan University. Before coming to his current position he was Dean of the School of Theology at Azusa Pacific University. Previously at Indiana Wesleyan University he served as Associate Professor of Intercultural Studies, Chair of the Department of Graduate Studies in Ministry, and Vice President for Adult and Graduate Studies.

Dr. Wright has a strong interest in international higher education having focused his doctoral studies on the social foundations of higher education as well as on international and comparative studies in education. He spent seven years working in educational capacities in Haiti and England. His areas of professional expertise include higher education policy, the design and administration of non-traditional and online programs, and higher education leadership.

Dr. Wright holds the Bachelor of Arts degree in Christian Ministries from Indiana Wesleyan University, the Master of Arts in Biblical Studies from George Fox University, and the Ph.D. in Educational Policy Studies and Evaluation from the University of Kentucky. He has published two books with Zondervan Publishing House, *Finding Freedom From Fear: A Contemporary Study from the Psalms,* and *Wisdom as a Lifestyle: Building Biblical Life-codes*, as well as numerous articles.